Praise for
MIRRORS IN THE EARTH

"Suler's sense of wonder is infectious, and her prose exudes her boundless reverence for nature . . . Spiritual nature lovers will treasure this meditative volume."

—*PUBLISHERS WEEKLY*

"I am in awe of how one small book can hold so much wisdom. Every paragraph is beautifully written and more importantly so deeply meaningful. Insightful, uplifting, and life affirming, *Mirrors in the Earth* reaches deep and stretches high. As much about ecological healing as personal healing, this book offers the reader a pathway back to self-acceptance, interconnection, and belonging and empowers one along the way to make a stand for the Earth."

—ROSEMARY GLADSTAR, herbalist and
author of *Medicinal Herbs*

"Asia Suler's heart shines forth as she guides and inspires the reader to look inside themselves and into the mirror of Nature to deepen their compassion for themselves. Suler shares stories of her personal transformation, including the painful parts, with clarity, warmth, and vulnerability. This beautiful book ultimately invites the reader to see and experience how our individual healing brings healing to our world. *Mirrors in the Earth* is offered as an antidote for despair; it is grounded in ecology and the author's love of the world."

—ROBIN ROSE BENNETT, author of
Healing Magic

"If you seek to heal the land, awaken sacred spaces, or regenerate nature, this book will bring you to the origin of your connection with the world. This is the place to start."

"Asia Suler's writing is very literally medicinal: her words bear the healing properties of the Earth. This is a book to live by—a book to bring you back home. Part personal healing journey, part prose poem in praise of the living world, and part wisdom teaching, *Mirrors in the Earth* is the wildly compassionate, fiercely loving map we all need in these times to guide us back to our innate and joyful wholeness."

"Asia Suler lays a cloak of pine boughs upon your shoulders, takes your hand, and guides you to an inner sanctum of spring ephemerals, ancient moonlit groves, and resurrecting webs of mycelium. You'll emerge transformed, your pockets full of jade-green insights about the natural world, and your heart gleaming with the truth of your wildness and earthy-soft goodness. Asia has created a keepsake, one that will serve as an intrepid and tender guide for the ages."

"This revelatory treasure of a book guides readers on a healing journey back to the Earth wisdom available to us all—whether in a fleck of mountain mica or the geological memory of ancient meteoric encounters. With her wide-ranging experience and elegant writing, Asia Suler helps us to recover an intimate, loving, and generous relationship with the natural world. This is a book I will return to and pass along, urging my friends to read it now."

"It's not unusual for books about eco consciousness to leave the reader stranded somewhere between helplessness and despair. What a refreshing relief, then, to find a book that guides us toward mutual healing for both ourselves and the Earth through the seemingly simple act of cultivating a deep and abiding relationship with the landscape around us. From the delightful introduction to the detailed descriptions of trout lilies ('like tiny faeries, gazing closely at the moss around their feet'), beech trees ('round and elegant as a brandy bottle'), and the particular shimmer of mica ('like the Milky Way, spilled generously across dark soil'), Suler weaves an ecosystem of healing in which both humans and the natural world play important roles. With personal stories of mending from both disease and trauma, as well as exercises to guide the reader in their own explorations, *Mirrors in the Earth* offers a living example of how to reestablish communion and balance."

—MAIA TOLL, author of the *Wild Wisdom* podcast series

"Asia Suler's exquisite ability to create rich and vibrant images with her metaphors placed me in the center of my belonging which felt like a homecoming. Sometimes raw, but always tender and honest, Suler's experiences are like a beacon lighting the way to the reflecting pool where nature serves not only as a mirror but as a benevolent teacher. This book is a gem you will want to read over and over as each time brings another polishing of Earth's mirrors."

—PAM MONTGOMERY, herbalist, teacher, and author of *Plant Spirit Healing*

"Asia's words are comforting and instructive in equal measure. Even in the darkest of times, her work has a way of illuminating the inner landscape and revealing to us a path where before there was none. Miraculously, she offers us not just stories, but spells, which weave their way through our world and leave our lives so much brighter than before. The book you hold within your hands is a true treasure whose gifts will live within you and guide you on your way long after you've turned the final page."

—SOPHIA ROSE, herbalist and writer

"*Mirrors in the Earth* is a beautiful reminder that walking the path of nature initiation is a lifelong apprenticeship. As someone who was projected onto more than mirrored as a child, it was so validating to hear Asia Suler speak about nature as our eternal mirror. She offers a unique glimpse into the journey that allowed this divine truth to move from being just an idea into something that is tangible, personal, and real for her. We are reminded that we each have a unique relationship with our birth mothers, the same is true about the Great Mother. This book awakens us to the remembrance that a relationship with nature is both personal and universal at the same time."

—MARYAM HASNAA AT-TAUHIDI,
founder of New Earth Mystery School
and Resonance Apothecary

"Read Asia Suler's lovely book and your world will tilt. You'll not only see that the world is your mirror but that the world is looking at you. You will learn from willow that what breaks can give birth and from beech that it may be okay to hold onto your leaves for longer than the almanac says. Now she comes with a willow twig between her teeth to help us to heal by making our confessions to the forgiving land, by aligning ourselves with Earth cycles of regeneration, and by recalling that the plots of our lives, like gardens, require boundaries. A beloved herbalist and Earth keeper, Suler reveals herself as an enchanting poet of consciousness who rouses us to heal our lives by telling better stories about them."

—ROBERT MOSS, best-selling author of
Dreaming the Soul Back Home

"*Mirrors in the Earth* is a poetic and heartfelt exploration of our healing journey as humans toward self-acceptance, overcoming our trauma, and most importantly, remembering that the first place toward healing the Earth begins with ourselves. Asia artfully guides the reader on the pathway to reigniting our memory that we are a part of the Earth and the Earth is a part of us, and that healing is the most important work we can be doing at this time."

—SAJAH POPHAM, author of *Evolutionary Herbalism*

"*Mirrors in the Earth* is a book of hope in times that feel hopeless, a nature-blessed call to healing and sacred action. Asia's gentle spirit shows us the way to transform and align ourselves, not separate from the world, but in service with the world. You will emerge from the ceremony of this book rewoven into the tapestry of nature, and deeply allied with our mutual healing."

—HEATHERASH AMARA, author of
Warrior Goddess Training

MIRRORS IN THE EARTH

MIRRORS IN THE EARTH

REFLECTIONS ON SELF-HEALING
FROM THE LIVING WORLD

ASIA SULER

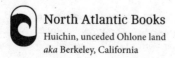

North Atlantic Books
Huichin, unceded Ohlone land
aka Berkeley, California

Published by
North Atlantic Books
Huichin, unceded Ohlone land
aka Berkeley, California

Cover art © bluejayphoto via Getty Images
Cover design by Jasmine Hromjak
Book design by Happenstance Type-O-Rama

Printed in Canada

Mirrors in the Earth: Reflections on Self-Healing from the Living World is sponsored and published by North Atlantic Books, an educational nonprofit based in the unceded Ohlone land Huichin (*aka* Berkeley, CA), that collaborates with partners to develop cross-cultural perspectives, nurture holistic views of art, science, the humanities, and healing, and seed personal and global transformation by publishing work on the relationship of body, spirit, and nature.

North Atlantic Books' publications are distributed to the US trade and internationally by Penguin Random House Publisher Services. For further information, visit our website at www.northatlanticbooks.com.

Library of Congress Cataloging-in-Publication Data

Names: Suler, Asia– author.
Title: Mirrors in the earth : reflections on self-healing from the living
    world / by Asia Suler.
Description: Huichin, unceded Ohlone land aka Berkeley, California : North
    Atlantic Books, [2022] | Includes bibliographical references and index.
Identifiers: LCCN 2021057736 (print) | LCCN 2021057737 (ebook) | ISBN
    9781623176914 (trade paperback) | ISBN 9781623176921 (ebook)
Subjects: LCSH: Self-acceptance. | Compassion. | Nature—Psychological
    aspects.
Classification: LCC BF575.S37 S85 2022 (print) | LCC BF575.S37 (ebook) |
    DDC 158.1—dc23/eng/20220223
LC record available at https://lccn.loc.gov/2021057736
LC ebook record available at https://lccn.loc.gov/2021057737
https://lccn.loc.gov/2020003933

2 3 4 5 6 7 8 9 MARQUIS 27 26 25 24 23 22

This book includes recycled material and material from well-managed forests. North Atlantic Books is committed to the protection of our environment. We print on recycled paper whenever possible and partner with printers who strive to use environmentally responsible practices.

At the center of the Earth, there is a spring, rising clear as rain. Emerging from soft forest soil, this spring has been running since the beginning of time and will continue to flow long after we have gone.

At the center of the Earth is a stream of benevolence.

And you are being invited to come drink again.

Contents

PREFACE   xv

INTRODUCTION: A Book of Mica   1

PART ONE: The Glimmer (Seeing Yourself)   17

CHAPTER 1: Garden Edges and Paradise on Earth   19

CHAPTER 2: Florida Inner Worlds   43

CHAPTER 3: The Seasons of Trauma   65

CHAPTER 4: Those That Keep Their Leaves   89

PART TWO: The Mirror (Appreciating Yourself)   103

CHAPTER 5: Tender Spring   105

CHAPTER 6: Drop Dosages   125

CHAPTER 7: The World Sees You   147

CHAPTER 8: Young Forests   167

PART THREE: The Glow (Giving Yourself to the World)   187

CHAPTER 9: Willow Water   189

CHAPTER 10: The Sugar Bees   207

CHAPTER 11: Chestnut Groves and the Resprouting of Hope   221

CHAPTER 12: The Reishi Tree   243

ACKNOWLEDGMENTS 267

NOTES 269

INDEX 279

ABOUT THE AUTHOR 295

Preface

BOOKS TAKE YOU on a journey. I've always known this as a reader but had no idea how deep that journey could go when I was the one doing the writing. The call to start this book arrived nearly ten years ago. It began as a gentle nudging, like a breeze through a screen window. Over time, it became more persistent. For a long stretch, the urge to write felt like waking up every morning to a cat curled on my chest—warm, insistent, weighty, undeterred. Yet every time I sat down, I found myself at a loss, unsure exactly *what* this book was meant to be about.

In those early days, I spent countless hours squinting in front of the arched glass windows of our small-town library, my computer idling in front of me. It took me years to realize that the reason I struggled to write this book pressing inside of me was the very reason I *needed* to write this book. Even though the book showed up every single morning, as self-assured as a cat, I couldn't truly begin because, deep down, I didn't believe in my ability to do so. I had to take the very journey of self-acceptance outlined in these chapters in order to see myself clearly enough to understand what was trying to come through and to let it arrive. In the process, I *became* the person who could write *Mirrors in the Earth*.

The stories in this book are a record of my own journey of realization—a roadmap of epiphanies—as precious to me as a string of rubies. Gathered from the rich hardwood coves of Appalachia, from the wild springs of Florida, from the hidden parks of New York City, and from a whole constellation of wild places in between, these stories are the parables that helped me come home to my belonging on Earth and trust the part I was here to play in the overall healing.

Finally, after five years of starting and discarding drafts, I had a life-changing experience of self-forgiveness among a bank of river willows. The message of that day—which appears later in this book—helped me realize what I had been writing toward all this time. This is not just a collection of comforting stories from the natural world or a lyrical guide to ecological learning. It is a book with a radical premise of both personal and ecological healing. It is the book I have been *living* all along.

Over the course of the following years I collected my most pivotal moments of earth-given revelation—and experienced a few more en route. Through writing, I re-created the same journey of learning self-compassion that the Earth had taken me on so that I could walk it again whenever I needed to. So that I could walk it again with *you*.

We make our paths by walking them—and *this* is the new pathway our Earth wants us to create. A pathway back to self-acceptance, interconnection, belonging, and benevolence. A journey that leads to a world in which all of life is seen as precious—and each one of us can wake up to the profound gifts we have to share.

Because your gifts are exactly what will make this next passage on Earth possible.

I used to think I needed a seismic experience of healing to become the kind of person who felt grounded enough, in her gifts and her grit, to write a book about self-compassion. But now, after having walked this dirt-softened path, dotted by flowers and moss and soothed by the sound of the creek, I know that the medicine we long for is right here beneath our feet; all you need to do is look down.

Gaze into the mirrors of the Earth and healing will rise to greet you.

Introduction:
A Book of Mica

IT'S MIDSUMMER IN the Southern Appalachian Mountains, and the air has substance. You can feel the water carried on the wind as it brushes past you, like breath on silk. I'm walking in the forest, barefoot and slow. The dense heat has been gentled by the thick canopy, and the soles of my feet are cool against the soil. As I walk, my steps grow slower until I am finally stopped by wonder. Standing stock still, I look down at the forest floor beneath me and feel the world turn over. Part of my mind knows I am gazing down at the dirt, but a sudden delicious sense of vertigo makes me feel as if Earth has been flipped and I am falling upward, into the starlit cosmos. Glittering, glinting, everywhere—billions upon billions of flecks of mica wink throughout the forest floor. It looks just like the Milky Way, spilled generously across dark soil. I am barefoot in the forest, walking among the stars.

If you drive north from Asheville into the heart of the Blue Ridge Mountains of North Carolina and then hang a hard right, holding on for another half hour of spiderweb turns into the folds of the mountains, you will find yourself at the old mica mine. Mica has a deep history in this part of Appalachia; mining for this mineral was once big business in these mountains. Mica has a unique chemical structure that makes it both an insulator—keeping heat in—and a conductor—letting it pass through. Place a sheet of mica between a hot coal and a cone of incense, and it will transform that tower of herbs into perfectly uncharred ashes. Marketed as *isinglass*, mica was used to make windows in woodstoves and paneling for the faces of kerosene lamps throughout the nineteenth and early twentieth centuries.[1]

For millennia before this, mica was an important ceremonial item among the Indigenous peoples of these mountains, including the people of the area now known as Asheville—the *Tsalagi* or Cherokee. Carried via pilgrimage and trade routes, mica from the Southern Appalachians has been found as far away as the legendary Hopewell mounds in Ohio.[2] Buried two thousand years ago within those enormous manmade earthworks are pieces of Appalachian mica, carved into claws, arrows, human bodies, bears, and ovals. Some archeologists hypothesize that the circular-shaped pieces of mica might have been made for *mirror-gazing*, a divinatory practice that involves peering into a reflective surface to seek visions from the beyond.

By the time I made this trip to the mica mine, I had been living in the mountains of Western North Carolina for several years, working as an herbalist. Fascinated by all aspects of nature's medicine, I had come to the woods that day with an amiable class of rockhounds to look for a variety of precious stones, including aquamarines and garnets. But as my companions splayed further over the hillside to search through the tailings of the old mine, I couldn't stop gazing into the mica at my feet.

Standing there in the forest, a gentle breeze picked up the edges of my faded, cotton-tiered skirt. The braid of my hair, sturdy as rope down my left shoulder, reached toward the earth. Slowly, I bent down, my skirt pooling like a waterfall around me, and picked up a shard of starlight from the ground. I pried the mica out of its small crater in the soil. It was the thickest specimen I had ever seen, with odd layers sticking out the sides like the pages of a beloved old book. In my palm, its top glinted like a vintage mirror, reflecting the diffuse forest light onto my face. As I turned it ever so slightly, the stone twinkled at me, and I flushed with a kind of child-like pride. It felt like getting a wink from my granny while digging in the dirt in my Sunday best.

In that moment, I became aware of two things—the heaviness of the self-doubt that had been hiding within me and the fact that the remedy was sprinkled all around. It felt as if the grandmotherly presence of the mica was whispering in my ear—"Don't worry, you are *good*, my girl." Nearly all my classmates were out of sight by this point looking for more exotic specimens, but I couldn't put down this piece of mica. It was a mirror, and the self-acceptance I saw within it was exactly what I needed in order to heal.

The breeze lifted the leaves of the maples and ruffled the hair at the back of my neck. My feet, planted in the same place, had warmed the surface of the earth to the temperature of my body so I could no longer tell the difference between my soles and the soil. The mica in my hand winked like Morse code and I received the message—it was so brilliant and simple I could weep.

The Earth *wants* us to see our goodness—because this is where the healing begins.

What Brought You Here?

Several years before my encounter with the mica, I had packed my car with everything I could fit from my tiny apartment in Brooklyn and had driven all day through a torrential spring rain to reach the Blue Ridge Mountains by nightfall. Having been accepted to the Chestnut School of Herbal Medicine, I left my whole life in the city to begin anew down south. At the time, I thought I understood what herbalism was. Looking back now, I realize I didn't have a clue. That first day in school, I was the only one in class who didn't know what a tincture was or how to make a cup of loose-leaf tea. I remember sitting awkwardly at the potluck lunch, balancing a full plate of food on my lap, barely able to eat. It was only a matter of time, I thought, before someone figured out I was a fraud. Looking back, I can still feel how strong my self-doubt was. Luckily, my fire to learn was even stronger. As I settled into the mountains, I dove headfirst into school, dedicating myself to an apprenticeship with Earth that would become a bridge into my life's work.

After graduating from herbal school, I started a small products business called One Willow Apothecaries. For the first few years, I sold herbal medicines and offered consultations out of my home. As I grew, the business grew as well—transforming from a straightforward herbal products business into a multidisciplinary school where people could learn to access their own soulful connection with the Earth. Into my teaching, I incorporated everything I was learning about how to connect with the living world—ecology, mycology, geology, and Earth-based mystic traditions. Soon, I began speaking at conferences across the country, submitting those first applications to present with only a few years of teaching under my belt, but with a passion as direct and distilled as an essential oil. I led retreats and took people out into the woods for immersive workshops. Eventually, I launched an online school. Today, over a decade since my first awkward day in class, One Willow has become an international center for education. And I have found my true calling as a guide, someone who helps people tap into their own profound connection with the Earth—and the ground of their deepest selves.

As my work evolved over the years, I kept encountering the same question: *How did you get here*? Whenever someone asked me this, I knew what they were really wondering: *How did you get to this place of making a livelihood from communing with the natural world? And how can I too?* But I can never answer this question without first talking about those early days in the mountains. And I can't speak to how I ended up in the mountains, bare-souled and seeking connection as if my life depended on it, without talking about what came before.

Everything you've experienced in your life is like the seashells ground to sand, that windswept shoreline that has led you to this moment. As strange and winding as the path sometimes seems, dipping in and out of the tide or disappearing into the surf, in the end, the path is always perfect because you arrived. Normally, when people ask me what brought me here, I say that I moved to the mountains to study the plants and stones—to be close to the Earth. The deeper truth is that I came to these mountains, and to this life devoted to the natural world, because I was in desperate need of healing.

After that long, rain-soaked drive down south to start a new life, I lived in a hostel for a week before I found the falling-down rental on the edge of town that would be my home for the next four years—a little blue cottage from the 1920s with a floor sunk so precipitously that I couldn't put a pencil down on the kitchen table without it rolling off. To me, the place was heaven. The cottage came with a quarter acre of grassy hillside into which I could dig a garden, a quiet bedroom for studying, and a view of the folding ridgeline above the valley floor—a horizon that would become my touchstone as I began healing from the exhaustion of everything I had been through in my transition to adulthood.

Although I was only in my mid-twenties when I rolled out my sleeping bag that first night in the blue cottage, a week before herbal school began, I had already experienced hard things in my life. A series of abusive relationships and trauma had marked my teen years, followed closely by debilitating health issues, including a chronic pain condition called vulvodynia. Affecting the muscles and nerves of the vulva and pelvic bowl, vulvodynia can range anywhere from mild discomfort to excruciating dysfunction. Unfortunately, I was on the extreme edge of that spectrum. I was in the middle of college when I was first diagnosed. Sitting in class most days felt like being perched on a bed of nails. I counted down the minutes until I could head to the woods to be alone, lying on the earth to cry and gather my strength for the next day. For the entire duration of my undergraduate years, you could say I was in two schools—Vassar College and the Healing

Academy of Nature. My time in the lecture halls of Vassar was intellectually stimulating, and I never lost sight of what a privilege it was to be a student there, but my time outdoors was my balm, my safe place, and my soul's classroom.

As a child of the Philadelphia suburbs, I didn't grow up intimately connected with nature. I knew that you could eat onion grass, and that bees stung, and that dark clouds meant a possible thunderstorm, but mostly it was just one indistinct watercolor to me. When I first developed chronic health issues, my interaction with everyone and everything changed—including with nature. When the pain was the worst, the only time I ever felt truly comforted was when I was in the woods. My wounds, though invisible to most people, were seen by the living world. With the trees and the creeks I could be my full self—aching, confused, searching, and sorrowful. I went to the woods as a wounded creature, and the forest embraced me as if I had never been anything but whole. The more connected I became, the more I could perceive the magnificent wisdom of the Earth. A life-long veil lifted from my eyes. With it gone, I saw that the more-than-human world was more sentient, intelligent, benevolent, and alive than I had ever realized.[3]

Now, after working with thousands of students and clients from around the world, I know this is often how we begin to heal our connection to the Earth. Disaster hits, trauma ensues, the hardship of life gets flaked into a point too sharp to bear on our own, and our spirit, seeking solace, flies straight through the screen doors that separate us from the wider world. When healing is needed at the deepest level, nature will always call us back home—not only to the oak woods or water-filled coves, but to the homes within ourselves that we've been alienated from. When speaking about those days of chronic pain, I often say that the world inside my body was so uncomfortable, I had to go outside. But I know now that the intelligence of my body was pushing me into the woods because it understood that if I visited the bright ponds lined with willows, these mirrors within the Earth, I would come home to myself. My body knew that this homecoming was the first step to healing—for myself, and for the world.

A Cheerleader for the Soul

There is an interesting ecological kinship between eastern China and Appalachia. Whenever this topic comes up, botanists will knowingly nod at each other. "The forests of eastern Asia and southern Appalachia are so similar," ecologist George Constantz remarks, "that if you were swept from one to the other you would be hard-pressed to tell them apart."[4] Some people hypothesize that the similarity goes back to the days of the super continent Laurasia, when these two areas of the world were close neighbors.[5] Despite being pulled apart by tectonic plates, these twin ecologies remained so similar over the millennia that many transplants from China do quite well here, including Japanese maples, wasabi, and Asian ginseng.

As it turns out, very ancient Chinese healing traditions flourish here as well. Still living in my blue cottage two years after I graduated from herbal school, I stumbled across a lineage of Daoist stone medicine that was also a transplant to these mountains. Carried into the coves here by Jeffrey Yuen, an elder teacher and eighty-eighth generation Daoist priest, the Jade Purity lineage of Chinese medicine endures as a unique gem in the tradition of Chinese healing. I was in my first year of Daoist stone medicine training with Sarah Thomas—a beloved local acupuncturist and teacher of the lineage—when I visited the old mica mine and found the bedrock message of my life: *The Earth wants us to see our goodness because healing self-judgement is integral to the overall healing of the world.*

The day after we visited the mine, Sarah's whole class met for a lecture. Spread out across a dark living room in the middle of a summer heatwave, twenty-five students were poised with their pens on the page, ready to record the *Ben Cao* for mica. Called a *materia medica* in the western world, a Ben Cao is the collected, written wisdom about a given medicine—in this case, a stone. Often culled from many different sources—including clinical experience, scientific studies, and ancient texts—the information in a Ben Cao can stretch back thousands of years. We had already received the Ben Cao of a dozen other stones; today we were going to talk about mica. With her students nestled together on the couch, Sarah began to illuminate just why mica is so medicinal. In Chinese medicine, healing is holistic; there is no division between the body, spirit, and mind. Stones are given as a prescription, just like herbs, and each stone has its own healing affinity. Mica's expertise, we soon learned, is its ability to reflect back to us our own goodness.

Called *Mo Xi Shi*, or Membrane into the Source Stone, mica helps us remember our divine nature, dusting away the cobwebs that distort our ability to see our own self-worth. Mica is a mirror, and what it shows us is our true selves. "Place a piece of mica on a client during a treatment," Sarah revealed, "and it will remind them that no matter how hard the journey has been, they're never going to forget who they are—a divine being who is inherently good." Like a cheerleader for the soul, mica reminds us that just by being who we are, we bring light to the Earth. Used in an acupuncture treatment, mica can act as a rebirth stone, bringing new beginnings to a beleaguered soul and a weary world. As Sarah spoke, I wrote as fast as I could, holding back tears. It couldn't have been a more perfect confirmation of what I had felt the previous day out in that mica-dotted forest. It was the affirmation my spirit had been seeking for a long time.

If I had been asked, during those earlier years of chronic pain, where the greatest ache was, I would have pointed to the fried nerves and muscle fibers of my pelvic bowl. No matter how much physical pain we are in, however, most hurts have their roots in our emotional soil.

When I first received the diagnosis of vulvodynia in college, doctors said my only recourse was to have surgery to remove nerve endings from this area of my body. After having spent all those afternoons in the woods—witnessing how the Earth healed itself after hard rains or hoar frost—I declined the surgery and decided to go my own way. It was a rocky, multifaceted road of healing that involved physical therapy, dietary changes, trauma integration, and the non-stop nurturance of the living world, but by the time I arrived at my little blue cottage in the mountains nearly five years later, I was pain-free.

The evaporation of the physical pain was a miracle, but even after arriving in Appalachia, a part of me knew that, like mica in all its many sheets, there were still layers to be healed. In the herbal world, we talk about the spiral path of healing. As you walk deeper into your path, uncovering the source of your strength and the gifts you were meant to bring to this world, you will revisit the same lessons over and over again. With each spiral, you reach a new level of completion, compassion, and understanding. True healing isn't linear; it's a labyrinth. As we walk, we have the ability to approach the old wound with new-found perspectives and matured strengths, accessing a new level of healing with each turn.

When we're holding a belief that isn't conducive to the overall growth of our souls, our spirits will try to get our attention through our bodies—sometimes with a condition or accident that is so overt we can no longer ignore what is going on within us. From there, we are taken on a journey through the layers of our emotional wounds, all the way down to the root where it all began—that first unaligned belief.

Standing in the forest that day at the mine, with a constellation of mica at my feet, I had what you call a light-bulb moment. I picked up that small mirror and retrieved a part of my soul. With it came the truth that I had been unable to admit to myself in the aftermath of my rough early adulthood, in the wake of my diagnosis, and through the years of healing that followed. Falling into pieces like the stars embedded in the soil, I finally saw what that hidden belief was—a thoughtform like a burr, stuck so deep in the fibers of my being it had, until now, been unconscious.

Somewhere inside of me I believed I wasn't good.

The Parent-Mirror of the Earth

There are many reasons someone might start believing they are not good. A sense of inner defect can expand malignantly with overt oppression, abuse, bullying, or neglect, but it can also grow subtly, fed from a million covert sources—from religious upbringings to social media. Most of us have had experiences in life that left us questioning our basic goodness, from not fitting in at school or failing to get affirmation from a parent, to experiencing a troll on social media or losing our jobs. For those of us who care deeply about social issues or the environment, simply looking at the reality of human-precipitated injustice can cause us to doubt not only our own virtue, but the basic goodness of humankind. At the center of many movements for repair is an implicit pessimism—an unspoken belief that humans, by our very nature, inevitably cause disharmony.

Even though I had come so far with my healing—from New York City to Appalachia, to the other side of chronic pain and down those first steps on my path as a teacher—looking into the mirror of that mica, I glimpsed the seed of my hurt. I saw the part of me that believed I was unworthy, unlovable, deficient, and hopelessly flawed—and I felt deep tenderness for this newly exposed piece of myself. I recognized with a shock how this belief in my own unworthiness was at the heart of all the hurt I experienced in my life, including my willingness to accept abuse, isolation, and overwhelm. I also recognized that I wasn't alone.

Whether we realize it or not, many of us spend much of our lives thinking we aren't enough. Underneath so many of the hardships we experience as humans is this erroneous belief. On a deep and very private level, we doubt our goodness, and that quiet worry is the very conclusion that has evicted us from our belonging—first to ourselves, and then to the Earth.

Before mirrored glass was invented, the only way we could catch a glimpse of our own image was through the natural world—calm waters, mica flakes, the onyx in someone else's eyes. Though today we have mirrors, cameras, and selfies, we still lack the ability to see who we truly are. With nature, however, there remains a place where it's possible to come into direct, caring contact with our soul. We need only look into the benevolent mirror of the Earth.

In healthy parenting, part of a caregiver's role is to mirror their child. When children begin to have an emotional experience of themselves as individuals, a parent's job is to reflect these feelings, along with the child's innate goodness, back to them so they can build self-worth along with necessary life skills. Many of us didn't experience enough of this early phase of healthy reflection. But no matter what our family of origin was like, we all continue to have access to this essential source of nurturance, because nature is the parent-mirror that will never forsake us.

On a very tangible level, nature is our lifelong caregiver. It is the source from which our lives are made possible, a mirror here to help us when we have lost sight of ourselves. Whenever we peek out from our hard places and hiding spaces, nature will reflect back to us the depth of our goodness—not because the denizens of nature are objects onto which we project ourselves, or because the more-than-human world lacks its own personalities and sentience, but because the beings of the natural world are our kin, our elders, and our teachers. As Potawatomi author and botanist Robin Wall Kimmerer recounts in her book *Braiding Sweetgrass*, "In some Native languages, the term for plants translates to 'those who take care of us.'"[6] We are the youngest children of creation. When we see ourselves in the wider world, we remember who we are.

Living in the purely human world is unnaturally hard on the spirit. The way our neighborhoods and communities are built today, we rarely get to be with the kind elders and mirrors of the more-than-human world. Is it any wonder that our self-perception has become so distorted? Meanwhile, the wider world has never stopped trying to show us who we are.

Some people think that nature is indifferent to humans, but I have found—through my own experiences, the stories of my students, and the wisdom handed down from nearly all Indigenous cultures around the world—that this simply isn't true. Nature is conscious, and it is caring. It *wants* to instill a healthy sense of self-compassion within us, because when self-love is intact, we truly become better citizens of the world.

In a recent study, researchers found that self-compassion actually increases our sense of responsibility, morality, and empathy toward others.[7] Stable self-esteem is also positively correlated with things like curiosity and a desire to challenge ourselves.[8] The ability to recognize our goodness is essential to becoming creative, compassionate, and inspired forces of change in the world. Seeing ourselves in the mirror of the Earth empowers us to take care of this place we call home and bring forth our gifts for the benefit of the whole. The Earth is asking us to look to the trees, the rivers, and the stones; because when we see ourselves reflected there, we become a part of everything once more.

In recent years, interest in natural medicines has exploded, but the deepest healing comes from the *relationships* the Earth is asking us to reforge. When I first started going to the woods with my pain, I wasn't just calmed by the aromatic chemical compounds of the trees; I was healed by the way they reached out to me. I still remember one tree in particular, a sprawling middle-aged maple that had been stunted from years of climbing students. I would visit this tree nearly every day, bringing small gifts like feathers I found, or stones shaped like hearts. I carried pieces of leather to try to mend branches that had been broken by climbers. When no one was around, I sang to the tree. Then, one day, I was walking the familiar trail when I felt a great ball of energy bound down the path and jump straight into my chest, like I was catching a puppy in the full throttle of a happy homecoming greeting. The feeling was so visceral it made the hair on the back of my neck stand up. For a split second I actually looked around for a dog or a person; the energy was that tangible. Then I glanced down the path and realized—it was the maple. My friend knew I was coming, and not only was the tree greeting me, it was welcoming me back. I felt something inside of me soften. *How could I possibly be bad, when I was so loved by this world? How could anything or anyone on this Earth be truly bad, when this world is so miraculously good?*

A Book of Mirrors

Everywhere on Earth there are mirrors, clear as mica, that will show you your goodness once more. No matter where you are—in the midst of your intricate self-doubt, your spiraling path of self-recognition—there will be welcome reflections, bringing you home like lighthouse beacons. Take a peek into your backyard—stories are there to hold you, comfort you, bring you back into the fold. Go looking for yourself, and eventually you will find mica. Common, spectacular, radiant, and familiar. Something many layered and made to translate the light. A being who is able to withstand the heat of these times and conduct the gifts you have been given into this life. You are so much more brilliant than you realize.

This book of essays that you hold in your hands is a palm stone of mica. Each page is a reflective layer here to help you see yourself. Crafted from stories in the more-than-human world, each essay is an affirmation from the Earth, a small mirror that will show you who you are and how deeply you are beloved. Every day we are handed messages that imply something is unnatural or dysfunctional about us—whether it's shame over how long it takes us to bounce back from loss, the belief that our sensitivity is a blight, the worry that we are too small to create change, or the fear that our traumas have damaged us beyond repair. Like a mica mirror, this book and the exercises that accompany each chapter are here to reflect back your worthiness, dissolving any man-made shame so you can begin to see how profoundly welcome you are in this world.

At the heart of this book is the belief that seeing our own goodness again is a crucial part of correcting course. The Earth is sharing these reflective stories with us, clear as quartz chips, because *self-compassion is a force of ecological healing for the world.*

Underlying these stories is an understanding that the central wound of our culture—the hurt that has caused us to distance ourselves from the Earth and create poisonous hierarchies of worth—is not the result of some fault in the human psyche, but the byproduct of trauma and self-judgement. As I once heard the Indigenous scholar and community organizer Lyla June share—paraphrasing the wisdom of her elder Patricia Davis—"[In our culture] we say that people are born not in original sin, but in original beauty."[9]

So many of us assume that if we want to change the world, we must first change ourselves, but this book proffers the belief that self-acceptance is the missing piece to healing. Only when we approach ourselves with compassionate understanding can we begin to access the latent energy, ideas, innovations, and revelations that will bring us back into communion with the Earth. When we begin to live from our original beauty, instead of the wounds that mire us in self-doubt, we bring the undeniable power of our creativity back into alignment with the wider dream of the world.

In this book we go on a three-part, mica-lit journey. *The Glimmer* from the natural world catches our eye and invites us to see ourselves more clearly, *The Mirror* guides this self-recognition into the gleam of self-appreciation, and *The Glow* enables us to embody a radiating self-compassion, a quality that is key to navigating this time of ecological hardship and cultivating the gifts we were meant to bring to this world.

At the center of this book is a question answered more simply than I could have imagined when I first pulled that glowing piece of mica from the ground. In an era of such deep ecological hurt, a time when all the traumas of our disconnection are rising to the surface, what are the gifts that we, as vulnerable, fallible, and incredibly caring humans, can bring to change the tide? Within this book of essays is the answer that this world is reflecting back to us, bright as a constellation of mica flakes within the soil.

Self-compassion *is* a gift for this world.

PART ONE
THE GLIMMER

Seeing Yourself

1

GARDEN EDGES AND PARADISE ON EARTH

SHE GLANCED NERVOUSLY around the room before raising her hand. Her arm was shaky, and I could tell that this was one of those questions that might come out with a few tears. She began her carefully rehearsed query, but by the end of the first few words I knew exactly what she was asking—and how to answer her. Every time I teach my Intuitive Plant Medicine program, a course where students learn how to connect to the consciousness of the green world, this question arises.

I often know it's coming because I can feel the worry rolling toward me like thunderclouds. Normally the confession goes something like this—"I love growing a garden, but since connecting to the plants on a deeper level, I feel so much guilt every time I try to weed or prune. What can I do?" Whenever I get this question I always smile warmly and send a wave of understanding. I know exactly how they feel— how many times have I, too, wondered if it's my place to pull an over- grown shrub or weed a dandelion root? The next thing I do, however, is give them the answer they didn't know they needed. Among their many benefits, beauties, and benedictions, gardens are here to teach us boundaries.

People say that gardening is not for the sensitive soul, and in some ways they're right. On the surface, gardening looks like all daffodils and days in the sunshine, but behind every flourishing flower bed is hard labor and even harder decisions. Pulling up weeds, pruning vigorous growers, controlling invasive species—gorgeous gardens are built upon boundaries and the difficult decisions they entail. In this respect, however, gardening is actually the *perfect* medicine for the sensitive soul. Gardens are graduate schools in the art of learning boundaries. I don't know any place where it is easier, or more obvious, to learn one of the core lessons of physical existence—that boundaries are what help us flourish.

So many of us were raised in a culture where we have no idea what good boundaries look like—or how lifegiving they can be. For the kind of soft-hearted people who are naturally drawn to activities like gardening, knowing how to draw a boundary between self and non-self is even harder. Open to the whims, wonder, and rich watercolors of existence, people who are sensitive are naturally less boundaried than others. Whenever someone warily raises their hand in my class to ask this question, I normally get excited to talk to them, because I know that I'm speaking to a highly sensitive and deeply compassionate person who is ready to work on their boundaries with help from the more-than-human world.

On the journey of realizing our own goodness, we will often be asked to start with defining, and holding, our boundaries. After all, how can we have compassion for ourselves, or recognize the immense care this world has for us, if we do not know how to delineate our self from others? How can we be a container for all the gifts that want to flow though us if we do not know how to shape the soft clay edges of our vessel? As much as spiritual traditions espouse the values of oneness, we can't ascend to such elevations until we first know how to cherish our own individual selves—the unique person we came to this world to be. You aren't just a self; you *have* a self. Though our unique souls are eternal, our bodies are a part of nature, on loan to us for the duration of our time here. When we can value and care for the selves we've been handed in this lifetime, we nourish and honor the creative earthen impulse that made us. This Earth wants to show you just how worthy you truly are—but first, you must learn how to tend the garden of the self.

A Garden Grows in Brooklyn

I first started gardening in an old tenement building a block away from the L train in Brooklyn, New York. Although my roommate and I lived on the second floor, beneath us was a tiny postage stamp of a backyard—a weedy, beaten, flat-baked place that was full of bricks and dirt the color of concrete. To us, however, the backyard was an oasis. From up on our fire escape, we'd gaze down at the spindly weeds and dream together of what it would look like with pink flowers, bell peppers, and bunches of basil.

One day we finally got up the courage to ask our landlord Mary if we could start a small garden. Mary lived on the first floor, so the entirety of the backyard was her domain. Already well into her eighties by the time we moved in, Mary was a veritable Brooklyn elder. Whenever someone asked her where she was from, she'd say that she lived on North 8th Street now, but that she was actually from North 7th—the distinction was incredibly important. Mary met her husband, the son of Italian immigrants, in the 1930s. I imagine the rendezvous must have happened somewhere in the no man's land between North 7th and 8th. Her soon-to-be husband had grown up in what was now our tiny one-bedroom apartment with all nine of his siblings, as well as both parents and grandparents. My roommate and I could barely fit our full-sized beds into the place, but somehow fourteen people had lived in this apartment. When she was betrothed, Mary left her land of origin to live with her husband's people, moving onto the first floor of the building on North 8th. I'm honestly not sure she ever got over it. With her husband gone, Mary was now the sole landlord of the house.

Mary was reluctant at first to give us her blessing, but we had seen that coming. Change wasn't Mary's favorite thing—how many times did we hear about how the new martial arts building across the street had once been the place to buy both hay and "powders"?—but after a few innocent smiles from us and a promise that she could have the final say in everything we did, the matriarch of North 8th Street gave us her blessing.

It took a long day of digging before we hit anything that remotely resembled dirt, and still we would have to bring in bags of clean topsoil for the new beds. Mary peered out periodically from between the cream curtains at her back window—curious, wary, but mostly just nosy in that gloriously Brooklyn way. Right from the get-go, there were treasures to be discovered. As we dug, we found the remnants of an old victory garden as well as hand-stamped bricks from the turn of the century, likely cast not too far away from our front door.

Even though I had spent the previous summer on a farm in Hawaii, I was still relatively new to gardening. Like most beginnings, I had sunflower-high hopes and enough pluck to forge ahead, despite knowing next to nothing about the actual skills required. With the help of some friends down the street, we built six small raised beds and got to work placing our herbs in their new homes. We seeded lettuce and marigolds and, having both all the confidence in the world and no hope whatsoever that this endeavor would actually work, we were stunned when everything began to grow. As they flowered and stretched toward the sun, each plant was a kind of miracle. We cherished them so much, in fact, that we began to neglect the cardinal rule of gardening by refusing to trim anything at all.

As any gardener knows, deadheading flowers and giving haircuts to your basil is essential if you want a bushy armful of abundance. But we were so in awe of the preciousness of these plants growing in the midst of all that Brooklyn concrete, we left them to their own devices. We watched them from the fire escape as if they were our children, let loose in the backyard without a bedtime. Everything grew leggy and wane, falling to seed by early August.

Amazingly, Mary became one of the garden's biggest fans—not that she didn't eschew any opportunity to complain about all the water being used or the tools left out in view. But really, it takes a hard heart not to go at least a little bit soft when a giant bush of bleeding hearts is blooming right outside your window. Even though we had won over our land-lady, I still felt like we had missed a crucial step in this whole gardening business. I was confused as to why our robust plot had called it quits so soon. In the intervening years I would learn that gardening requires equal amounts of precious reverence and powerful boundary holding.

If you want a truly lush garden, a space that produces at its full potential of abundance and growth, you need to prune and weed and cut and cull. I got one or two small harvests of herbs that first year; at the time I thought this was normal. Now, I know that you can make pesto nearly all season long if you simply keep trimming your basil. In fact, the more daring you are in cutting back the excess, the more you will be rewarded with growth. We started a garden because we wanted to learn how to take care of plants, but we ended up finding out even more about how to care for ourselves.

Gardening is something that humans have been doing for at least ten thousand years—even before the agricultural fields of the fertile crescent, humans practiced forest gardening and Indigenous land man-agement techniques now known as *permaculture*.[1] Interacting with the environment—weeding, seeding, and setting fire to underbrush—is a part of our collective heritage. When done in the spirit of respect and co-creation with the world, gardening is like being handed a small corner of the Earth's canvas and being given permission to create.

When you let go of the results and become devotees of the practice itself, gardening can be one of our greatest human joys—and one of our biggest teachers. Gardening took a short hiatus as a popular pastime after the victory gardens of WWII, but today, gardens are back in vogue with nearly everyone, Brooklynites included. The timing of this resur-gent interest in gardening couldn't be more impeccable, because of all the lessons gardening can bring to us—collaboration, plant communication, time management, and a sense of the cycles of life—perhaps the most potent teaching of all is the one we seem to struggle with the most in our world today: boundaries.

Bright Lights and Applesauce

For as long as I can remember, I've known I was sensitive. When I was a newborn, my pediatrician tested my "level of responsiveness" and declared to my parents, after the fifteen-minute series of prompts, that I was literally off the chart. Luckily for me, I had parents who honored my sensitivity as a physical reality of my body, rather than something that had to be trained out of me—my only wish is that every sensitive could have such a soft landing.

My parents rolled with the punches of my emotional maelstroms and dramatic reactions to everyday things. They still laugh about the time they fed me my first solid food—applesauce. Upon first taste, my eyes went wide as silver dollars and my whole body shook. They wondered if I was having an allergic reaction to this new introduction—until I opened my mouth greedily for another taste. Apparently, I did this with every single one of the next twenty bites, my nervous system lit up like a Christmas tree from so much novelty.

From an early age, it was normal for me to have my entire life colored by deep emotions—not just my own, but other people's as well. I was hyperaware that the things I did or said affected other people. I was cognizant of this because whatever they felt, I felt it too. This made me very quiet and observant while in school, only to let my hair down once I got back home to my comfort zone. Whenever my parents got report cards that described me as a reserved and mature participant in the classroom, they would wonder who these teachers were talking about.

My sensitivity often functioned as a kind of lodestone, drawing in peers—and later, partners—who were dealing with heavy emotions, mental instability, or weighty issues at home. At first, I thought everyone, like me, worked as a kind of grounding rod for the turbulent emotions of their friends. Then I felt like this was my special duty to perform, a belief that got me embroiled in a whole line of relationships—romantic and otherwise—that were entirely based on the amount of emotional sponging I was capable of doing. My sensitivity was a huge part of how I ended up in a series of abusive relationships throughout my early adulthood and what led my body to start manifesting health issues in the wake of those traumas. Depending on the situation, sensitivity can be both a gift and a challenge, but it is nearly always a vivid communicator. As natural empaths, sensitive people make excellent listeners, counselors, and healers. The problem is that without learning how to hold good boundaries, sensitives often end up attracting people and situations that drain their batteries.

In our society, we are often taught that sensitivity is a kind of character flaw. Many sensitive folks grow up thinking that something is wrong with them, when the truth is that sensitivity is a part of nature itself. In her groundbreaking book *The Highly Sensitive Person*, psychologist Elaine Aron shows that high sensitivity (or, as it is called in scientific circles, Sensory Processing Sensitivity) is a largely genetic trait marked by an innately more responsive nervous system. This trait exists in about 20 percent of the human population and can be found in over one hundred different species around the world. In her book, Aron highlights the essential qualities that define a highly sensitive person (or HSP)—a disposition toward deep thinking, emotionality, a brain that can process a lot of information at once, a high degree of self-awareness, sensitivity to complex sensory experiences like bright lights and loud music, and empathy.

In our stimulating modern world, these traits of high sensitivity can sometimes feel like a hindrance rather than a help, but according to Aron's research, having high sensitivity in the genetic pool is evolutionarily advantageous. HSPs, who are finely attuned to subtleties, are often the first to notice small signs of danger, as well as the budding of new opportunities. Highly sensitive people are also primed to perform the more subtle or esoteric roles in societies. Many HSPs are naturals in the role of shaman, priestess, seer, healer, or diviner.

For all their gifts, however, highly sensitive people spend much of their lives learning how to deal with the wide-open gates of their bodies, navigating the inevitable overwhelm of having more nebulous boundaries. An overwhelmed nervous system can look like many things depending on the person and their life experiences. In people socialized as women, one common reaction to overwhelm is tears or other forms of emoting. In those brought up male, however, overwhelm can look different. Because they are so often told that displays of emotions are "unmanly," from a young age, when sensitive men get overwhelmed, they may tend toward shutting down.

I'll never forget when I first started seeing my partner, John. We had been on several dates already and had stayed up late into the night talking about our childhood, family dynamics, and previous relationships. He shared with me that people in his life, particularly former partners, often got upset with him for being emotionally insensitive. I almost laughed out loud. In the handful of dates we'd been on, I already knew enough about this man to understand that the *exact opposite* was true, and I told him so.

"You know," I said, "I think you are actually *highly* sensitive. Maybe what your previous partners read as indifference was actually you in a state of overwhelm." It was like the blinds were pulled back, illuminating a whole room he had never explored. Needless to say, coming to understand that he was actually a sensitive person who was prone to nervous system overwhelm, and not an indifferent oaf, completely changed his life, as well as our life together. Today we call our home The Highly Sensitive Sanctuary, and one of our main goals is to create a space where we can both feel safe to be our wonderfully sensitive selves.

Even though I grew up in a family that accepted, and was aware of, my sensitivity, finding Aron's work validated me in a way that gave me strength to be myself and encouragement to begin the work of fortifying my naturally porous boundaries. Once I clued into the deeper realities of my sensitivity, I looked back and found that my tango with boundaries was at the core of many of the issues that plagued my life, including anxiety, overwhelm, insomnia, and toxic relationships. I began to recognize that, like many sensitive people, I had developed a strategy of self-preservation that was actually working against me—namely, saying *yes* when I really wanted to say *no*.

When you feel other people's emotions so intensely, acquiescing to someone's requests for your energy can feel easier than dealing with the fallout of saying no. This protection strategy, however, is a kind of slow-motion self-sabotage. When I was younger, I said yes to all kinds of things I actually, on a deeper level, wanted to say no to—jobs, friendships, parties, social roles, and romantic entanglements. Being so naturally boundary-less, I often had trouble understanding what it was I actually wanted. I was so focused on creating feelings of ease and affirmation in my surroundings that I lost connection to my own inner desires. It felt easier to just go where other people's strong emotions were pointing me and figure out how to untangle my truth from the mess sometime later. Through the process, I ended up getting lost in the weeds.

As a sensitive person, your inner sanctum is like an open-air temple: it is naturally more accessible to the winds of the world. In order to protect the sanctity (and the sanity) of our inner places, we need to learn how to be discerning gatekeepers. The word *garden* comes from the Middle English *gardin*, meaning "a walled place or enclosure." If you are someone who identifies as sensitive, empathic, or compassionate, learning how to erect positive boundaries is the only way to nurture the garden within, to create a space where you can experience the depth of your goodness and the flowering of your gifts.

What Is Not You and Does Not Belong in Your Space

Looking back, the entire decade of my twenties seems like one big Operation board game—*how can I extricate myself from all these draining relationships without touching a nerve or triggering the alarm?* After such a long stint of being a people pleaser, the energetic surgery of shifting my relationships caused a lot of waves, but through the process I became dexterous. As I worked in the garden, both within and without, I began to understand how beautiful a boundaried life could be. The word *paradise*, after all, comes from the modified Greek word *paradeisos*, which means "enclosed park or garden." In the end, boundaries don't hem us in; they set us free.

I still remember the first time I actually felt my own boundaries. In my sophomore year of college, a local Reiki practitioner rented out the top floor of a Victorian building on campus to offer training to interested students. A Japanese healing technique that involves channeling energy through your body and into another person, *Reiki* is similar to the Christian concept of the laying on of hands. After so many Western medical treatments failed to bring relief for my chronic pelvic floor pain, I was intrigued by the idea of energetic healing.

To help us get a sense of what energy *felt* like, the teacher asked us to rub our hands together to create friction and then slowly, palms facing one another, pull our hands apart. I felt as silly as a first grader in a clapping game, but I swallowed my pride and rubbed my hands together with vigor. I didn't expect to feel much as I started to inch my hands apart but was stunned to have the distinct sense of a rubbery fullness in the space between them. Later, we did the same thing, except we turned our palms outward so we could feel the edge of our own personal energy. Unsurprisingly, this one was a bit harder for me to feel, but eventually, hands hovering about a foot away from my body, I could sense a subtle ripple, like the tension on the surface of water. This, the teacher told us, was our *own* energy field, something we would need to learn how to take care of if we were going to do work with other people.

I once heard an Andean shaman describe evil as "anything that is not you and doesn't belong in your space." When we come to recognize our boundaries, we get clear on what is actually life-giving, versus what is life-draining, for our particular selves. During the intervening years of learning boundaries—years where I would eventually go deep into the subtleties of what was helping me flower versus what was stunting my growth—my gardens would become my greatest teachers.

When an emotional or energetic issue needs our attention, like our boundaries, it will often make itself known through the body. One of my clients calls this her "storyteller body." Our bodies are experts at communicating, sometimes quite loudly, when an issue needs addressing. In his book *When the Body Says No*, renowned physician Gabor Maté talks about this connection between emotional stress and physical illness, pointing out that a lack of healthy boundaries can create so much stress in our system that we become vulnerable to chronic conditions.[2] As Maté summarizes succinctly—"if you don't know how to say no when you need to, your body will say it for you in the form of chronic illness."[3]

After Brooklyn, I moved to five different places over the next ten years in Appalachia, planting and leaving a garden in each one. By the time I was on my third garden in the mountains, I had healed my chronic pain and had ended most of the majorly draining relationships in my life, but I was still working on the more subtle particulars of what it actually meant to have life-giving boundaries. Looking back, this was the perfect time for me to contract Lyme disease.

After a long camping trip in Minnesota, I came back home to Appalachia with some odd symptoms including strange bodily aches and a sense like my mind was a helicopter that couldn't land. Within a few weeks I was diagnosed with Lyme disease and began a treatment protocol that would last several years.

Lyme disease is a tick-born infection caused by an ancient bacterium called a *spirochete*. Spirochetes are unique because they can cross bodily boundaries that regular bacteria can't—like the blood/brain barrier. According to some researchers, within a week of infection, the bacteria that cause Lyme disease can move into your brain. To this day I maintain that there is no better way to learn about boundaries than to meet a spirochete.

One of the things I noticed early on when dealing with Lyme was that when I did the things I *wanted* to do, *when* I wanted to do them,

I always had enough energy. The moment I tried to make myself do something I didn't really want to do—have another phone conversation with a friend who needed to unload, answer emails, attend a birthday party—my energy tanked. During those years, the only things I could do that wouldn't wipe me out were more self-focused activities, especially reading, writing, meditating, and gardening. At first it was hard for me to accept that I was allowed to take care of myself before I tended to others, but as I learned the subtlety of what my body, my energy, and my boundaries truly required, I began to heal.

I had already learned the power of saying no to things that were clearly taxing my energy, but I had needed a teacher as potent as Lyme disease to help me learn more about the subtle nos—the ones that are just a shade more colorful than the yeses, those nos that are like butterfly wings, unfolding for a moment to reveal the color that lies on the other side of this decisive moment, before disappearing again into the tiniest pen-line of possibility. The truth is, those subtle nos are often the hardest to say yes to. Luckily, when it comes to teaching us about the gradients of boundaries, the hard, and soft, contours of the garden offer no better place to learn.

Reclaiming the Garden

The land was quiet under a quilt of snow as I huffed all my belongings up the two flights of stairs toward home. It was midwinter, and I was finally moving into what I hoped would be my final home in Appalachia. I bought the house right before the new year, and by the time I got back from visiting my family for the holidays, the pipes had frozen. That first day I had to haul buckets of water up from the creek in order to clean the floors. I was alone, the house was frigid, and I couldn't have been more delighted. After a decade of moving from place to place, I finally found a space where I could plant a forever garden. Set in the elegant V of a lush holler, just a few acres from the top of a mountain ridge, the land was everything I could have dreamed of. I couldn't wait for spring to come.

Where I live in Appalachia is the definition of lush in the warmer months. Old-timers say that on a hot day, you can literally watch the kudzu grow across the pavement. It is a place that is full of water, light, ancient soil, life—and some of the greatest diversity in the temperate world. In some ways, growing a garden here is easy; the valleys are full of fertility and the hills are soaked in the summertime by near-daily thunderstorms. If you don't wear a dress during the warm season, you'll likely find it in the back of your closet covered with a sheen of mold. The abundance of water makes life unstoppable here, but it also makes gardening the ultimate master class in boundary holding. Gardening, boiled down to its minerals, is a process of deciding what you would like to cultivate and letting the world know that you are claiming this space for growth. In a place where there are so many opportunities for life to take hold, it is the task of a lifetime to learn how to draw a line in the sand and say no.

That winter, I began to walk the contours of the land, dreaming of what would grow there once spring softened into being. Soon after I moved in, I found a dented folio in the back of a closet with an old edition of *Southern Living* magazine. Opening to the page marked by a faded Post-it note, I found myself staring at my house. Or, more accurately, the spectacular gardens that used to surround it. Skirting the creek and spiraling out from the north side of the cove was a rare woodland flower garden, breathtaking enough to have been featured in this distinguished periodical.

The original owners of the house had started what would become their masterpiece nearly twenty years ago. Squinting out the window, I could still see the edges of the stone walls they had built. I matched them with the photos to imagine how the land might look come spring. Those first early days of warmth did not disappoint. My small cove was filled with tiny flowers, gentle daubs of blue and yellow. But pretty soon I realized that this was not the same well-tended Eden captured in the glossy magazine photos. The impeccable lushness I saw in the pictures, the diversity and color and communities of rare plants, didn't just happen on its own—it had been cultivated.

In the interim years, after the original owners had moved on, a couple from Florida bought the home as a rental property, and the garden was left untended. The new owners had hired a landscaper to keep the grass mowed and the paths mulched, but no one made the subtle, everyday decisions needed to keep the garden. No one decided that the hydrangeas were becoming overgrown or that the hostas needed more space to thrive. The result was that the pushiest plants overtook large swaths of what had been a diverse wonderland. Come June, I realized that the beautiful garden from the magazine was now an overgrown tangle of giant-sized shrubs and waist-high weeds—I had a lot of work ahead of me.

The Soft and the Hard

In landscaping, as well as in ecology, there are two types of boundaries— hard and soft. Hard boundaries are things like stone walls or fences, large boulders in the earth, or a stream bed. They are semipermanent and difficult to cross. Soft boundaries are a bit more malleable. In the garden, a soft boundary can be created by amending one half of a bed to house acidic-loving plants or cordoning off a section of your yard to grow roses. Weeding creates a soft boundary, as does planting a thick groundcover or a shade tree.

Well-planned gardens almost always begin with setting down hard boundaries—any landscaper knows that hardscaping comes first. Deciding where certain walls or features should go makes the rest of the garden flow like water from a fountain, naturally finding its contours. In the bounds of a human life, our early years are usually when we learn about how to set down those first hard boundaries— what we deem acceptable, the kind of behavior we will allow, or the requests we feel obliged to fulfill. The way we were tended, as well as the way our families and communities modeled boundaries, are all a part of the hardscaping of our life—and an intrinsic aspect of the living world. Boundaries are everywhere in nature. They are the soft curve of a wren's nest, a mountain range, the bee's sting, a wolf's bark, and a bear's scent. Boundaries are how nature not only protects itself but creates so many different niches of diversity. The boundary of the Appalachian Mountains, after all, is what prevented the last glaciers from stretching further south, allowing these coves to become a nursery for all the plants that would eventually reseed the northern part of the country. Learning boundaries is an innate part of nature's upbringing.

Through experiences that both compromise and clarify the territory of our own being, we learn to set down the boundaries needed to define the contours of our particular garden. Depending on our life experiences, the hardscaping of those boundaries can look quite different. Some folks reach adulthood and their gardens are deeply welcoming, but overwhelmingly undefined. Others reach maturity and their gardens are a bit like mine in Brooklyn, full of a few feet of soil but surrounded by nearly impenetrable concrete. It can be discouraging to find out just how loose, or inflexible, your hard boundaries have become. Like the boulders in the middle of the garden, however, hard boundaries aren't forever; they simply take more effort and elbow grease to move around.

When I started developing relationships with people outside my family, including my first love interests, I was clear about my hard boundaries—I knew I wouldn't stay in a relationship in which I was being physically harmed—but I was pretty unclear about what my soft boundaries were. This hazy understanding of my soft boundaries led to a string of early relationships in which emotional abuse crept in like weeds at the corners, choking out the seedlings of my self-esteem and confusing me about the strength of what I had thought were my boundaries.

When I first moved into my new home, I assumed the hard boundaries of the garden were relatively intact, if only a bit buried by overgrown plants. There were boulders featured in the center of the garden, stone walls, and a large barn that offset the rest of the landscape. As spring crept onward, I began to realize just how compromised the hard boundaries of the garden had become when all those soft boundaries had gone untended. The stacked stone walls were dotted with thick hedgehogs of fern roots, and exposed boulders had become hidden under years of uncleared leaves and saplings. Buried a foot down in the soil were the remnants of what was once a stone lined path—I used a digging bar to pry each rock up. Through the garden, I worked on rebuilding the stone walls of my boundaries, stacking them straight again so I could truly thrive. Hard boundaries and soft boundaries are both important, but often it is the soft incursions—the daily subtleties of what we want to cultivate in our space and what we do not—that define whether a garden is a garden or just an overgrown patch of weeds.

Soft boundaries are subtle boundaries—those that are more easily crossed—but creating them is what allows us to become true artists in the garden. Interacting with soft boundaries gives us the opportunity to decide what exactly we want to grow in our life. Soft boundaries don't ask: *What does your forever yes or no look like?* They ask: *How do you feel today? What is the no for this moment, for this week, or for this season?* I may pull up a whole tangled root system of a hydrangea because I am feeling a no for that particular season and then I may decide to reintroduce that same plant there next year. It doesn't change the fact that I don't want it now.

They say that the soft landscape is the *living* aspect of your garden. Just like weeding, tending the soft boundaries of our lives entails making decisions on the day-to-day details of how we want to live. They are the subtle decisions about what we want to spend our energy on—like whether to call back a friend or go for a quiet walk instead—and every time we make one, we cultivate our lives. As the writer Annie Dillard says, "How we spend our days is, of course, how we spend our lives." When our boundaries are too soft, when we allow any seedling to take root in our soil, we rob ourselves of the space and time we need to grow into our true potential.

Cultivating the Life You Want to Live

That first year in the garden was chock full of hard choices. Large mats of the original plantings, like celandine poppy and epimedium, had grown over many of the more delicate communities. Invasive species like garlic mustard had colonized the hillsides, and hydrangea bushes had taken over every sunny spot as far as the eye could see. Part of me didn't want to touch a hair on anyone's head, and another part of me realized that if I wanted a garden that was full of beauty, diversity, and delicacy, I would need to set some boundaries.

Even though I was clear on the precious lesson this garden was handing me, it was still hard to pull out a certain plant, especially when I enjoyed its flowers or knew its medicinal benefits. Sometimes I would leave the plants where they were, even though I was irked by the space they took up. Just like my wonderfully sensitive students, I still struggle at times with the feeling that I don't have a right to decide who stays and who goes. That first year, I left whole swaths of the garden over-grown. But inevitably I returned—months, or even years later—to get more heavy-handed. Afterward, I always breathed a sigh of relief. We often need to do more pruning and culling than we think.

Your life is your garden, and you are the one who decides what grows in it. As much as lawn care companies would like you to believe that there are "good" and "bad" plants, there is actually no such thing. A weed is only a plant that is growing in a place where you'd like space for something else. The same is true for all the many soft bound-aries we have to set down in our lives. Each opportunity you have to say yes or no is an invitation to learn more about yourself—who are you? What do you desire? Creating boundaries is the way we begin to understand what the gardener within us wants to cultivate in this life.

The decisions we make surrounding our boundaries can be a grad-ual process—we don't need to get everything right on the first go. Before implementing a permaculture design, permaculture teachers often recommend that you spend the first year in a new landscape simply observing. Similarly, we need to spend time with ourselves in order to understand the subtleties of our own slope and sunlight and desire. We need to give ourselves space to explore our inner terrains so we can begin the lifelong task of learning our boundaries and asking questions of ourselves: What is mine? What isn't? What do I want to cultivate here? Boundary definition is an ongoing art.

When it comes to the garden of our lives, we cannot control what seeds blow in on the wind, or which perennials, planted long ago, return. But we can control who stays. We can make a decision based on what we desire and what, ultimately, feeds us. Whenever a student raises their hand to ask me the inevitable question about pruning and weeding, I get excited, because I know exactly what they are *actually* asking—Do I have permission to hold a boundary? Can I really grow what I want to in this lifetime? Am I allowed to take up space on this Earth? Am I worthy enough to claim the resources I need to flourish?

And the answer is, always, *yes. Yes, you are.*

We are the gardeners of our life. The Earth has given us each a small plot to cultivate so we can learn how to become empowered co-creators on Earth. When European settlers first arrived to Turtle Island, they assumed they were walking into the Garden of Eden, and they were— but not because the continent was an untouched place. What those first colonialists saw as unspoiled wilderness were actually finely maintained and soulfully tended gardens. Ample evidence has surfaced in recent years that our most beloved "wilderness" spaces could be more accurately described as native gardens—places of abundance that were expertly managed by the Indigenous peoples who have called this land home since the beginning. Even the rainforest, the epitome of wilderness in the Western mind, is likely one giant permaculture garden. As humans, we have a distinct ability to help create paradise on Earth, but it begins with tending the enclosures of our own beings and recognizing that our innate sensitivity is the gift that allows us to hear what the world wants to create with us.

Chop Wood, Carry Flowers

While the end results of our efforts are rewarding, gardening isn't really about fruit yields or flower counts; it is about the joy of the process. For the first few years I gardened, I thought the measure of my success was how many cans of tomatoes I put up or how many pole beans I plucked. It was an exhausting relay in which I never crossed the finish line. Soul-nourishing, boundary-revealing, and deeply healing gardening, however, isn't about reaching a final destination, as it is about experiencing the curative effects of ongoing cultivation. As the old Zen saying goes—"Before enlightenment, chop wood, carry water. After enlightenment, chop wood, carry water." Gardening is a lesson in finding peace amid the long journey of growing into the person you came here to become.

That first summer in my new home, in the midst of all my weeding, I had the roof redone. I knew immediately who I was going to call. Fernando had once been my neighbor when I lived further out in the county. A highly skilled and singularly good-natured man, Fernando had immigrated from Mexico to one of the most insular communities of these mountains long before I had ever even heard of the Blue Ridge. It's not easy to be any kind of outsider in these hills, but it is a particularly hard climb if you are a person of color. The welcome has gotten warmer over the years, but in the past, these tucked-away communities were notorious for their distrust of newcomers. When I think about it, I'm awed by the sheer strength of will, and self-belief, it must have taken for Fernando to move here during a time when virtually no outsiders were welcome—to start a business and become so successful that he was eventually able to bring over his entire family.

Smooth-faced into his fifties with a smile that lights up both eyes, Fernando is a bit of a Buddha. Calm and even-handed, he has an inborn ability to see the long view, though perhaps this is just the nature of an expert roofer. While his nephews worked on the shingles, we chatted about our various house projects, his infamous yearly empanada party, and our forays into homesteading. In the middle of our conversation, he pointed to the yard and exclaimed with authentic joy, "what a beautiful garden!" My first reaction, of course, was to try to downplay his enthusiasm, going over in detail what the garden *could be* and my efforts to help it transform. He listened to my whole anxious tirade and nodded. With a peaceful smile, he shrugged and said with equanimity, "Give it five years."

Five years. Five years! In a world where we want a website to load in less than a second and financial transactions of millions go through on the same day, five years feels like an eon—but the moment he said this, I felt liberated. Five years meant I could take my time. Five years meant I didn't have to do anything now. Five years meant that it was not about some end goal of having the perfect garden, the perfect life, the perfect boundaries, or perfect self-knowledge. It meant that the journey itself was a gift that I could experience.

It takes a while to build soil. It takes a while to figure out the best place to plant a rose bush—and how to prune it. It takes a while to create a garden that feels like it is a true reflection of your soul. But when we say yes to tending the boundaries of our life, slowly, with sensitivity and connection, we begin to transform our reality.

Setting Boundaries to Change Your Reality

The better I got at weeding, the more the flowers flourished. The more time I spent in the garden, the more I learned how to root in myself. Over time, gardening taught me to feel more comfortable saying no to the subtle encroachments on my space—emails, social engagements, overwhelming media, and my own people-pleasing tendencies.

I had expected to feel good once I fortified the gates of my inner garden. I knew I'd have more free time and probably be less stressed and more nourished by all the nos I was proffering—but what I didn't expect was for my entire perception of reality to change.

Sensitivity is a door that swings both ways. On one side of the hinge, it is easy to become overwhelmed. On the other is a world full of vivid aliveness, fed by the deeply emotional beauty of existence. When I protect my outer borders, I have more inner space to actually experience the world around me. With better boundaries, my nervous system is free to take in all the subtle, sensuous details of life. The more I focus on these fine aspects of existence, the more my reality changes. Time slows down. The days seem slower and more luxurious. I am less worried about where I'm going and more apt to buy an ice cream and sit by the creek. I find myself stopping to admire a flower, wondering how I never noticed the technicolor joy of it all. The constant quiet stream of self-doubt ebbs away and surprising springs of self-contentment bubble to the surface.

When I create a walled paradise in which my sensitive self can thrive, I am quicker to laugh and to forgive myself for my foibles. Life seems infinitely brighter, more charming, and full of humor. All of the shifts I have always wanted to make—to slow down and enjoy the moment, to let go of future tripping and embrace my goodness—come into focus. It is as easy (and as difficult) as making a boundary.

I remember back to the self who began that Brooklyn garden—the one who had no idea of the importance of hard and soft boundaries, the girl who was still embroiled in draining relationships, in the midst of healing from chronic pain, and just a few years away from contracting Lyme disease—and I know she would be so amazed to see where she has ended up.

Two years after arriving at my new home and rebuilding the walls of the garden, I felt ready to expand the inner sanctum I had created. John, my highly sensitive sweetheart, moved in with me, and a whole new life-giving chapter of my life began. The Highly Sensitive Sanctuary was born.

When we set boundaries in our lives, we reclaim our lifeforce. We say to the world that we deserve to be here and that we will carve out the space and time that we need so our gifts can flourish. When we set boundaries, we bring vividness and color not only to our own lives but to the lives of all those around us.

Boundaries open the door to coming into a reciprocal relationship with nature itself. When we learn how to protect and enshrine our own selves, we naturally develop a healthy respect for the agency, autonomy, and boundaries of all beings—creating spaces where every creature's sovereignty is recognized. When you honor your boundaries, you naturally cultivate respect for others. When you care for your own personhood, you open your eyes to seeing the world as a collection of animate individuals who deserve the same kind of enshrinement. In a culture where a lack of understanding and respect for boundaries can be seen everywhere—from how big business tramples the landscape, to the colonialism that colors our history—learning how to hold good boundaries is a kind of repair-work that can help heal the world. If we, as a culture, knew good boundaries, would we still frack mountains or dig under the mantle of the earth for oil? *Boundary making isn't a selfish endeavor, it is a lifegiving reorientation for the Earth.*

Inside of you is a power. That power is made of the gifts that you were meant to bring to this world—your sensitivity, your compassion, and the bright brilliance of your caring heart. Nourish the walls of your own inner paradise, and like hothouse roses blooming all season long, there will be no end to the bounty of what you can offer this Earth. Set your boundaries, and you will become a gardener, not only for your life, but for a world that is coming home to itself.

EXERCISE:

Cultivating Your Garden

The following exercise can help you begin to recognize the contours of your own garden—what needs to be weeded and what wants to be lovingly encouraged. Be brave, be honest. Step into your role as the head gardener of your life.

1. We all have people in our "inner circle," those people we spend the most time with or who take up the most bandwidth of thought or care in our lives. Make a list of the top ten people who come to mind.

   Beginning with the first person on your list, imagine that this person just called you or showed up at your door for a visit. Write down your immediate visceral or emotional reaction to seeing them. Be sure to use feeling words as well as physical descriptions of any sensations inside your body.

2. With this information in tow, create a physical map of all these people in your life. Place yourself in the middle, like a shade tree at the center of the garden. Intuitively place each of the ten people somewhere in the surrounding landscape. Where are they in relation to you? Where are they in relation to each other? Get creative with colored pencils or objects on a tabletop. Now step back and look. . . . How do you feel about this garden constellation?

3. Try moving people around in the garden. In front, behind, out to the edges, closer. This will tell you who to set boundaries with. Notice how you feel with each move. Imagine this is a map of your dream garden and each person is a plant. Where should they be?

4. Make a note next to each person who you decided to move further away from you. Write down what actions you could take to help them find their proper place in your garden. Whenever guilt comes up, try telling yourself, "I am the gardener of my life, and the living world is fed by any boundary I make that supports my own light."

5. Anytime you need to, you can redraw this constellation or create it with objects somewhere in your home. Move the people and plants around, and know that these small representational gestures will create a ripple in your larger reality.

Try doing this exercise with anything else in your life where you need to clarify your boundaries, including work projects, home improvements, and so on.

2

FLORIDA INNER WORLDS

IN CALM WATERS it's possible, with the right turn of oar, to move as quietly as the current itself. Navigating the lazy ripple of the Florida springs, I practiced dipping the paddle in and out of the river. Beneath our canoe, fish swam inside water the color of sky. Herons took to the treetops as we passed. Every once in a while, we'd catch the eye of an alligator or the playful tail of a river otter slipping like a ribbon into the bright bowl of the water. It was mid-February and I was stripped down to a t-shirt. I was alive, and the day was so brilliant it felt like it was ringing.

Hours prior, my small troupe of friends and I had arrived at the public boat launch to begin our three nights of canoe camping. These particular friends come down to Northern Florida—the ancestral lands of the Timucua, and later, the Creek people—every winter for at least a few weeks of birding, swimming, botanizing, and citrus eating. Many of them spend large chunks of their year camping and living off the land. I was comforted by the depth of their wilderness know-how—one of them only allowed himself a smoke if he started the fire by friction. These are deeply skilled human beings. I, on the other hand, brought a bag of store-bought snacks, my fresh enthusiasm, and a willingness to hold a paddle. Luckily, for my friends, this was sufficient.

As per usual on the weekend, the dock was busy with families toting coolers and big-muscled sports boats. Small fish dallied in the shallows just a step away from old wrappers scattered like sea foam along the shore. It was both jovial and saddening to be among the crowds—to see the happiness of people enjoying nature, but also to be faced with the upsetting reality of humanity's trash, trampling, and noise. We, with our cotillion of canoes, were eager to start the journey.

Sitting atop a field of limestone, Florida has a particular porousness that lends itself to the champagne rise of vast amounts of crystal-clear water. Some of these natural springs are so profuse they form wide rivers, while others trickle in as corridors and can be paddled for miles, the close-fitting vegetation creating an emerald cave over the water. The headwaters of some springs are so clear, you can see straight to the bottom of their eight-foot caves; divers can regularly be found plunging into their depths. In winter, cold-intolerant West Indian manatees migrate to the springs as well, luxuriating in the constant seventy-two degrees Fahrenheit of the earth-warmed waters. For someone who grew up just a short drive from the silty, cold, mid-Atlantic shore, these crystalline springs were a revelation, and I couldn't wait to enter their world.

Gathering our camping gear, we put our boats into the water and began to paddle. Just a few miles downriver from the dock, things quieted dramatically. The mind of humanity began to thin as the forest grew thicker. The birds became more frequent, and even the river seemed to deepen, as if it were more full of its own being. Developed Florida, the parts that humans have claimed and made into strip malls and amusement parks, can feel as spiritually flattened as a sandbar. But paddle out into the middle of the wild Floridian springs, and you will find a dimensional paradise that never ceased to belong to itself.

My love affair with Florida had begun several years prior to this camping trip, when I was in herbal school. As a class, we took a trip down to the North Central woodlands to study the plants. It was the first time I had ever visited an undeveloped part of Florida, and it felt like crossing through the gates into heaven. Growing up, I only knew Florida as the land of Mickey Mouse, retirement complexes, and air conditioners. The one time my family visited, we flew into Orlando, went to Disney World, and then headed right back home. I had no idea that these breathtaking wild places even existed, or that Florida's nature is so mind-blowingly diverse.

Often, we are handed half-stories about a place, person, or culture. We see the part, and we assume we know the whole. The moment we think that a half story is the full picture, however, is the moment we lose touch with the truth of how magnificently complex every being truly is. We can no more *know* an entire place than we can understand the experience of every denizen that lives there. World of river canyon and dune, whale song and bee dance—the complexity of the worlds that we inhabit is staggering.

Florida, wild Florida, holds many worlds. The evergreen oaks and hidden rivers, tropical flower forests, and life-soaked everglades. This thin peninsula, with a gulf on one side and an ocean on the other, is one of the most ecologically diverse places in the United States. Each niche in Florida is a rich tableau of color, perspective, and diversity—wild citrus groves and dolphin-filled coves, abalone-colored beaches, and ancient shell middens the size of white-columned estates. The sheer uniqueness within the diversity of Florida's ecology sets the heart spinning. From the panhandle to the everglades, this long state holds a dizzying array of habitats, including estuaries, sandhills, tropical hammocks, scrub, and upland and bottomland hardwoods. Florida is listed as a global biodiverse hot spot, which means it has over fifteen hundred endemic species. It also means that it has lost over 70 percent of its original habitat.[1] Florida has been described by many as an ecological treasure that is slowly being lost to saltwater and a sea of humanity.

From where I live in the mountains of Western North Carolina, it's just an eight-hour drive in midwinter to go from snow-dusted hillsides to the subtropical haven of Florida's northern interior. In the winter, mountain folks head down to Florida to get a break from the cold, and in the summer the Floridians come up to escape the heat and mosquitos. Both places are geologically connected as well. Once upon a time, the Appalachian Mountains were as high as the Himalayas and tipped with quartz. Over millennia that quartz eroded across the entire southern part of the country, washing down the thousand-mile watershed to become sand on the beaches of northern Florida. Sometimes I wonder, as I sift the blonde grains through my hands, what this quartz, like the crystals at the center of our computers, might still remember from those early days of this continent.

Florida in winter is a stained-glass heaven backlit by hibiscus and ripe oranges. Every February, I make a pilgrimage here because it is a place where I can glimpse the diversity of worlds that still live inside this world—the places that never stopped belonging to themselves. I come because, when I immerse myself in these unique spaces, I remember the preciousness of my own inner terrain. Being in the Florida springs is a kind of baptism. Wading into their crystalline waters, I wash away the over-culture I feel expected to fit into and go skinny-dipping in the clarity of my own being. In Florida, in the thick of winter, I come home to my inner world.

The Hillsides of the Mind

As a child I lived entirely in my own world. I was always a dreamy kid, liable to twirl off into fantasy from the springboard of any moment. Many highly sensitive children are described as "being in their own world," both because their own worlds can be a respite from the overwhelm of the wider world, and because they tend to have vivid imaginations. For me, my own world was not only where I decompressed from the stress of everyday life, it was also where I mined inspiration and creativity. When I look back on those early childhood days, they seem to shimmer with wonder and confidence. All this began to change as I grew older and more enculturated. Over the years of schoolmates exclaiming "Earth-to-Asia" or my teachers remarking on my unfocused daydreaming, I began to feel ashamed of my inner terrain. Observing the expectations of my culture, I started to realize that wandering in the hillsides of your mind was seen as antisocial, odd, and perhaps most sinful of all, unproductive.

Like many children, the message I received was that there is only *one* world—the "real" world—and that I would be remiss if I didn't join it. As I grew up, I began to understand that remaining in my own world was seen as not only dysfunctional, but distinctly selfish. By the time I entered high school, arriving with that particularly pain-tipped teenage desire to fit in, I had abandoned my inner home. It would be years before I remembered the truth—that we do not live in *one* world, we live in *many worlds*, and that this multitude of worlds is what makes our planet so distinctly special.

I still remember when I made the conscious decision to shelve my inner world for good. I was in ninth grade and knew that, starting that year, every academic move I made would count toward my application to college. I always knew that attending higher education was important to me, so I wrote a sign, misspelled, that said "colege" on my desk and purposefully put away the daydreams so I could learn how to concentrate on what was right in front of me.

Looking back, I recognize this willful dedication as a blessing—it taught me how to work steadily and maintain focus—but I also see it as a time of distinct loss. In order to excel in school, I purposefully discarded the visionary depths and distractions of my inner world. While academia rewarded my single-minded dedication, my spirit never stopped crying for me to come home. I distinctly remember this moment. What I don't remember, however, are all the unconscious inputs that first led me to believe that leaving my own world was necessary, not only for academic success, but in order to be a "good person."

At some point in my early years, I picked up the belief that residing in my own world was unforgivably self-absorbed. The deeper this belief rooted in my being, the more I worried that being ensconced in my own inner experiences would signal a lack of true care for others. For a sensitive person, the idea of being seen as selfish or uncaring felt like a death knell, so I slowly abandoned my own world. The more I forsook my inner experiences, the more my sensitivity became hyperfocused on the people around me. As a natural empath, I became an ever-vigilant spider on a web that was not of my own making. Along with finally learning how to study, I spent much of my adolescent years training myself to be so delicately in tune with the experiences of others that I often forgot the soil-deep sensation of what it felt like to inhabit my own terrain.

I thought that the most caring thing I could do for the world was to put myself as wholly as I could in someone else's shoes, forsaking my own inner experience so I could better understand theirs. As a result, I ended up in relationships with people who were hurting and wanted to escape their world by handing it over to someone else. Outside of class time, I threw myself into social justice work and running various charitable clubs until I had whittled down my nighttime to just a few hours of sleep. I thought that this kind of world-adoption was the only way you could help someone heal or be of service to the one "true world." The moment I decided I would adopt another person's world, however, was the moment I orphaned my own. It would take me years, and a quiet paddle down Florida's wild springs, to understand that there was a way to honor and care for all worlds, but that it always began with honoring the niche that is your beautifully intricate inner terrain.

Campus Rambles and Coming Home

By the time I got to college I had forgotten what it felt like to be rooted in my own experience. I became the kind of person who, when asked, couldn't decide where to go for dinner because I was so distanced from my own desires. Unsurprisingly, the further I departed from my own world, the more I suffered. Through my newfound focus, I had made it to a venerable, high-powered college with excellent academics and a beautiful campus. But less than a year after I arrived, I began suffering from the chronic pain symptoms that would eventually lead to my diagnosis of vulvodynia. Living in other peoples' worlds was literally draining me of the energy I needed to maintain my own. The sicker I got, the more I realized that I wouldn't get better until I could, very literally, come home to take care of myself.

Deciding to come back to myself was like returning to my hometown and finding that what had once been a field was now a forest—I had to reacquaint myself with my terrain. I started meditating and journaling. I read spiritual books outside of class time and went for long walks in the woods to assuage my chronic pain. Though the school itself was an arboretum, my favorite walks took place across the street from main campus, on the four-hundred-acre stretch of ecological preserve called The Farm. There, among the white pines and walnuts, I first began to see my own experiences mirrored in the Earth. I stumbled across deer in the early nubs of spring and tracked long-legged herons to the pond. I learned to nibble spicebush berries in the winter and catch the flying seeds of jewelweed in the fall. Once a barred owl watched me from a midday perch before flying off in full silence.

The more I left main campus to connect with all the alternate realities that surrounded me, the more I realized that there was no end to the number of worlds that we live among—and that each one is incredibly important. The deer and jewelweed showed me, through the flash of tail and the burst of seed, that the idea of only one world was not only woefully inaccurate but was a source of damage for the Earth. Our disregard for the multitude of worlds is part of what justifies the short-sighted rational of filling in a swamp to build a housing development, or bulldozing a forest to build a strip mall. In a culture where the worlds of hawthorn or heron doesn't count for much, we cease to see just what we, and the Earth, are losing when those worlds disappear.

Walking at The Farm, I saw that I lived in a world of many worlds—the worlds of sassafras and spider, cloud and creek—and that *my* world was equally as important and ecologically sacred. The maples and mushrooms that grew there helped me realize that taking care of my world wasn't selfish—it was a vital act of ecological tending.

Amazingly, the more I gave myself permission to be in my own world and to do the repair work needed to feel at home there, the more easily I could meet the many worlds around me—being in my own world gave me incredible respect for every being's reality.

I'll never forget the day that I realized, with a shocking thrill, that my experience of the magnificent many-armed oak outside my window was completely different from that of the gray-eared squirrels that collected the tree's acorns. That year I had won a coveted single room with a view out the third floor of my dorm building. From that vantage point, I saw the oak as a distant hydra, an ancient sea creature poised among the green grass. From a squirrel's vantage point, however, the tree was an ocean of bark, limbs like horizons and a latticework of perches leading up into the sky. When we see something differently, we develop completely different experiences of, and relationships to, reality. The tree I knew was not the same tree that the squirrels saw, which was different still than the tree's own experience of itself.

There isn't one world, one perspective, or one truth—there are only the precious many. Experiencing this naturally unfolding epiphany, I began to see how this recognition of the many worlds, including my own, wasn't a hindrance to justice, societal healing, or interpersonal understanding—it was the only real way to connect. When we can honor difference as being sacred, and our interaction with difference as being a distinct privilege, so many of the rifts in our society can heal. When we value diversity, we make space for all worlds to be equally seen and valued.

We can never fully know what it is like to live in another person's world, but the more securely we can root in a love for our own world, the more we can interact with others from a place of true humility and awe, carrying an awareness of just how special each world is. We don't live in one world, but many, and this manifold world is asking us to recognize the generative power of our own unique ways of being.

Returning to our inner worlds is a kind of ecological revolution. It is an important step in inoculating our culture with belief systems that honor all life on Earth, protecting diversity in all its forms. In every moment, the denizens of this world are co-creating together. We can only become effective collaborators, however, when we cherish all the worlds we encounter—beginning with our own. *Ecology* is often defined as the study of the relationship between organisms and their environment, but I think it is more accurate to describe this branch of science as the observation of the relationships between *living beings* and the *living land*. I didn't know it at the time, but my off-campus rambles were the beginnings of my understanding of what a true ecology is—a complex map of living consciousnesses, overlapping, interacting, and dreaming a wider whole.

Creating at the Wellspring

I often do my best writing when traveling. Untethered by all the tiny tugs at my attention, I can put down the fishing line of my mind, and its tendency to cast itself into the streams of other people's lives, to find my own flow. Camping in nature is one of the easiest ways for me to return home to this inner river—even better if I get to a particular campsite by boating down a quiet, bucolic stream.

After a full day of paddling the Florida springs, stopping to eat lunch under a watery canopy of Spanish moss, we set up camp that first night in an abandoned citrus grove. We shook out our tents and got a pot of wild rice boiling over the fire. Everyone opened their knapsacks to put together a meal, and we ended the evening by eating a small mountain of tangelos, scattered like carnelians everywhere underfoot.

The next morning, I snuck away with my journal to write before the day fully rose.

Early morning is my favorite time to be on the water in Florida. The spring-fed rivers maintain the temperature of a perfect early-spring afternoon, no matter what the time of day. On cold mornings a fog-like steam rises from the warm body of the water, floating ethereally across the crystal surface. Being among the vapors feels like walking between the worlds. Every time you glimpse an ibis wading through the mist, it is as if you witnessed a thought become tangible. That morning I nestled against the buttress of cypress roots, letting my feet touch the water's edge, and I wrote until the sun rose high enough to burn the surface clear again. My thoughts were like visions glimpsed through untouched waters. I watched excitedly as new ideas rose in a well-spring to the surface.

Back in Appalachia, I had been struggling creatively. The ideas for this book were pinging around somewhere in my consciousness, but like pet parrots set loose into the woods, they had become too wild to capture. I had spent a few frustrating days before I left trying to get some words down, ending up with a single page that I soon scrapped. But on that misty morning, nestled into a very writerly chair of cypress roots, I was being given access to the menagerie within again. I had turned my attention to the depth of my inner world, and the possibilities now seemed—like sun dapple on the water's length—endless.

When asked, most authors and artists will tell you the same thing— if you are creating with other people in mind, crafting your artwork to appease or perform, the work will inevitably be hollow. By contrast, if you create from a place of deep connection to the muse of your own personal terrain, your work will be something the world has never seen before. Our creativity is intricately tied to our ability to allow ourselves to be in our own inner worlds. It is from here that we can begin, in collaboration with the rich imagination of the other beings with whom we share this planet, to co-create another world. Letting yourself be fully immersed in the weather-whims of your own organic way of knowing and experiencing is more than just a luxury of individuality; it is a radical act of reclamation, and the first step in the process of re-wilding our world.

An Animate World

If we want to see the world around us return to life, we must first be able to recognize all the artisans that *give* it life. There is no better way to open your eyes to the masterpiece of all worlds, including the one within, than to revive the ancient worldview of animism. *Animism* is the heritage belief system of humankind. Though animism disappeared in some parts of the world with the arrival of human-centric religions, in other places, especially land still tended by its Indigenous peoples, animist belief systems continue to underpin entire societies. In animism, everything is seen to be awake and alive, animated by an intangible essence that one might call *Qi*, spirit, soul, sentience, or simply lifeforce. Everything from baskets to stones and ideas to archetypes is seen as having its own self and inner being. Animism is, in essence, a religion of personhood. It is a belief system that acknowledges our world as a co-creation among equals. As scholar Graham Harvey succinctly summarizes, "Animists are people who recognize that the world is full of persons, only some of whom are human, and that life is always lived in relationships with others."[2] Animism recognizes that our Earth is not defined by a single artisan but by a complex weave of creators, each with their own distinct sentience. Within this framework, it is only a gentle leap to understand the core tenant of many animistic belief systems—that consciousness *itself* is what creates the world.

Within many animistic cultures, the idea of mind over matter would sound like a silly transmutation of the truth—mind *creates* matter. On Earth, the amazing variety of consciousness is what gives life to the diverse tapestry of our world. From an animist perspective, the consciousnesses, or inner worlds, of all the beings on Earth co-create this reality. It is one giant weaving, and each of us has a strand. This tapestry is made with even more intricacy when we are able to cherish the uniqueness of our own consciousness and its amazing world-creating abilities.

Many people yearn to see a great change on Earth, hoping that we will be able to step off the path of ecological harm and shift back toward a more life-honoring, environmentally conscious way of living. This change, however, will only happen with some deeply creative thinking—the kind of thinking that only arises when we are committed to the wisdom and imagination that exists within. In animism, the world that we co-create with our unique geniuses is a kind of beautiful dream that each and every one of us gets to participate in. But our power as dreamers of a new reality requires being willing to surrender as deeply as we do in sleep to the currents of our own inner visions.

Dreaming into Being

For as long as I can remember I've been a vivid dreamer. Every morning I awake with at least one remembered story from sleep, and my mind naturally dips into daydreaming. Growing up, I swallowed the cultural fable that such inner wanderings were the simple fiddlings of my subconscious mind, so I never saw them as the incredible storehouse of creative material that they could be. From an animistic perspective—one that values consciousness as the driving life force behind the creation of physical reality—dreaming is not simply the random firing of our brains; it is a remembrance of our time dwelling in an intangible, but very real, realm of being. As visionary dream teacher Robert Moss summarizes, "Dreaming is traveling. We journey effortlessly beyond body and brain, into realms beyond the fields we know in ordinary life."[3] Dreams, including daydreams and reveries, are the way we zoom out to the edge of our consciousness, learning to feel its texture and possibilities. Dreaming is a direct line into the very part of ourselves that is helping to dream our lives, and this world, into existence.

Our dreaming selves are our most creative visionaries. Many famous artists, leaders, and inventors have cited their dreams for some of their most brilliant work. The famous Beatles song "Yesterday" came to Paul McCartney through a dream. Einstein credits one of his dreams with inspiring the theory of relativity. Harriett Tubman led seventy people to freedom with the help of her visionary, prophetic dreams, and Niels Bohr, the father of quantum physics, first saw the structure of an atom while he was asleep; he was later awarded the Nobel prize for this discovery. Even daytime dreams are valuable points of connection with our wider consciousness. Research shows that daydreaming, once deemed a childlike character flaw, is linked to greater creativity, as well as the ability to find novel solutions to problems, receive insight, and increase productivity.[4]

I can attest that, in writing this chapter, I have spent quite a lot of time staring out the window and daydreaming in the midst of tackling a particularly tricky paragraph. After allowing my mind to wander for a spell, I return with just the right phrase. Dreaming, in all its forms, is an invaluable way to connect to our own inner worlds and the creations that wish to move through us. When we dream, we wake up to the truth of our larger reality—that we are beings of consciousness on a deeply creative journey.

In Western culture we've begun to call the layer of consciousness that we explore through dreams the *dreamtime*, a term borrowed from the Aboriginal cultures of Australia. Known by many names in the over 250 different Aboriginal languages, the Aboriginal concept of the Dreamtime is an entire epistemology that includes cosmological order, creation stories, lifeways, and ancestral law.[5] For those of us who did not grow up in an Aboriginal culture, it's impossible to comprehend the incredible complexity of the Dreamtime. That said, like a seed that traveled across oceans to help re-diversify a depleted world, the word *dreamtime* has become planted in the Western imagination, and it is helping us understand a very elementary aspect of life—*that dreaming is an access point to consciousness*, and that this realm of the spirit is as real as the hull of my canoe pushing through calm Florida waters.

In English, Aboriginal words for the Dreamtime are often translated as "the eternal or uncreated" or, even, the "all-at-once." In Aboriginal belief systems, The Dreaming is how our world was created and how it continues to be made anew every day. Dreaming created boulder opals and marsupial wolfs, dolphins, and unique species of bush flowers that bloom in only one place on Earth. Dreaming created me, and it created you, and it created the unique world you inhabit, including the creative gifts that you alone were meant to bring to this planet.

Once upon a time, every niche of our Earth was a land dreaming itself into being, living in its own exquisite world. The desert and its loom-patterned sand; the high mountains with their icy howl; the swamp-lands with their long-legged egrets, cypress knees, and warm-centered storms. This world was a multitude of worlds, and that multitude was what made this Earth magnificent. One day human beings appeared and, as I believe all of our ancestors would tell it, we too became a part of the dreaming of this world. For a long time, this is how we both lived and defined ourselves.

We still live in a world of deep diversity, dreams that are as variant and symbiotic as a murmuration of starlings. Yet so many human beings today fail to recognize the agency and potency of such worlds because we were not taught to honor our own. We were created to be dreamers, and that dreaming is most powerful when we occupy the small space that is *ourselves* in the multitudinous whole. We have dimmed our ability to dream, and so we have forgotten how to nurture the dream of this world. But all of that changes when we finally come home to our own inner shores.

Dancing Teacups and Talking Toasters

Hanging out with my Florida flock of friends never fails to make me feel like a kid again. Maybe it's all the orange juice, or the skinny dipping, or the fact that I get to play nearly all day, but I always come back home from a paddle trip in Florida full of spirited joy. On the last day of the trip, we spotted a star lily on the shoreline and spent a humorous few minutes trying to maneuver our flotilla closer to get a look. During our paddle to our campsite for the night we had to get out and portage over a fallen tree in the river, and one person's pup, eager to get a look at a heron up ahead, fell with a splash out of the boat. Later, as the stars began to come out, we fed dried palmetto fronds to the fire and one of my friends initiated a sing-along. By the time the Pleiades were visible, we were all harmonizing. Living alongside the multitude of worlds that exists in nature—world of frog, of fern, of fungi, each one adding to the perfection of the overall chorus—you are fully released to be exactly who you are. No matter where I am in the world, every time I let myself be in my *own* world, I return to that childlike elation of recognizing that I am a part of the wider family of life and that my voice is important.

All of us began our lives on Earth in our own worlds. If you've ever been around a young child, you can recognize immediately how entirely, and wondrously, ensconced they are in their own imaginative experience. Many of us think back on our early childhood with nostalgia because we remember how supremely good it feels to inhabit that world. When we reminiscence about our childhoods, we sometimes get a pang of homesickness because we miss the way that world felt.

Our culture tells us that living in these imaginal realms is incongruent with the realities of growing up, but what if our first responsibility as adults was to *reclaim* our inner worlds? What if the true marker of adulthood is the maturity to be able to acknowledge your own experience so completely that you could authentically honor all other individuals on Earth as the subjects in their own stories as well? When we know what it is like to inhabit our own world, we can begin to imagine what it might be like to live in the world of a loon, an elm, a tumbled stone, and we can start courting a relationship with these neighbors.

Children are masters at accepting the living world around them. They know they themselves are alive—people with feelings, emotions, and desires—and so they innately assume all other beings are as well. Without being taught to doubt the value of their own subjective experience, kids naturally live in an unquestioned world of subjects who also have their own personalities, preferences, and perceptions. Toasters that talk and teacups that dance and trees that are our best friends.

Slowly, however, most children learn that subjectivity is viewed in our culture as innately flawed.

The debate over *subjectivity* (the idea that everything we know is innately influenced by our inner experience) versus *objectivity* (the concept that there is one knowable truth that exists outside of our personal experience) has been going on in the Western world ever since we had terms to describe both viewpoints. Today, children learn early on that if they want to understand how the world truly works, they need to leave their own subjective realities behind. But taking ourselves out of our own world in order to know the truth of the wider world simply isn't possible. We live inside of a self, with a unique brain chemistry, life history, and positioning in the gyres of cultural and political systems. We can pretend we don't live in our own particular world, resist that world, dim it, quiet it, or strive to be somewhere else, but we never actually leave the globe of our own beings—not fully.

I remember being frustrated as a child with this whole concept of objective truth—I struggled with subjects, like math, that demanded a single answer. Even though I was a voracious reader, sometimes I failed the state-wide tests because I couldn't believe the comprehension questions weren't an invitation to do some creative writing. If I wanted to succeed on tests, as well as within society, I learned that I would need to leave my own world behind—but it turns out that there are a multitude of cultures on Earth that get along brilliantly, and with much more well-being than our own, through harnessing the power of our innate subjectivity.

Animism naturally espouses an intersubjective worldview, one that sees reality itself as existing in the relationships formed between beings. What is *real* is not some objective truth, but the lived experience of what is shared in the space between subjects. Life itself is an experience, as scholar Elina Helander-Renvall writes, of "a subject-to-subject sharing of presence."[6] In many Indigenous cultures, which are largely animistic, people learn about a particular plant or environmental process, not by removing themselves from the equation, but by being fully in their own relationship *to* it.

From this standpoint, the truly important task of adulthood is not to become more objective but to embrace our subjectivity as the very thing that makes these relationships possible. By firmly rooting ourselves in our own wonderfully subjective worldview, we acknowledge that every being on Earth has their own truth. We naturally begin to honor all forms of diversity—ecological, biological, religious, racial, cultural, and experiential.

In a culture that has so esteemed the ideals of objectivity, and the world of lifeless objects it breeds, is it any wonder that we have drained and paved and built over so many worlds? When we come home to our own inner worlds, the world as we know it changes. All the things we thought were just imaginary fantasies—the dissolving of injustice, the healing of ecological scars, the harmonization of the human and more-than-human communities—could become reality.

The Tenderness of the Return

We tried to make the last hours of our trip as long as possible. After paddling halfway back to the landing dock, we pulled our boats over into a particularly scenic sea glass–colored cove and took out a set of snorkels. Happy to push our arrival back a few hours, we all spent the afternoon floating with our faces down, gazing into another world.

Even though my lungs are made to be bellows for the air, I have always felt like my spirit could breathe easier beneath the waves. Watching schools of fish float by in silver and blue, I forgot about the upper world altogether, letting the back of my neck go red under the sun's gaze. I tried to remember to reapply my sunscreen as I kicked along in the cove, taking breaks from looking into the world below to float face up, arms out like a starfish.

Held by the water, connected by its very molecules to every other creature who was also being touched by its flow, I closed my eyes. Swathed in afternoon warmth, a soft pink cocoon of light, I began to think about all the years I had spent denying myself this pleasure. The years of trying so hard to care for everyone else's worlds that I left my own behind. Those years where I so deeply, so dearly, missed my home. Tears slipped unseen from the corner of my eyes, the wellspring inside of me joining with the flow of the river itself. I seemed to feel everything—the gift of this time, the longing to remain here forever, an ache over the state of the world, all the suffering each of us experiences, the bliss and the communion that have been here for us all along.

I cried for the manatees who are wounded by motorboats and yet keep swimming, visiting us like mothers on the rivers, so forgiving, gentle, and kind. I cried for the land itself, all those worlds lost to development. I cried for what Florida once was—exquisite, diverse, and multitudinous—and I cried for the unbelievable beauty that still remains. I cried to know that I was invited, exactly as I was, to participate in this gorgeous collective of dreaming worlds.

I belonged. I belonged with manatees and pure spring water. I belonged in my world. I belonged to this world. I had come home and would never leave again.

I would be returning to my normal life in just a few short hours, but I felt ready. Rooted in my own world once more, I saw possibility shimmering everywhere around me. I allowed my imagination to light the path ahead like sunrise on the water. In a dreaming world, a conscious world, in a world so full of worlds, healing is not only possible, it's inevitable.

This business of returning home to our inner worlds is a tender one. Just like revisiting our childhood, coming home to ourselves can bring up a whole swirl of emotions—hope, elation, activation, and grief. Sometimes people worry that if they let themselves be fully in their own world, they won't be able to feel, or empathize, anymore with the wider world. But I've found the exact opposite to be true. When I am in my own world, I am even more open to the tenderness of all worlds.

Being in your own experience doesn't mean you won't feel the feelings of others or experience heartbreak over the plight of this Earth.

It means you can feel it like the Everglades can feel a storm. You can embrace it fully because you have the resources to bear it. You have not drained your swamps or turned your inner terrain into a plantation for sugar cane—all sweetness, and flatness and one-dimensionality for the sake of societal demands. When your world is strong enough and complex enough, you can face anything. When you allow yourself to ground in your own inner being, you have enough roots and wind breaks, hollows, and sheltering coves to bear any storm.

With this wider and deeper perspective, we are able to participate in writing a new creation story now—one that talks about how we, as humans, learned to come home again and take our place as co-dreamers in this world. Inside each of us is a creative seed that we are being asked to bring to the wider world. As George Bernard Shaw wrote, "Imagination is the beginning of creation." Each of us was born with the imaginal ability to help bring a new world into focus. All we must do is allow the transformation to take place.

Inside every caterpillar's body is a set of cells that holds the DNA codes for the butterfly—scientists call these cells *imaginal cells*. After climbing inside the cocoon, a caterpillar's body completely dissolves, becoming a soupy ocean of DNA. The imaginal cells arise out of this chaos with the keys to the caterpillar's winged transformation. Curiously, when these cells first get to work, the immune system of the caterpillar attacks them, thinking they are alien invaders. The previous incarnation of the caterpillar does not recognize these imaginal cells as a part of its own being, who they are becoming. Ultimately, however, the imaginal cells establish their foothold, and the caterpillar transforms into a butterfly.

As we begin to transform ourselves into a people who enshrine our own beauty alongside the generous collaborative nature of reality, a part of us, or our culture, will doubt, block, judge, or resist such a shift in vision. But this transformation of becoming *even more ourselves* has never been more needed on this planet. Your world is more important than you could ever know. The tools, strategies, dreams, and creations that are meant to help us move forward are embedded like rubies in the matrix of our unique soil. So give yourself all the time you need to daydream, to envision, to come home. It is not selfish to go within; it is an act of regeneration akin to undamning a river.

We, as a world, are in a time of deep metamorphosis. The things we see falling apart are indicators that it is time for our imaginal cells to come forward with the plans they have been incubating all this time. Every act of dissolution is an act of beginning, and inside of you exist the keys to help envision, support, and birth this reincarnation. Allow yourself the tenderness of returning to your own world and there, if you let it, will be all the tools you need to help give our future wings.

A Reverie

Have you forgotten what it feels like to be in your own world? Have you spent too long sojourning in other people's universes to know what your own ecology even feels like anymore? Here is a soft reverie to help you remember.

You are floating on your back in a cove of crystal-clear water under-neath the gaze of the sky. The sun settles down upon your chest, warm as honey. Each limb is weightless. Nearby are river otters—you see them diving and fishing and moving like playful angels among the cathedral-arched roots of the cypress. Beneath you in the shallow, sun-warmed water is white sand and grass that waves like music. The seventy-two-degree water that is moving past you now has lived inside the earth for thousands of years. You are the first human this particular upwelling has ever touched. It holds you, cleans you, and loves you as equally as it loves the star lilies blooming like spinning fireworks by the bank. There is nowhere to be but here with yourself among your kin, among the fellow dreamers known as *otter, grass, sunlight, water*. There is nothing to think about but your experience of all this buoyancy, beauty, and light. You are whole, in a world where every single being is born whole as well. You know, in your bones as hollow and weightless as bird feathers, that you have given all you need to be a part of this beautiful world. And in this moment—perfect, light-filled, weightless, and held—you are home.

EXERCISE:

Childhood Worlds

Sometimes we need to go back to a time before our imagination got paved over to access our own inner world once again. Take some quiet time to sit and reflect with a pen and paper on the following questions.*

1. Remember a time in your childhood when you felt safe being in your own world. Where were you physically or in your imagination?

2. What did you like to do in your world? How did you feel there? Try to use as many descriptor words as possible.

3. What beings from nature were in your world? Plants, animals, clouds, and rivers? How did you interact with them? In what way did they enrich your world?

4. What were some of your most common daydreams as a child?

5. If the child you were then could say anything to you now, what would they share?

Note: If it doesn't feel comfortable to go back to your childhood, try reimagining your experience as a loving adult who can offer your inner little one space and safety to dream. You can give your inner child now, in your imaginings, what you would have liked to have had then.

3

THE SEASONS OF TRAUMA

IT'S LATE OCTOBER, and the maples stretching over the deck have finally faded to gold. I know more colors are to come—pumpkin orange, deep ochre, and ember—but today the change is just beginning. I take a break from writing this chapter to look out the window, my mind needing a moment to stretch from the page like a cat rising from sleep. As I watch, a single leaf falls, lazy as a snowflake. I can see my kitten Tula on the porch, her tiny tortoise-shell face turned upward, watching the trees with interest. I have to remind myself of how precious these moments are. A thousand leaves may fall this season, but for this one leaf, this is its first time in flight. In moments like these, when I am fully present to the minute details of the Earth's turning, I can't help but appreciate how miraculous the seasons are.

One of the greatest blessings of living in these mountains is watching them change—from snow blanket to wildflowers, thick summer canopies to brilliant fall ridgelines that fade into the blue of winter again. I don't remember noticing the seasons much when I was a child.

They were simply a part of the background of my experience, like a soundtrack you never listen to closely enough to pick out the lyrics. But when I reconnected with the Earth as an adult, I began to relish the seasons as that which gave texture, meaning, and rhythm to my life—not to mention untold beauty. I know of no greater joy than the turning of the seasonal wheel. After the long slog of winter, those first flowers of spring seem like angels. On the heels of April rains, my bones are truly ready for the heat lamp of summer. The cool of fall is a balm after the sunburn of August, and winter's quietude gives me lasting peace after such a busy season of harvest.

If there is any topic that will never go out of style among poets, my mountain neighbors, or ecologists, it is the seasons. As the cadence that shapes all of life, the seasons are the very foundation of our experience on this planet—but it was never a given that we would have such beautiful diversity woven into our lives here. If it hadn't been for a major disruption in the early days of the Earth's growth, we would never have known the changing symphony of winter, spring, summer, and fall. Nor would we be able to experience the more nuanced tides of olive, humpback whale, apple cider, and cherry blossom season. None of these seasons, so celebrated and essential, would exist if it weren't for a singular trauma, an upset so great it changed the Earth forever.

The Impacts That Shape Us

The early days of planet formation are a hectic time. In those first eons, fledgling planets are endlessly knocking together in a dance of forge and collision. The last of these dances, called the giant impact phase, is often what gives a planet its final character. Earth experienced ten different major collisions with other astronomical bodies over this time, each one shaping our planet. According to the Theia impact theory, however, the last collision took the cake. Around 4.5 billion years ago, Theia, a massive rocky orb the size of Mars, hit our Earth with such force that the planet turned spontaneously molten and was knocked so far off-balance that the tilt of our globe was permanently shifted. Today, instead of spinning upright, Earth leans at 23.5 degrees, a cant that sets the globe rotating at an angle in the sun's light. As our planet dips her crown toward and away from the sun, the resulting dance of shadow and warmth births the variations known as the seasons.

With the exception of a narrow band around the equator that is nearly seasonless, all of Earth's life is defined by seasonal shifts. Sugar maples burn into embers as they sense the sun's changing. Geese fly north in broken necklaces as summer sets in. Peepers tinkle the tiny bells of their voices as spring begins. The sheer profusion of habitats, niches, flowers, fruit, migration patterns, species, and subspecies is all due to this tender tilt in the Earth's gait.

If we were in ballet class, this kind of off-centered pirouette would be seen as an imperfection, but our tilt is what makes Earth the incredible place of diversity it is today. In fact, if we had stayed turning in a perfectly upright axis, most species we know wouldn't exist. Russel Foster, a professor of circadian neuroscience at the University of Oxford, hypothesizes that, without our tilt, life as we know it would be entirely different. "[There would be] fewer species with much less diversity in form and behavior," Foster speculates, "It is also possible that life would not exist at all. As we have a huge diversity of life-forms, there has always been some species that have been able to bounce back after major extinction events."[1] Without our seasons, Earth may never have become the ocean-blue planet of life that it is today.

When it first happened, this collision was a catastrophe for our planet, but Earth's meeting with Theia ended up being the impact that gave us life. The seasons that are so essential to our thrival here on Earth are the result of trauma—and its subsequent healing. They are the aftermath of an impact so immense it changed everything, and yet it was this very event that set us on our journey. The way our planet carries herself in the wake of healing from this literally earth-shattering event is what has given us this precious gift known as life. Her resiliency has much to teach us in the wake of the collisions that have colored our own lives.

Trauma is a natural part of being alive, yet so many of us have shame around the things that have hurt and changed us. We assume that what we experienced shouldn't warrant the dislocation we feel. Or we worry that our alteredness somehow makes us less lovable. Our traumas, however, are not the things that have damaged us beyond repair, but the impacts that have gifted us our unique dimensionality.

What if our personal traumas were not just the boulders that threw us off track—but the very encounters that gave us our gorgeous season-ality? What if those impacts, and the natural grace of how your body, heart, and mind have learned to heal, are responsible for the sheer diversity and depth of the gifts you embody today? As Peter Levine, author of *Waking the Tiger* and founder of Somatic Experiencing writes, "Trauma has the potential to be one of the most significant forces for psychological, social and spiritual awakening and evolution."[2] When we lean into the gravity of the Earth's own story, we see that the most devastating impacts on our existence never came to destroy us but to show us the beauty that can sprout from how we regenerate in the wake of these life-changing events.

When the World Flips Upside Down

It was the last few weeks of November. We had yet to have a true cold crack, but the afternoon's steady rain had turned into a light flurry by sundown. The cozy part of me wanted to curl up and enjoy this first dusting of winter, but I had plans to meet my partner John's family in town for dinner, so I rallied. I pulled on my hiking boots and stowed a pair of nicer evening shoes in a tote bag. I turned on the porch light for when I would come home later and stepped out into the gray glow of evening.

I should have known to turn back as soon as my feet hit the steps. Underneath the cotton-thin layer of snow the rain had hardened in a glittery sheen over the wooden planks of the porch. I caught myself roughly on the railing as one of my feet slipped out from underneath me. *Whew!* I thought, *that was a close call.*

Once at the car, a sturdy Subaru that had seen many years of navigating these mountain roads, I blasted the heat as I used an ice scraper to clear the front window. I remember thinking I'd never seen ice quite so stubborn. Looking back, there are often signs, no matter how subtle or explicit, that let you know something big is coming. Like the flash of light before the crack of thunder. Reflecting on my own life, I don't necessarily think these signs were meant to get me to change direction, though that does happen sometimes. Rather, I see these signs as angels, coming to let me know that—even though I couldn't see what was coming—some wider and kinder force did, and that force sent a bit of its benevolence to be by my side.

I have a small felted wool angel hanging from the rear-view mirror of my car. Something inside of me must have known the road was more dangerous than it looked under the dusting of snow ahead because as I kicked the car into gear, I touched the bit of white wool and said out loud, "Angels, please help me get down this hill tonight." Little did I know that they would, but I probably should have been a bit more specific in my prayer.

The winding gravel road up to my house was one of the first things I noticed when I visited the property with my realtor. Technically maintained by the state, the road was still pretty rough, with two blind curves and a steep drop down into a forest gully for most of its length. I loved the road because it meant very few cars would wander past my house and it would be safe to walk anytime of the day. I also knew that living up a road like this would mean extra precautions, especially in the cold months.

As soon as I navigated my car out of the driveway and began the rocky descent, I realized why I had thought to proffer a prayer—and hoped with every fiber of my being that it had been heard. The gravel beneath the snow had been smoothed into a thick skin of ice. The road, pitched at a steep angle nearly all the way down, had turned into a slip-and-slide, and there was nothing I could do once the car started down the treacherous path but use every skill in my toolkit to keep myself on the road.

I lured my eyes away from the scarily steep ravine to my left and put the car into a five-mile-per-hour crawl. Time slowed down to match my pace. Everything stood out in crisp detail—the outlines of a snowflake on the windshield, the blowing light in front of my head-lights, the fading smear of blue on the horizon as twilight dissolved into night.

After I made the first blind curve, I let out a brief sigh of relief, even though everything else in my body stayed as frozenly focused as the gravel beneath my wheels. I would still need to make the next curve, the final one before I hit the pavement and the warmer temperatures of the valley below. I was almost to the last curve when I slid onto the part of the road where the spring flows. Spilling darkly over the gravel nearly all times of the year, the water had frozen in a solid estu-ary of black ice. My car, with its year-round tires just a season away from being worn out, didn't stand a chance.

It's interesting how, in moments like these, time comes to a com-plete standstill. It reminds me of when I was in my early twenties and took mushrooms with friends at the beach. As my trip hit its peak, I started practicing handstands in the soft sand. Every time I kicked up, it seemed like I was upside down for an eternity, as if I lived there then, in that upside-down world. I couldn't believe how long I was able to maintain that gymnastic feat. Looking back, I probably stayed up no longer than my normal few seconds, but my brain, under the influence of such novel chemicals, registered time differently. Now, as my car began to fish-tail, I experienced a completely different set of chemicals rushing through my brain. The hourglass of time stopped. I entered a suspended state of pure lucidity. In the span of a millisecond, a decision had to be made.

Do I purposely crash the car into a snowbank, risking the chance that I might plow right through it and plunge off the road and down into the creek? Or do I try to lean into the skid, get past the curve, and just pray that I regain control on the other side? In that millisecond I had time to review the intricate viability of both options—and chose the latter. Amazingly, I made it around the curve, but by this time, the car had gained enough speed that there was no way I was going to get it back under control. In the last seconds of having my wheels on the road, I was able to steer myself away from my neighbor's shed, their parked car, and their mailbox—swinging left, right, and left again—before the nose of the Subaru hit the ditch hard and my car flipped, end over end.

Suddenly, I was upside down. My hair was swishing along the ceiling with Christmas music still playing from the glowing stereo. I tried to undo the seat buckle but couldn't because of my body weight. After a frantic second I figured out how to push myself up from the roof to release the belt and fell to the ceiling with a thud. Living in a kind of unreality, I found my phone, hanging by its charging cord, and called John, who was already in town with his family.

The first thing I told him was, "I got into an accident, and my car is upside down." The first thing he asked was "where are you?" to which I replied, not really thinking, "on the ceiling." He guided me to turn off the car and start figuring out how I was going to get out. Amazingly, no windows had smashed, but the car had wedged itself perfectly between the sides of the steep ditch. Eventually I realized that I could wedge one of the back doors open just enough to squeeze my body out.

A few days before I had put a full-length mirror in the back of my car, planning to drop it off at the thrift shop the next time I was in town. In the flip, the mirror had shattered into a million bright pieces. I climbed gingerly over the broken glass, as well as the spare tire that had fallen out from its well and all the various other contents of my car, now jumbled in an incomprehensible pile on the ceiling. Jamming the door as far open as I could into the snowy hillside, I squeezed through the narrow gap and scooped myself out into the cold night air.

As I walked away down the unlit road to the bright illumination of a nearby house, I was thankful that I had worn my boots for the drive instead of my dinner shoes. A sheepdog barked at me as I knocked on the unfamiliar door, introducing myself and asking if I could wait in the warmth while John drove the forty minutes from town to come pick me up. The tow truck would come tomorrow. I was just one of the many calls they had to attend to that night; the unexpected ice had caught many people off guard.

I was familiar with the symptoms of trauma. Because I grew up with an EMDR (eye movement desensitization and reprocessing)-trained psychologist as a mother, the signs and aftereffects of trauma were a part of everyday conversation in our house. I had also worked with enough clients myself to see how trauma tends to play out. First, I would be running on the fumes of adrenaline, amped up enough that I wouldn't feel much at all. I watched myself curiously as I made bubbly conversation with my neighbors. I continued to observe myself in this state of shock as John picked me up and I waved a big-smiled goodbye. We went to the grocery store to get something to eat for dinner and I watched myself as I went for only two things: wine and potato chips.

John was still living in a house close to town at that point in our relationship, so we headed back to his place where the roads were still clear. Once we got back, I logged on to social media, intent on finishing filming a video series I had started earlier that day. John peered incredulously at me from the other room, but I just waved him off.

I called my parents and drank two glasses of wine without feeling any effect. John and I watched a few episodes of a funny sitcom and stoked the fire before we went to bed around midnight. I knew I was probably still in shock but, in the absence of feeling anything, I wondered if maybe I was actually fine? It wasn't until after the lights were out and the dog was snoring that the reality of what had just happened began to process through my body. It felt like a wave crashing through the surface of my numbness. While John slept, I began to decompress, my whole body shaking in the darkness.

Trauma Is What Happens after the Crash

A teacher of mine once gave me this simple definition—"trauma is any-thing that happens to you that violates your trust." You thought some-thing was going to be one way, and then it was different, and that one moment of having your unspoken trust turned upside down forever changes the way you interact with life.

In the dictionary, *trauma* is defined as a distressing or disturbing experience or event, but anyone who works intimately with trauma, and its lived results, knows that trauma is much more than a noun. Trauma is not what happened in the past, but what continues to live in our present. Trauma is how things reverberate within us, changing our behavior, our awareness, our thoughts about ourselves, and our per-spective of the world. Rather than just being a singular event, trauma is the way our body, heart, and mind continue to react to an experience as if it is still happening. Because, on the level of our nervous system, it is.

Trauma is not actually the impact itself; it is the aftershocks. As Peter Levine summarizes in his book, "Traumatic symptoms are not caused by the 'triggering' event itself. They stem from the frozen resi-due of energy that has not been resolved and discharged; this residue remains trapped in the nervous system where it can wreak havoc on our bodies and spirits."[3] It can also wreak havoc on a planetary level. When Theia collided with Earth, the stuck energy of that impact was so intense, it turned the entire planet molten. Our Earth had a lot of healing to do to discharge all that energy, but as she healed, something incredible happened—Earth found her destiny.

Our Earth, unlike all the other planets in our solar system, has become a bastion of life unknown anywhere else in the galaxy. A place of ocean depths and amphibians, waterlilies, spruce trees, eagles, amanita mushrooms, and aquamarines. As Levine writes, "While trauma can be hell on earth, trauma resolved is a gift of the gods—a heroic journey that belongs to each of us."[4] Though the reverberations of trauma may be the farthest thing from beauty, the healing that can come after—the pirouette of our resiliency, the way we integrate that learning to become the people we were meant to be—is perhaps the most beautiful and transcendent force on Earth.

The morning after my accident, John and I went out to meet the tow truck. I was startled when I began to cry as they dragged my car, belly-up, out of the ditch. Though my neck was stiff, amazingly, I had no injuries. Even more incredibly, the car, although badly beaten, was still able to run. The Subaru and I had been very lucky that night; our time on the ice could have ended in a much worse way. The road was still frozen solid. Not wanting to risk John's truck, we hiked on foot together up the road to my house. I went into the bathroom to wash my face, and pure silence spilled out of the faucet. The ridge had seen its first night in the single digits, and the pipes had frozen solid. I decided to pack a bag and hike down to stay with John in town. It would take a while before I felt like I could truly come back home.

When the Thaw Comes

In Chinese medicine it's said that whenever we experience a trauma, our blood freezes. Blood, as the foundation of our lifeforce and personal power, is essential to nourishing and enlivening our body. Similar to Levine's view on the way trauma lives in our nervous system, Chinese healers believe that when a trauma happens, a part of us literally freezes in that moment, unable to move on.

In Chinese medicine, the marker of true vitality is good blood. When we have healthy, freely moving blood, we aren't as suspectable to damaging inputs from the outside—including bacteria and viruses, as well as the pathogens of outer judgements or draining attachments. To be fully in our own power, we need to get these pockets of stagnant blood moving again, thawing the pieces of our lifeforce that have gotten frozen with them. In the aftermath of a traumatic event, animals often go into full-corporal shakes, their body discharging the energy that was mobilized to meet the threat. Amazingly, when animals allow their bodies to complete this process, they don't show any signs of lingering trauma or distress. As humans, we often resist this impulse to shake because it scares us or the people we're around. But shaking, and getting the blood moving again, is an integral part of what helps our nervous system complete its process.

In the midst of a traumatic event, we normally go through a series of experiences. First, our fight impulse is mobilized. During my accident, this was the part of me that decided, once my wheels were irrevocably on the road, that I would get down that mountain come hell or high water. If fight isn't an option, we turn to flee. Once I started slipping, I knew my only chance was to try to get away from the slickest part of the road as deftly as I could. But once the threat is inevitable, we go into the deepest survival response of all—we freeze. When I think back to the moment my car actually flipped, I see myself as an ice sculpture locked immovably to the seat. On the other side of a traumatic event, our nervous system has to deal with the immense amount of energy we just generated, energy that was put into lockdown once we froze. When the event ends, this is when our body wants to begin its process of release. By allowing the stored energy to move, perhaps with bodily shaking, or crying, interspersed with laughter and relief, we begin to thaw from the freeze and reclaim our power again.

For about a week after the accident, I felt like I was orbiting my body. I gave myself as much space as I could. I made time for meditating and journaling. I purposefully exercised and took long baths in the evenings. Every day I told myself, and my nervous system, that I was safe. At the end of the week I scheduled a massage. After a blissful ninety minutes, I couldn't believe how much more present I felt. It was like going from living in black and white to color again. The massage undoubtedly helped to get my blood moving, but I could sense that there was still some unresolved energy inside me.

By Christmas, I was feeling much more myself again, but some things were simply different. I had had all the confidence in the world about driving to town before the accident. Now, I worried nearly every time I left the house. I drove down the hill at a crawl, no matter the weather. When there was even a hint of snow, I refused to leave at all. In my mind, I knew the accident was over, but my body was the one who had experienced the trauma, and it wasn't eager to let me get into a situation like that again. In trauma-informed circles, this is called *hypervigilance*, an enhanced state of sensitivity to threat that can cause undue anxiety. Trauma doesn't just shock you in the moment; it can also wear you out slowly over time.

Once the new year arrived, I decided I would give in to my impulse to stay at home and spend as much time as I could outside. I passed the rest of that winter walking, learning the roads again through my feet, visiting the trees, and becoming present with the cold in a way that felt distinctly cathartic. Being with nature is innately healing for our nervous systems. The amazing thing about trauma is that it's not actually healed by revisiting the past. In trauma-informed therapy, the goal of healing is actually quite simple—to become present. The nature of trauma keeps us frozen in the past, floating somewhere outside of the moment we are currently inhabiting. When we become fully present, however, we can begin to recognize where we are and how strong we've always been. Connecting with nature is one of the easiest and most effective ways to "be here now." *Ecotherapy*, as it is called in the field of psychology, can help reduce depression, relieve stress, and promote profound feelings of well-being. Studies show that nature immersion can be immensely helpful for a wide range of trauma symptoms, including PTSD.[5]

That winter I slowed down to watch all the subtle changes happening around me. The way the rhododendron leaves drooped in the cold of the morning and then picked themselves back up again in the afternoon's light. The ice crystals that grew from the water dripping down the rocky hillsides, melting again into puddles as the days lengthened. The flash of a cardinal on fading snow. By the time spring's thaw arrived, my heart no longer raced when I got into the car. One day I even drove all the way down the gravel road, marveling at the early buds of the magnolias, before I realized that I hadn't had a single moment of anxiety. Dropping back into my connection with nature and its seasons helped me reground in the moment and release the pent-up trauma of my accident. By rooting in the Earth's strength, I found my resiliency.

In the world of trauma therapy, resilience comes from our ability to feel safe, to trust that we are lovable and that we belong. Weathering the storms of life means finely honing our resiliency. But resiliency isn't just the health of our coping mechanisms or our capacity to self soothe; it is the ability to celebrate our own seasons, to embrace our changing selves and our diverse emotions, as a part of our own natural cycles. Nature is the greatest teacher of resiliency. No matter what is thrown at our Earth, she finds a new rhythm of grace. In nature, resiliency is everywhere—the way a forest grows back after it's cut, the tenacity of a frog surviving drought, the adaptability of a bear living on the edge of suburbia. It is the autumn hardening into winter, and winter softening once again into spring.

By the time the cherry blossoms had faded on my street, I was back home. My previous paranoia had become a healthy respect for the weather on the mountain. My anxiety had transformed into a wonderfully alive feeling of awareness every time I drove. I took more time in my commute now, noticing the changing seasons of the valley through which I rode. I gave thanks to my car more often and felt what can only be described as awe for this miracle of technology. After the accident, I wouldn't be who I was before, but I recognized the immense beauty of who I had become.

The Tilt That Gives Us Life

The famous Persian poet Rumi once said, "the wound is the place where the Light enters you." Despite how piercingly lovely this truth is, most of us still spend our lives attempting to avoid trauma. We craft situations so we can control the uncontrollable, but the unexpected still remains a built-in part of existence. Trauma is as innate to the human story as it is to the spin of the planet we live on. It cannot be expunged from our experience any more than the seasons can.

Some kids grow up afraid of monsters under the bed or giant spiders. I grew up afraid of trauma. As the child of two psychologists, one of whom devoted her career to helping people with their trauma, from a young age, I was aware that bad things could happen to you—things you did not deserve and that you had no control over—and that those bad things could change your experience of life forever. As a child I was acutely aware of how lucky I was to have a loving family, a stable home, and a safe community, but I was also deeply cognizant of the fact that, out of the blue, anything could change. That was just the very nature of trauma. It was as unexpected as a morning earthquake.

What I didn't know then, but would find out in due time, was that trauma is inevitable. Experiencing trauma doesn't mean you didn't do a good job of keeping yourself safe or that something is wrong with you. It simply means that you spent some time here on Earth. Early in life I resolved to keep myself safe from trauma, not realizing that trauma is the very narrative arc that gives shape to our lives.

In the intervening years between that childhood resolution and now, I have inevitably encountered traumatic events—abusive relationships, chronic pain and illness, car accidents, the death of loved ones, an allergic reaction on the subway. Eventually, I came to the realization that even though I would have opted out of these particular traumas if given the choice, without them, I wouldn't be who I am today—a person with incredible pith, pluck, compassion, and resilience; someone with the drive to help others navigate the bumps of life because I know just how rough the road can feel. Working through my traumas helped me understand the diverse intelligence of my inner world and find the undiminished goodness within me. In the end, my traumas brought me back down into the earth of myself as surely as a leaf in autumn returns to the soil.

People often think of trauma in big newsletter headlines—murder, assault, natural disaster, genocide—but trauma is often more nuanced. There is no objective explanation of what makes an event traumatic. Because trauma is defined by how our bodies and nervous systems react, trauma is entirely subjective. What is traumatic for one person will not be for another, and what rolls off one person's back might haunt someone else for decades.

We all carry trauma, regardless of whether or not we can name it. Negative feedback from a mentor, a fall off the slide, or a word said in anger can all create trauma in our lives. If we want to start the healing process, the first thing we need to do is recognize this and let go of the harm that we subconsciously perpetuate when we minimize our own trauma. No matter what it is that you experienced, if it continues to reverberate through your life, it is trauma. It's not only okay to name it as such, it's often distinctly lifegiving to simply call a spade a spade. When I first drafted this chapter, I was surprised to find myself crying as I crafted the description of my accident. Even though it had been years, my body still needed to process the last leftover energy from that cold night. It felt like pure cathartic completion. I let the tears fall with as much freedom as the maple leaves twirling past my window.

Sometimes, we can feel ashamed that something in our life has affected us so deeply. But when we recognize that trauma is subjective, that it is not just one moment but the ongoing tilt that we adopt in the wake of such an impactful event, we see that there is no shame in the way traumas continue to affect our lives. In fact, this is exactly what trauma was designed to do.

Caroline Casey, a trickster astrologer, visionary activist, and mythologist, calls trauma "our beautiful, dangerous assignment."[6] We are the heroes on our own journey, and the traumas that come to shake our lives are the very things that hand us our greatest gifts, the assignments of healing that ultimately teach us how to turn around and help others. Each one of us is born inlaid with gifts, whole as a geode. Trauma helps us crack open, so we can find the crystals within.

I wouldn't be writing this book, or doing the work I am in this world, without my own beautiful, dangerous assignments. That is the nature of surviving, and healing, from trauma—it brings dimensionality, depth, courage, compassion, and dedication into your life. Some of the greatest works of art—painting, poetry, dance, song—have come out of life's most tragic losses. Maya Angelou's *I Know Why the Caged Bird Sings*, the paintings of Frida Kahlo, the perfect heartache of every Billie Holiday song. Even the artwork we take for granted as natural facets of the earth—the apples of autumn, the pureness of winter's snow, daffodils in spring, wood thrush songs, summer strawberries, and coyote howls—are the exquisite ripples of the beautiful, dangerous assignment we are all a part of.

When we claim our gifts, the full beauty of who we have become in the wake of our unique assignments, we naturally start to release the haunts of the past. When we can recognize, with the level clarity of a blue autumn sky, that everything that knocks us off balance ends up deepening the meaning of our lives, the world takes on the most outrageously spectacular hues. When you are able to understand that, even though what happened was *not* okay, the way you responded was as brilliant, adaptive, and life-givingly gorgeous as the autumn itself, the path forward becomes as unclouded as the moon—and every lost part of your self can find the way back home.

The Moon Guides You Home

I still remember, clear as starlight, the first time I ever spoke to the moon. I was in my senior year of college and had already been dealing with chronic pain and health issues for several years. I had recently begun losing my hair and was starting to get eruptive breakouts on both sides of my jaw. After three years of health issues I felt like I was spiraling—I didn't know how to heal myself, but I knew I needed help. In my attempts to manage both the physical pain as well as the deeper emotional traumas underlying them, nature had become my solace. One night, I decided to venture into the woods to sit with the full moon. I had just started tracking the moon's cycle, and I wanted to feel a deeper connection to its rhythm.

I packed a bottle of water, my journal, and a bit of sweetgrass to burn. I closed the front door quietly and stepped into the small stand of woods separating our ring of senior housing from the rest of the campus. It was a scraggly stretch of forest, recently cut and still growing back in with skinny tulip poplars and sassafras shrubs. I found a tree big enough to rest against and leaned into the moon's light. In full gaze of the sky, I closed my eyes for a while and just breathed, noticing how it felt to have the moonlight touch me—comforting as a hand smoothing down my hair, patting the rough curve of my face.

I thought about all the ways I felt broken, just a few steps into adulthood. The weight of it felt like a glacial boulder, unmovable on the forest floor. Without knowing why, or from where the impulse arose, I opened my eyes and started speaking to the moon. Something was simply so inviting about her gaze. She looked like a grandmother, glowing with a deeply neutral love. I began to pour my heart out into her light. I told her about all the hurt inside me. All the places where I felt like I was broken beyond repair. I spoke out loud every hot, hard, angry shard of frustration and pain. I told her the things I didn't feel I could say to my friends, doctors, or family. With no one to judge me, no reason to feel ashamed, I let loose the depth of my despair. Tears rolled like pearls down my cheeks.

I heaved and grieved and, in the midst of my turmoil, I felt distinctly heard. I could sense her, this moon grandmother of mine, reaching out to soothe me, letting me know that everything would be okay. Able to see so much farther than me, she told me that the road ahead was much brighter than it now seemed. I laid on the ground, in a pool of her light, and just let myself be held. Each beam illuminated a forgotten piece of me, the parts that innately trusted in the goodness of the world, those parts that were still innocent and unhurt. In my mind's eye, I saw the child in me, the one who always trusted that life would take care of her, peek shyly from around the tree. The deeper I allowed this light to soak into me, the safer it felt to come back home.

In shamanic practice these moments of healing and reintegration are called *soul retrievals*. *Shamanism*, a word that comes from the Evenki people, a Tungusic tribe in Siberia, has become a buzzword in modern culture, but its roots are ancient. Commonly considered to be the ancestor of all religions, and intricately tied into animism, shamanism is a way of seeing and healing that revolves around interacting with the unseen energies that surround us. Though many shamanic traditions are culturally specific, similarities stretch across societies with techniques and beliefs that are near universal. At one point in time, all of our ancestors practiced a variety of what we now call shamanism. In its most basic form, shamanistic healing acknowledges the fact that our world is interwoven with a universe of the unseen and that, at times, we need to be able to work with what is invisible in order to experience healing.

From a shamanic perspective, any time we experience an upset so great that we cannot fully process it, a piece of ourselves steps away. It is not *lost*, exactly, but playing a serious game of hide-and-go-seek. Like a child who hears his parents fighting and stows away in the back of the coat closet, pieces of ourselves leave when being here is just too much to handle. Soul retrieval is a cross-cultural shamanic technique—found from Tibet to the Andes, to the isle of Ireland—that helps to bring back pieces of ourselves that we have lost during the course of our lifetime.

In psychological circles soul loss is called *dissociation*, and the process of retrieval is similar to reintegrating fragmented pieces of our personality. Just like soul loss, there is an inherent wisdom to dissociation. We dissociate so we don't have to bear the full brunt of that moment's pain, an impact that might shock our system beyond repair. With soul loss, a part of ourselves hides itself away to stay safe. The problem is, until we can retrieve those pieces, we miss out on all the vitality and power they hold. The object of a soul retrieval is not to change the past or erase the trauma, but to reconnect to the parts of ourselves that we lost in those moments so we can embrace the wholeness of ourselves again. Like pieces of a meteorite scattered around the world, our dispersed soul parts are waiting for us. Once we find them, we can begin to appreciate the sheer magnitude of what our spirit survived and recognize the transcendent beauty of who we are today.

After my moon-led soul retrieval, I snuck in the backdoor of our house; the moment felt too precious to have to explain to my roommates. I went straight into my bedroom, turned off the lights, and nursed myself in the wonder of the moon's light. A piece of me had returned, and with it came the renewed faith that healing was possible.

Wide Shining Light

The moon has been a source of wonder, mystery, myth, and homecoming for as long as humans have been gazing up into the sky. The moon is responsible for countless poems, symphonies, and soliloquies, as well as the tides. Gazing up at the moon's loveliness, we might never guess that she, too, is the result of trauma. When Theia hit our Earth 4.5 million years ago, not only did this huge upset create the seasons, but it also birthed our moon. As the hypothesis goes, after Theia's impact, the Earth was surrounded by a field of broken debris. Each piece was like a dislocated self, floating safely in the solar system as the Earth went molten from the shock. Overtime, these pieces came together to form what we know of as the moon.

Our precious moon, the lamp that guides us by night, the grandmother that holds us in her light, was created from the very same impact that set us askew. And yet, it is the moon that continues to stabilize our ability to nurture life. Without the moon, astronomers hypothesize, the Earth's tilt could vary as much as 85 degrees, causing climatic changes so dramatic that life wouldn't be possible. As it stands now, we shift only a degree or so over time. It is one of the most beautiful paradoxes of existence, that the same impact that sets us off course becomes the guiding light that helps us navigate the deeper callings of our life. In soul retrieval, whether it is spontaneous like my experience with the moon or guided by a practitioner, you call back all the pieces that have been dislocated by traumatic impact. When they return, they bring with them untold gifts. You can often see when a piece of someone's soul returns to them. It shines through their eyes.

Theia was named for the Greek Titan who was the mother of both the sun and the moon. On its own *Theia* means "goddess" or "divine," though her full name, *Theia Euryphaessa,* can be more closely translated as "wide shining."[7] Instead of darkness rising up to eclipse us, what if the things that have happened to us, no matter how hard, are emissaries that show us our wide shining light? What if the impacts that have shaken us to our core aren't meant to shatter us but to help us feel the truth of our inextinguishable brightness? Following our own inner light, over time, we can gather up each piece that once left us, finding them like mica flakes under the lamp of moonlight.

In Clarissa Pinkola Estés's book *Women Who Run with Wolves,* she retells the traditional Japanese myth of the Crescent Moon Bear. In the story, a woman's husband returns from war, but he is not the same person who left. This new person is moody, angry, volatile, and destructive—he returned home missing pieces of himself. The wife, wanting to help him, consults with a healer who tells her she needs to retrieve a single hair from the Crescent Moon Bear who lives up in the mountains.

It is a dangerous task. It takes her many days of bringing offerings, coaxing, calming, and courting the bear before he is willing to offer her a pure white hair from the moon at his chest. When she brings the hair back down, the healer throws it into the fire. It wasn't the hair the wife needed, but the experience of the kind of patient love, understanding, and generosity of spirit it takes to heal after trauma. Within all of us live both this profoundly hurt husband and that fiercely loving wife. We each contain a part that needs to rage at the injustice of the hurt we have suffered and a part that knows exactly what to do to bring back our light.

In astrology, the moon corresponds to our emotions, the inner tides that rule our lives. We have come to view emotions as burdens in our current culture, but the truth is that our emotions are like the seasons:

they are what give us diversity and depth. Emotions show us what our inner self needs, where our desires lead, and which moment in the cycle or season of life we are moving through.

One of the greatest ways we can heal is simply by letting ourselves go through our own seasons of feeling—whether those seasons move through you daily, monthly, or seem to come up during certain times of the year, like tough anniversaries. No matter how the seasons of your inner being present themselves, embrace them. Embrace the quiet winter of inner reflection. The new spring of tenderness. The passionate rush of summer, the aching nostalgia and settled longing of fall.

Your traumas were the great impacts that helped to create the planet that you are now. At some point in your days of formation, you too were knocked about, but now you are like the Earth, so beautiful in her regeneration. Just like our planet, you are made more whole by that which you have experienced, not less. As Levine so exquisitely captures, ultimately our healing journeys "propel us into the exhilarating ability to soar and fly, giving us a more complete view of our place in nature."[8] From this elevated perspective, you can see, with clarity, both your gifts and your belonging, tapping into a near-divine state of self-acceptance, gratitude, and aptitude for experiencing the ecstatic reality of life.

One mystery left behind by the Theia impact theory is the disappearance of Theia herself. If the Earth was hit by such a tremendously large planet, why can't we find any evidence of this planet's different chemical makeup? Some scientists have answered this by pointing to the Earth's core. We cannot find chemical evidence of Theia because it has become a very part of our planet. The core of our Earth is, apparently, much bigger than it should be for a planet our size. Looking at this fact, scientists have hypothesized that when Theia hit, she did not just glance the surface, but literally became a part of our planet, expanding the core of who we are.

Our traumas shape us. They are, in a sense, a part of our makeup, expanding our very core. In the wake of healing, our center point becomes larger, our hearts wider, our capacity for joy, innocence, delight, and trust that much bigger. As the aperture of our soul expands, our spirits are given access to that wide shining light.

The things that have shaken you have also delivered you. They have helped you become who you are and will, through working with them, show you just how unreservedly good you are. Trauma itself is hard to celebrate, but resiliency isn't. The perfect elegance and creativity of our response is worthy of admiration, adoration, and the same volumes of poetry that we ascribe to the flowers of spring, the fruit of summer, the color wash of fall, and the haiku of winter. So, the next time you feel the weight of your own traumas dragging you down, look up at the moon for help. Step outside and feel the gorgeousness of the Earth's tilt. Tell yourself, so the deepest part of you can hear, that you aren't damaged. You are simply a person with seasons—and those seasons are distinctly beautiful.

EXERCISE:
Resourcing in Nature

Our bodies instinctively know how to heal from trauma. When we spend time in nature, we allow those instincts to rise to the surface and guide us in our healing. This exercise is designed to help you feel resourced—distinctly centered, grounded, or held—through your connection to nature.

1. Set aside an hour to be outside in a natural setting. Choose a place that feels innately comfortable to you, like a local park or a beloved spot in the woods. Wear comfortable clothes and bring a warm shawl or blanket with you.

2. Find a place to be in this natural setting that feels private and safe. Make sure to keep your shawl or blanket with you in case you get cold. Begin by looking all around you. Use your neck to look to the right and left, up and down. When we engage our neck muscles, we are signaling to our body that it's safe for our gaze to wander.

3. After looking around, choose one thing in nature that feels distinctly comfortable to let your gaze settle on. This could be a tree, a stone, a flower, an acorn, or a stream. Notice everything you can about this being or object that you picked. What are its colors? Textures? How might you imagine it tastes or smells? How does it interact with the light, the breeze, the earth, or a passing pollinator?

4. Once you have taken in all the sensory details you can, from this comforting anchor point, turn your attention inward to the felt sense of your body. Try tuning into the pure sensations in your body, leaving behind the need to ascribe any meanings or emotions to them. Look for feelings, like "my chest feels tight, my stomach feels warm, my feet feel solid." Moving from the top of your head down to your feet, take an inventory of how you feel in each place on your body. Linger with your awareness on your feet, lower limbs, and pelvic bowl, noticing how they are resting against the solidity of the earth. Welcome every sensation you feel without judgment.

5. Find somewhere in your body that feels distinctly comforting to focus on. What is it about this area of your body that feels so good to bring your awareness to? Let yourself bask in the good feelings here.

6. Now, find a part of your body that feels less comforting. Perhaps an area where you have constriction, ache, or heaviness.

Notice first what happens when you simply sit with this sensation without trying to change it. Be curious to see if it might begin to shift as you sit with it. If you'd like, you can also ask the Earth to come help you dissolve some of the discomfort. See what happens if you let the Earth's loving energy flow into this part of you.

If at any point you feel too uncomfortable or are experiencing distress, just open your eyes and look back to your comforting gaze point in nature. Every step of this exercise is optional. You are the expert on your own healing.

7. Whenever you are ready, open your eyes and return to enjoying the nature around you. If you feel cold, pull the blanket or shawl over you. If you feel called to move or shake, let that impulse flow organically through you. With your eyes open now, you might even notice that your senses are stronger. Colors might be more vivid or the sense of the breeze more acute. Enjoy your experience of being held by nature, and rest here for as long as you'd like.

Note: Though I believe deeply in nature and our natural ability to heal, I am also a big proponent of working one-on-one with a trained therapist. If you are someone who is struggling with PTSD, trauma, or are feeling overwhelmed by your experience, please seek out the help of a professional. Therapy can be one of the greatest gifts you ever give yourself.

4

THOSE THAT KEEP
THEIR LEAVES

THE FROST-HARD GROUND crunched underfoot as I puffed my way up the path into the woods. It was mid-January, and the world outside was a globe of quiet. I'd been walking for a while but hadn't seen anyone on the trail. *Good,* I thought to myself, *now no one will know that I haven't bothered getting dressed today.* In the years after I came to the mountains, before I met John and we created our Highly Sensitive Sanctuary, I moved through as many different relationships as I did homes and gardens. Each time I thought the situation might be permanent, the lease—and relationship—would expire.

On this particular day, it had been a few months since I had survived the heart-wrenching breakup that had defined my fall season, but the messy aftermath had lingered and my interest in doing things like putting on pants was still dramatically diminished. Waking up close to noon, discombobulated and depressed, I had simply thrown on my jacket over my pajamas, yanked a hat onto my uncombed hair, and ventured outside. Sometimes, when I don't know what else to do, I walk. When I think back over the years it seems I've always had my most important revelations while walking. It began during those long rambles in college when I took solace among the trees. When I moved to Brooklyn, however, walking became a cornerstone of my daily routine.

My last winter in NYC, while the garden was asleep, I got a job as a dog walker. Ask any dog walker, and they'll likely tell you that winter is one of the most miserable times to start the job. A walker goes out no matter the weather—rain, shine, windstorm, snowfall, ice event, or downpour—if a dog's people are still going to work, then you are still on the schedule. My agency only did one walk at a time, so my seven-hour day was blocked out in half hour strolls, with just enough time to ride my bike across the city from one apartment to another.

Being a dog walker during a New York City winter is not for the faint of heart. If it isn't bone cold, it's wet and slushy. You've got to wear more layers than a snowman to stay comfortable, and at the end of the day, your clothes look like a Jackson Pollock from all the road-blackened snow spray. The job was gritty, unglamorous, and exhausting—and I absolutely loved it. Sure, most evenings I was dragging myself up the steps to my apartment, my whole body crying out for a hot bath, but I got to spend the entire day moving, visiting every park in a few-mile radius, and hanging out with a New Yorker's last remaining tether to wild nature—their pets. I always did my best thinking on those walks, dreaming into the future, puzzling out the hard pieces of my past, or simply enjoying the poetry of a winter-quiet street. My love for walking was borne in the gentle woods of the Hudson Valley, but it was sharpened and honed by the New York City streets.

Some essential part of my love for walking must have been forged during all those days beating the Brooklyn pavement, because my favorite time of the year to go rambling is when the leaves have fallen from the trees. There is a particular kind of rigor and joy to winter walking. The layers padded around my core and the near silence of the trees make me feel like I am insulated inside the imagination of the Earth. The cold air distills me, the sheer openness of the landscape sets me free, and with so little to focus on, my eye can pierce the glass of my thoughts more clearly. After I left Brooklyn and moved to the mountains, my love for walking was like a sapling that took root and grew exponentially. Even though I was in a completely new place, when I walked, I always felt like I was heading home. In this part of Appalachia, the mountains are folded like the fades of an old apron. In summer you can get lost in one pocket after another if you try to follow a holler to its end. In winter, however, the whole landscape becomes visible. Blue and hollow as a bowl, the once-dense coves open like a mind in meditation, asking to be explored.

Growing warm from my strenuous hike up the hill, I unbuttoned the wool of my jacket to let the winter air find its way into the PJs underneath. My knit hat perched slightly askew to allow the heat to escape, I walked past the old abandoned cabin and up to the overlook at the ridge. In summer this view is a tangle of grapevines and young trees, but in winter it opens up so you can see the blue folds of the mountains to the east. All winter long I had come up here when I needed perspective, a way to see through the tangle of my thoughts.

I stood, coat open to the wind, and let the mountains move straight through me. Gazing out from the knot of dark vines and trees bent by winter's weight, I let the heaviness of what I had been carrying drop down into the earth. I kneeled on the cold ground, unable to stay standing with the bending force of my grief, and began to cry. I cried for my hurting heart, for the person I had lost, and for the dream of a future that had died with that relationship. I cried for my loneliness and unwashed hair. I cried for the now-wet knees of my pajamas and for all the mornings I'd woken up feeling like I was trapped under a stone.

Once the floodgates opened, I realized that the heaviness I had been carrying was much older than this most recent hurt. I cried for all the unnamable weights that I continued to carry with me, no matter how old or wise I seemed to grow. I cried for the patterns I repeat, again and again. For the traumas that affect the way I walk through the world. I cried in frustration because I was here again, on this familiar overlook, gazing through a dark twist of vines and wondering if I'd ever get to the sunlit hills on the other side.

I knew this place, this summit of grief. I had been here many times before. I felt the frustration of self-judgement rising like heat, arguing with the pureness of my tears—how long does it take to process something, to let go? Was there something wrong with me that I was still dealing with the same kind of heartbreaks? Is there a timeline for grief or release? And if so, have I completely missed the boat?

I hadn't heard anyone come up the path, but as I wiped the hot tears from my cold cheeks, I heard someone nearby whisper, "susshhhh, shhhh." I turned around to look for the source of this deeply comforting voice. "Susshhhh, shhhh." It sounded like a mother acknowledging the hurt of a child, a loving affirmation that murmured, "I know, I know." I spun in a circle to find the source of the sound.

To my left was a beech tree, its leaves still curled, thin as ancient paper on the young skinny branches. As the wind moved it shook each bough and the leaves whispered again, this time directly in front of me. "Susshhh." I rose and walked up to the tree in wonder. Looking around, I saw it was the only one in the whole grove with any leaves. The buckeyes were bare, the maples only dotted here and there with an old brown remain, but this beech was lined with whispering gold. I had never noticed it until now, but I would soon learn that this tree was not an anomaly. It turns out, some trees keep their leaves, even after the bright flare of fall. I put my head against the bark and listened to the whispers. It sounded like someone saying, *everything will be just fine.*

Have you ever walked in a quiet wood in midwinter and heard the calming hush of old leaves on the wind? Have you seen those fawn-colored curls that linger despite the bareness of the forest's canopy? Within each of these trees is a story about letting go of the shame for what remains. If you listen, they will tell you a tale about living on your own timeline, regardless of the outer seasons. Inside the pages of their leaves is the assurance that, no matter what you are holding onto, the story is unfolding perfectly. Sitting with this beech tree, I first learned the parable of *those that keep their leaves.*

When Fall Isn't the End

Everybody loves the fanfare of fall in the deciduous world—the drama and colors and poetic dénouement. A bit like the grand finale of an opera, something is innately glamorous about the catharsis of autumn. With its bright pile of leaves and red-hued trees, autumn's release seems dramatic, clean, and complete. For anyone who has lived through fall in a part of the world where the trees set themselves on fire, you know it can be an ecstatic experience to join this ceremony of cremation—to sync up with the falling leaves and allow your burdens to dissolve along with them. But for all the perceived social, or ecological, pressure encouraging you to let go as the leaves whirl down from the trees, a quiet truth all too often goes unacknowledged—not every autumn is complete in its catharsis. Not every finale marks the end. Not every leaf will be ready to go when the winds turn cold. Not every tree will shed its weight when the day is done. No matter how vivid the fall, inevitably winter comes. The color fades. The ritual ends. And sometimes, even after the most elaborate ceremony, the old things remain.

So often, we're told that there is a right and wrong time to release. That there is a set season in which it is natural to grow or move on, and that if we stray beyond this time, we will become shamefully left behind. As with many things in our culture, there is a subconscious belief in a society-wide metronome of what a "normal" life looks like, when it is the "proper" time to do things.

We have a schedule for when we should go to school, fall in love, get married, have children, and retire. We also have expectations for how we are meant to move through grief, loss, self-doubt, or trauma, releasing the hardships of one phase so we can swiftly and efficiently move on to another. If you listen to this cultural narrative, it would seem that moving on should be as reliable as turning forward the clocks for daylight savings time, but the truth of organic growth and change is much more individual, undefinable, and diverse. If you only look outside your window, you will notice that nature has a much wider idea of how flexible these timelines are. As much as we view autumn as the ultimate season of release, it turns out that a whole population of deciduous trees goes about things much differently.

In grade school we learn that there are two kinds of trees in the temperate landscape: those that are fully deciduous—trees that shed all their leaves with the arrival of fall—and the conifers— those evergreen beings that hold on to their photosynthesizing parts throughout all seasons. But as often is the case, there is a third reality, a class of trees that falls somewhere in-between. Curiously, some deciduous trees aren't as deciduous as we think. Even after the autumn ends, these trees hold onto their leaves. A mysterious process, scientists have nevertheless given a name to this interesting characteristic—*marcescence*.

Marcescence is an ethereal word, one that sounds like an incantation. Coming from the Latin "to shrivel,"[1] marcescence is the technical term for a deciduous tree's peculiar tendency to retain its dead leaves throughout the winter. Though we assume nearly all deciduous trees drop their burdens at the end of autumn, if you simply look around, you'll see outliers everywhere. When we reflect on the things we continue to carry, we assume we must be misfits. But one glance at the forest will show you that you are in good company.

Every strategy adopted and sustained in the natural world has its advantages; otherwise, those strategies simply wouldn't exist. Curiously, when it comes to marcescence, ecologists still aren't sure why some trees evolved this time-tested tenacity. As marcescence most often appears in trees that are still young and working on attaining the fullness of their height, one hypothesis is that the remaining leaves help to disguise new tasty buds from browsers. It's also possible that retaining those leaves longer means a bigger dose of compost right when the tree needs it in early spring. While the ecologist may struggle to understand the purpose of such holding on, the poet, the walker in the woods, the one who grieves, understands innately.

We are told that we all must follow the same timetables of seed, plant, tend, reap, and compost. But when our own journeys don't conform to the larger cultural ethos, we feel as lost as the last oak leaf, left on the tree to spin solo. It is worthy, and good, to lives one's life by the rhythms of the natural world, but everywhere you look you will see a spectrum of existence that thrives on the sheer diversity of timelines. Microclimates, niches, the tiny shifts of daylight that make it so that a tree on the hilltop will act completely differently than one down in the cove. Marcescence reminds us that we navigate our particular cycles of birth and death by following the rhythm of our own inner metronome—and that no matter how baffling that timeline might seem, it is adaptive, sacred, and filled with hidden wisdom.

The Gift of Marcescence

Every fall, I attempt to join the festive regalia of letting go. As the bulk of the leaves drop, I try to bring myself into alignment with the season by stripping away the husks of old relationships, projects, losses, and blocks. Sometimes, I succeed. But sometimes, no matter how many piles of discard I make, or how many fires I burn down to ash, some stubborn leaves remain.

There have been many such times in my life when I have held onto the skeletons of the past long after the easy encouragement of autumn, clutching them as tightly as the beech instinctively holds the last dervishes of its leaves. There have been many seasons when I have needed a grace period of marcescence, the quietude of a long winter to fully process and let the old become compost. Sitting with the soft "sussshhh" of that slender beech with its gentle rattle of leaves, I was comforted to know that, while letting go is normal, holding on is natural too. Some things take a quick summer to process and are shed with the first orange seep of fall. But other things, the big things, the challenges that are here to help us truly *see* ourselves, need a bit more time. The longer it takes to let something go, odds are, the more profound its effects will be on your life.

The body is wise in what it decides to hold. Every second spent in the meditation of marcescence contains wisdom. Not a moment is wasted. From a scientific perspective, marcescence announces that the trees are not quite finished in their process. There are aspects of the past seasons that are still being completed. What is left, even after we have cleaned ourselves of all that we can in a single season, is important. Those remaining leaves, though mysterious, serve a function.

Marcescence speaks to us in winter-quiet tones: if you are still grieving, that grief is serving a purpose. If you seem to be circling around the same inner blocks, triggers, or issues, there is a reason why they stubbornly cling. If there is something that you seem to be perennially working with—trust the timing. Whatever you are holding onto is part of an unknown ritual of self-preservation and transformation. There is no shame in being the one who has kept their leaves a little bit longer. It is an adaptative quality that serves the Earth as surely as the rain.

It may not be a process that we always understand, but it persists as a strategy that is beloved by the world. The shimmer of beech leaves in the northlight of winter lifts the spirits when all else is bare. The perfect flower husks of a tulip poplar are a reminder of the eternal blooms within. The oak's steadfast leather curls remind you of your strength, undiminished. What you hold onto has an elegance, and importance, all its own.

Your Timeline Is Brilliant

All winter I hiked up to the ridge to hear the lullaby of that beech tree. At first, I was still struggling up in my coat-covered PJs and bed-tousled hair, but eventually I was hiking briskly in freshly washed leggings and a neat braid. I hiked on ice days and slush days. I hiked with scarf-light hope and a heart heavy as snow boots. I hiked up to sit with that mother-beech and to be with the understanding she preached. I hiked when I felt I was finally getting somewhere, and when I worried it would all just collapse again. Every time I got to the ridge I would listen to the tender "sushhh" of the leaves and be comforted—it was okay, in absolutely every way, to take as long as I needed.

We associate rattles with soothing newborn babes, but in some cultures, rattles are used as instruments to help facilitate a shaman's journey into the unseen, a pilgrimage taken to gain perspective and bring back medicine. Sitting underneath the softly *sushhing* rattle of that beech, I found myself able to journey into a wider mindset, flying above my moment of heartache and frustration to perceive the wisdom of taking the slow route. From that place of higher vision, I recognized the truth—everything is released at the right time.

All winter I sat on that ridge and allowed myself to be exactly as I was—tired, tender, and in process. Every day I gave myself this gentleness, and every day little things began to shift. Winter passed in a spiral of walking, and soon spring was beginning to bud. The first warmth of March always begins in the ground, with the soft chickweed and nettle greens. It takes weeks until spring finally reaches the canopy. In these mountains, the trees don't begin to leaf out until late April. By that time, I'm often so busy looking down that I forget to look up.

One day, as I was walking the hill, happy to spot new wildflowers along the winter-worn path, I realized with a shock that it had been weeks since I had last looked at the beech. I hiked with purpose around the bend. My light sweater gathered the sun to my back as I sought out the tree. But the beech I had grown so accustomed to over the winter had transformed. I couldn't pick her out at first. Finally, I found the tree by her shape—round and elegant as a brandy bottle. The empty rattle of the beech's leaves was gone, and the tiny folded fans of her new green had just begun.

Some years I wonder, will the leaves of old ever keep the new ones from growing? Will the heaviness of what the tree carries prevent its fresh beginning? The answer is, always, no. When it is time, it is time. Eventually, as spring creeps near, even the most stubborn of leaves will let go as the new ones begin to grow. The old is never kept forever; it simply isn't possible. Everything falls away in the right moment.

The spell-word of marcescence whispers in our ears: It is truly okay to be on your own timeline. Spring is coming. You must only allow your process to follow its natural course.

I still remember the day I met my therapist. I was finally ready to begin addressing the trauma that had lingered from the abusive relationships of my teenage years. Despite having done so much healing on my own, it was time to reach out to a professional. Shannon was an effervescent, deeply warm woman with wild gray hair, owl-black eyeliner, and Kate Bush playing in the waiting room. I loved her immediately.

I had had an incident earlier that month that pushed me to finally reach out for help. After going back home and seeing old friends from that time in my life, I returned to the mountains feeling inexplicably shaken. I felt like I was living outside of my body. I was having flashbacks to memories of abuse and experiencing moments of heart-racing anxiety. Shannon helped me identify this as the effects of PTSD and worked with me to start gently approaching this old wound.

I remember exclaiming to her, with both exasperation and wonder, that I couldn't believe I could be so triggered by something that had happened half a lifetime ago—a part of me was shocked that I was still holding on so strongly. She smiled and began, in a voice as soothing as a baby rattle, to explain that this kind of holding on is a natural part of our inner adaptation system. When something is too big to process at once, we package it neatly and put it away to be released another day. Such holding on isn't a sign of our weakness—it is an indicator of our strength. Our wise bodies know when we are in a safe enough place to start releasing these things, and so they wait until spring is on the horizon. They begin to let go when a new era is already underway.

I started working with clients over a decade ago. I was only in my mid-twenties at the time, but I had already moved through so much and was eager to help. For all the different healing journeys I've accompanied people on, however, there is almost always one constant. Despite all those wondrous moments of realization, at the center of our life is a powerful theme, something that we are *meant* to spend a long season processing. Whether it's the wounds of childhood, self-criticism on loop, or grief over the state of the world—these big things are here to help us open up to the core gifts of our journey. For as bright and shiny as our more easily achieved revelations are, they aren't the stuff that makes for truly revolutionary change.

It is the things that are still rattling around inside us come wintertime that will inevitably deliver us into spring. The most powerfully healing remedies can take a long time to brew. The things you spend many seasons holding onto are not signs of your shortcomings, but indicators of the depths of your soul's journey—and an intricate part of the world's beauty.

One of the greatest joys of walking throughout the seasons is encountering all the diversity of timelines that make up the environment around me. I love noticing how the leaves at the top of the ridge turn red sooner than the leaves down by my home or how the winter settles more quickly on the north side of the cove. Gardening is the art of working with this timeline diversity. A variety of species, each one flowering at a different time, will make your yard breathtaking. In my front garden bed, I watch with glee as the crocuses fade into hyacinths, which let go in time for the irises, who make way for the day lilies, coneflowers, verbenas, and mums. It turns out that we need late bloomers—they are the ones that bring beauty to the Earth when all else grows dim. The Earth is an orchestra, and our own personal timing is what makes the symphony a true masterpiece.

When we do this work of allowing ourselves to be who we are naturally, we nourish the wider cycles of the world. By honoring our own internal rhythms, we revive a society that honors the animacy of all the Earth's diversity. When we sanction the perfection of our journeys of unfolding, we can create a culture that is wise enough, strong enough, slow enough, and self-forgiving enough to realign ourselves with the Earth's perfect wholeness.

Every spring I always try to wait and see—when exactly do the beeches lose their leaves? And the answer is always the same: in their own time. You are a globe, spinning in the seasons of its own year, and when it is time for spring, spring will come. Marcescence never lasts forever. If you simply fall into alignment with your own being, you will never be left behind.

EXERCISE:

Mark the Timelines of Your Life

This exercise is intended to help you recognize the seasons of your life. Creating a picture of your own unique timelines, you can recognize how far you've come and find gentleness for what you are still working through.

1. Get out a fresh sheet of paper. Placing it horizontally, draw a line from one side of the page to another. At the start of the line write your birth date. At the end write "now."

2. Fill in the timeline with each "era" that you can think of, marking it in a way that feels special to you. For each era, write in the major challenge that accompanied that time. Add in any special dates or landmarks as well.

3. When you are done, look over your timeline. Notice how, what was challenging for you in the past, nearly always dissolved when it was time. Can you find any ways in which the timing of what you let go of (a relationship, a job, a dream) was actually perfect for what then came next in your life? How have the things you held onto illuminated your gifts, talents, or strengths?

4. Moving to now, the present day on your timeline, write the following affirmation, inspired by poet and philosopher John O'Donohue. *"I live like a river flows, carried by the surprise of my own unfolding."* Notice how you feel in your body when you say this affirmation out loud. Give it time, and take your time. If you find yourself wanting to consider what you are still holding onto right now, go ahead. How might what you are holding onto be helping you to grow? Use your imagination to picture the best possible outcome and allow the unfolding.

PART TWO
THE MIRROR

Appreciating Yourself

5

TENDER SPRING

I PICKED UP THE dog-eared Post-it note with my packing list crammed onto every inch and glanced down at the pile of objects on the kitchen floor. A sleeping bag, my knife, a cookpot, a pillow, a plant identification book. Was I missing anything? I cracked open the front door to test the coolness of the air and promptly added a hat to the pile. In spring it can still get down to freezing in the mountains. I looked at the pile one last time and took out the pillow so I could add another wildflower ID book. No one could say I didn't have my priorities straight.

This was going to be my first time camping alone. The idea of it made my insides flutter. I was like a puppy in my enthusiasm—awkward, ungainly, and ready to sprint headlong into this new adventure. I had planned the expedition to coincide with the first flush of wildflowers known as the spring ephemerals. Short-lived perennials, *spring ephemerals,* are wildflowers that live the whole of their above-ground life in the short handspan of early spring. Many people are familiar with common garden ephemerals, such as daffodils or hyacinths, but there is a whole community of woodland ephemerals—rare, delicate, enchanting, and brief—that dot our native forests. All winter long I gaze like a card reader at the cold mountain soil, scrying into the duff to imagine what fantastical roots might be nestled between the trees. In spring, after a long wait, the unfurling of the ephemerals nearly knocks me off my feet.

For most of the year, woodland ephemerals live underground, but as soon as the soil warms, they begin their quick ascent to supply some of the first food, nectar, pollen, and medicine of spring. Often growing in forested north-facing coves, these rare species don't receive enough light in the thick of the growing season to thrive. But in those first few weeks of early spring, before the canopy closes, ample sunshine can sweep the forest floor to call the ephemerals up from their year-long sleep. In the time it takes for the maples and tulip poplars and basswoods to set out their leaves, these flowers go from bud to bloom, fruit and seed, dying back to the roots as the canopy finally flushes to fullness. In the deciduous belt of the Earth, where trees sleep like Persephone during the long winter, ephemeral wildflowers are the heralds that announce the return of the growing world. They are akin to the dawn chorus, rooted songbirds that celebrate the reawakening of a rich hardwood cove. It's hard *not* to be taken by them.

The first ephemeral of spring always catches you by surprise, as mysterious and discreet as only denizens of the underworld can be. You must attune yourself to the subtle, the unexpected, arising from bare forest floor. Once your eyes catch their contours, however, you will notice that the flowers come in waves, exotic as silk flags in the caravanning desert of early spring. Bloodroot, hepatica, spring beauties. Anemone, trout lily, trillium. Temporary miracles, each one. So gentle in petal, they seem to be able to break even the hardest heart, and soil, wide open.

I had never heard of woodland spring ephemerals until I came to the Blue Ridge. My first week in herbal school the entire class—awkward, eager, and very green at the edges—headed to Great Smoky Mountains National Park to meet these indelible heralds of spring. The Southern Appalachian Mountains are known for their spectacular show of ephemerals, the Smokies hosting the main attraction. For six hours, as our class rambled in the woods, I tried to keep up with my first plant walk. At the end of the day, I had written down a list of over forty different plants. "Many of these flowers," our teacher Juliet Blankespoor said, "will be completely gone within a week or two, so make sure you meet them while you can."

During a break, I wandered away from the group and bent down to the fragile white bloom of an ephemeral whose name I had just learned—*bloodroot*. I touched a newly emerged petal, knowing this flower would only last a few days before it fell away. Other bloodroots nearby were still emerging from the ground. Named for the red sap of their roots, bloodroot appears from the depths of the earth in the most fantastical way. Rising from the soil inside the tight scroll of a single leaf, the plant grows to its full height before the hand-like leaf unfurls, proffering a slender flower splayed like a miracle in its palm. With petals as thin as water, and color like sunlight on snow, bloodroots are so otherworldly beautiful they seem to glow. There is a part of us that feels, acutely, that first wildflower bloom—that sharp acknowledgment of just how much bravery it takes to blossom into the unknown.

Just a few weeks prior I had left behind my whole life in NYC, including my partner of five years and my entire community. As much as I had put on a brave face, most days I was terrified at how vulnerable this new beginning felt. As I looked at the white dapple of these delicate flowers, my mind wandered back to the previous fall, when I had been interviewing for herbal schools. At one school a student had cornered me to ask if I had a thick skin—apparently, ribald teasing was a part of the repartee at this particular establishment. I thought back with a tinge of humor on how, eager to be accepted, I immediately said, "Yes." At the time, I liked to imagine that living in the city had given me a harder edge, but the truth was that I would always be a sensitive person, my skin as naturally thin as bloodroot petals. Gazing at the wonder of these moon-hued blossoms, I was beginning to understand that maybe this tenderness wasn't such a bad thing.

Spring ephemerals are regarded as the lace glove of the flora world. They come and go as swiftly as a spring rain, often so diminutive you can walk by without even noticing them. Some ephemerals are so short-lived, their flowers only last a few days; others, like trillium, can take upward of seven years to even begin to bloom. There is a reason why ephemerals are so rare. These flowers make their appearance when temperatures are low, nutrients are scarce, and water uptake is slowed. Every time they bloom, they run the risk of being felled by a rogue snowstorm, and for most of the time that they're in flower, the rest of the pollinating world is still slumbering. Delicate and scarce, their exquisite gentleness can sometimes be mistaken for daintiness, but in the heart of the forest's own mythology, the story of spring ephemerals is a far cry from fragility. Spring ephemerals, though outwardly delicate, are some of the most resilient plants in the forest. As the very first flowers to bloom in spring, they are emblems of root-deep courage and true bravery. Surviving in some of the most tumultuous months of the season, ephemerals embody the truth of what strength really means.

We place so much emphasis on strength in our culture—strength that looks like fort walls, or indestructible egos, or tears held back until you're alone. Strength that is working fourteen-hour days without complaining or pushing yourself to the finish line even though your body asked you to stop miles ago. We idealize this kind of fortitude, but often the greatest marker of our strength is our ability to be fallible. In her groundbreaking research, social phenom and proud Texan Brené Brown found that not only is vulnerability the key ingredient to living a whole-hearted life, but it is the very definition of strength itself. As she writes in her book *Rising Strong*, "Vulnerability is not winning or losing;

it's having the courage to show up and be seen when we have no control over the outcome. Vulnerability is not weakness; it's our greatest measure of courage."[1]

I remembered how my previous partner in NYC—a distinctly daredevil, jump-off-a-waterfall sort of person—had once criticized me for not taking enough risks. At the time I felt slightly wounded by this observation, but later I realized that I didn't agree. I may not be interested in jumping out of planes or paragliding off mountains, but by loving the way I do, by feeling the depths of what I feel, by choosing to show up with undimmed enthusiasm for life, I take huge risks daily. Sometimes the bravest thing of all is just to allow yourself to be vulnerable.

Most of the year, the courage of ephemerals is invisible. From late spring onward they go dormant, nestled unseen beneath the earth. Still hidden, throughout the winter ephemerals steadily grow their roots, thriving underground in a time when most plants are asleep. By the time spring softens, they rise triumphantly, bearing a message that all gentle-hearted people need to hear, at least once in their life. Your tenderness is not a hindrance to your journey; it is a marker of your resilience. Your outer softness is an indicator of how strong your roots are. Sometimes you might feel as vulnerable and exposed as bloodroot in early spring, but every brave act of allowing yourself to be soft in the world enables you to give the flowers of your journey to this planet. Spring ephemerals remind us that one cannot happen without the other. The gifts you were meant to give to this world hinge on your willingness to endure one of the most gorgeously vulnerable processes on Earth—being yourself.

Still standing in my kitchen, eyeing my swelling pile of camping gear, I decided that I was ready. I stuffed the last wildflower book down into my backpack and hauled the load up to test its weight. It was heavy, but I was strong enough to carry it. It was mid-April, the birds were singing, and I was ready for my first solo camping trip.

Walking the Same Trail Twice

I sat in the small parking lot for a few minutes, summoning up the courage to start hiking as I marveled at the sprinkling of pink-headed spring beauties next to the trail. My friends had given me directions to a spot that was a few hours in, with all the amenities you could need for a stint in the wilderness—a creek, a copse of trees, and a spring. I went over the directions in my head again as I hitched the pack up onto my back. They seemed straightforward enough. I started up the trail with my heart bouncing in my chest.

I hiked slowly, my nervousness slowly dissolving in the wonder of the forest's depths. After an hour of steady walking, I hit a fork in the trail. My friends hadn't told me anything about a fork. I stood, shifting my weight from one foot to another, deciding what to do. Finally, I took the least traveled prong, reasoning that my friends had assured me this particular camping spot was a bit off the beaten path. As I walked, the trail got thinner and thinner until finally it petered out completely into the underbrush. My heart stopped still. I had clearly chosen the wrong path. I began to retrace my steps, turning off the main path to take what I thought was a shortcut back to the fork.

When I reached the trail again, I was relieved. I rigorously headed in the direction I thought would lead me back to the fork. It seemed a long way, but time moves oddly when you're in the forest. It was another half an hour of hiking before I realized, with a start, that I was going back the way I had come in. Knowing that I would need to retrace my steps yet again, redoing nearly all of the hard hiking I had just accomplished, I plunked my heavy pack dispiritedly to the ground, feeling distinctly embarrassed about my lack of wilderness skill. I considered giving up altogether; my shoulders were raw, and I still wasn't sure I could find the campsite. I slumped down next to my pack; I needed a moment to think. Dejected, I wrapped my arms protectively around my knees and laid my head down to rest. I took a few deep breaths, trying to relocate my enthusiasm for the trip. When I opened my eyes, I nearly jumped with delight—a pink lady's slipper orchid was blooming right beside me.

The moment you meet a pink lady's slipper, you know you have just experienced something spectacular. This rare ephemeral's appearance first begins with its leaves, two long tongues unfurling from the ground. Then the stalk rises, sturdy and impossibly straight. Finally, the flower emerges, a tiny plum that billows into an incredible flounce of pink. All orchids seem to boggle the mind with their otherworldly appearance— and pink lady's slippers are no exception. With a color like a deep rosé, the flower is shaped more like a shell than a blossom, with an intricate sea-creature fold called a labellum leading to a glowing space within. Strikingly vulvic, lady's slippers attract people and pollinators alike, a quality that is integral to their reproductive strategy.

Part of why orchids look so exotic is because their pollination depends on their beauty. Most insect-pollinated flowers offer nectar to passersby. Orchids only offer their loveliness. Drawn by their exquisite colors and shapes, an insect will crawl into an orchid looking for its bound-to-be-fantastic nectar. Meanwhile, as they search, the opportunistic orchid pollen hitches a ride on this pollinator to find the next flower. Our local pink lady's slippers are specifically designed to entice our native bumble bee. After crawling inquisitively inside her folds, the blustering, empty-handed bee must then squeeze his way out the top, bopping his head on the flower's reproductive organs and inadvertently carrying its single pollen globule away to greener pastures.

Lady's slippers are rare flowers, in part because they only produce one of these pollen packages a season. In order for another flower to be fertilized, that same bumble bee must be bamboozled enough to retrace his steps and try yet another lady's slipper. Amazingly, it happens. The bee's eager naivete means that lady's slippers continue to propagate. Looking down at the lady's slipper next to me, I saw the same hint of trickster humor in my own situation. Lifting my head to look down the trail, I couldn't help but laugh at myself. Shrugging my sore shoulders good naturedly, I lifted my pack and began down the path once more.

I may have felt silly for getting so mixed up and having to retrace my steps but, I reasoned with myself, the world is mysterious. Who knows, maybe this moment of enthusiastic backtracking would end up being as helpful to the Earth as the zig-zag of an eager bumblebee.

Throughout my life I've fallen for jokes that branded me as gullible or far-fetched ideas that made my friends shake their heads. At times, my innocence has been labeled as naivete. But what others sometimes see as foolishness is a conscious choice that I make anew every day. No matter what happens in my life, I choose to believe in the unseen goodness. I choose to trust the world—even if it sometimes means I end up taking the wrong path for a bit. In some branches of my family, complaining is considered an Olympic sport. Even though sarcastic grumbling was one of the core ways we knew how to find common ground, as I grew older, I noticed the limits of cynicism. In school, as well as in my community, skepticism was often painted as a form of intellectualism, but I also noticed that it was one of the fastest, and easiest, ways to drain the mystery out of things. When we assume the worst, we conclude nothing better is going to come along. When we think we cannot change things, we stop ourselves before we even start. There have been times that choosing to trust has meant that I have needed to walk the same trail over again. But I still prefer this to waiting at the trailhead and never getting started.

When I began experiencing chronic pain, these different ways of seeing the world were brought to the forefront. Dealing with such a stark challenge, it was clear that I had two options. I could either crumple into the victimhood of my hurt, believing that my pain was happening *to me*, or I could decide that everything was happening *for me*, even when it was incredibly hard to see. It wasn't easier to choose the second option, but it was infinitely more life-giving. When I chose to approach life this way, I could recognize the medicine in all things. I trusted that there was, indeed, a wider wisdom. And even though it sometimes meant giving up my certitude, it also meant being delighted, over and over again, by the unexpected support life can bring. As Albert Einstein once said, "There are only two ways to live your life: as though nothing is a miracle, or as though everything is a miracle."

Hiking the familiar path back down to the fork, I hooked my thumbs under my pack straps to relieve some of the weight from my shoulders. My thoughts wandered to my ancestors. I could feel them in my feet as I stepped joyfully into the wilderness. In recent years, psychology has explored our brain's tendency to focus and fixate on negative experiences, an innately adaptive quality called the *negativity bias*. In a world where survival is based, at least in part, on avoiding threat, our negativity bias helps us remember what to avoid in the future. Hiking with a lilt in my step, I wondered, however, if this was the full story. As the sun streamed down onto the flower-dappled path, I had a hunch that optimism has been as inherent to our species' success as our need to be cautious. If our ancestors weren't willing to be idealistically trusting, how could they have done things like cross oceans in canoes, or hike into the arctic circle, or eat a mushroom to see what would happen? What if the fact that we are here at all is a testament to our willingness to be enthusiastic about life's possibilities?

After my grandmother died, my mom was the one who carefully went through all of her things. There were lots of treasured items, but the most unexpected of all was just a little slip of paper. Written in my grandmother's hand and tucked into the back of her day planner, the small notecard said, "*everything is always working out for me.*" My mom donated many things, but the note became an heirloom. Since then, it's become a kind of mantra in our family, especially when things seem like they are decidedly *not* working out for us—which has the lovely side effect of also helping us to laugh in tough moments.

Believing in the good things coming feeds something incredibly important inside of us. In one Harvard study, researchers found that *dispositional optimism*, a mindset in which you tend to expect positive outcomes for the future, has been shown to have a wide variety of health benefits including a reduced risk of cancer, heart disease, stroke, and infection, and it even contributes to a longer life span.[2] Optimists literally live longer to see all those positive projections for the future unfold.

Such tender optimism isn't frivolity or naivete. It's a lifesaving, world-saving, sanity-saving magic—and, I believe, a core ingredient in rescuing the grace of our collective destiny as human beings. When we are trusting enough to believe in new possibilities, untold generosity and healing can flower in the world. When we allow ourselves to be our tender, sensitive, and vulnerable selves, we literally open our hearts to experience more meaning on Earth.

I was humming to myself when I reached the fork in the trail once more. This time, I knew exactly which path to choose. It had taken a few extra hours, and some nicks to my pride, but I felt so much more alive for the detour and delighted about the days ahead.

Setting Up Camp for the First Time

To keep the weight down in my bag, I had packed only a light tarp for cover. The week before my trip I had practiced my knots every day, wanting to perfect the set-up and reassure myself that I could actually do this. The campsite my friends had pointed me toward was a soft shelf of soil just a few paces up from the creek bed. It was private, sheltered, and full of the water's music. I slung the tarp between two trees and secured it at a slant so I could see the creek from where I slept. I dug a fire pit just outside the edge of the tarp and collected small pieces of wood, no thicker than my wrist, to cook with. I dug out the dried wild rice, hard boiled eggs, and nuts I had packed. I wanted to keep the food simple, foraging for greens to add to my one-bowl meals.

Finishing the camp set-up, I rolled out my thin sleeping pad and looked up into the canopy. The forest was dotted with a pointillist-type of hope, the bright green as refreshing to the eye as key limes in a cold glass of water. Within a few weeks the small buds of the canopy would already be hand-sized, as floppy in their newness as a puppy with too-large paws. But for now, it was the height of ephemeral season and the trees were lit with the gentlest daubs of green. Spending time in the forest during this small window in early spring is deeply revitalizing. Like being with an infant or a litter of kittens, it cleanses the soul to be among such newness.

When I first came down to Appalachia to study plants I was the very definition of a babe in the woods. Looking back on it now, I am moved by how innocently I undertook the whole endeavor. I had left my life behind to start a career in something I knew next-to nothing about. It was an act of wild, wide-eyed naivete, and yet it worked out. At the time of this camping trip, I was already a few years into creating my herbal products business and growing my practice. I had started teaching at local events, and my products were well known throughout the community. With no shortage of clients, I was making a decent living from my business. Despite all these outward signs of success, however, the sense of imposter syndrome still followed me like a shadow. It was there, suffocating and familiar, whenever I put out my newsletter or taught a new crop of students.

My first few years in the mountains, I spent a lot of time hanging out at a local punk house. Everything about the house and its inhabitants was new to me. The people who lived there dumpster dove for food and made zines. They gave each other stick-and-poke tattoos and cordoned off the bathroom so you could only poop in a composting toilet up the hill. They were, in summation, very cool. I was deeply intimidated at first. I had arrived there tattoo-less and clueless, still dressing in New York fashions, as bright-eyed and bushy-tailed as they come. Right off the bat, certain members of the house decided they didn't trust me one lick. They eyed me suspiciously whenever I came around, as if my tidy dresses were a dangerous contagion introduced into the safe sea of black cut-offs and brown faded t-shirts. I was dating one of their new roommates, so my presence was inevitable—much to these housemate's chagrin and my own nervousness. It didn't take me long to realize that trying to be like them wouldn't work. It was like fitting a square peg into a round hole. But neither could I just be as nice and agreeable as possible. In the crusty world of punk, sweetness itself was suspect. So I decided to just be me, as completely and totally *me* as possible.

I didn't damp down my spirit, my enthusiasm, or my newness. I got excited about celebrating holidays. I brought over Christmas lights to decorate and party hats for birthdays. I asked a lot of questions—when the housemates made bone broth, or harvested mushrooms, or brought home roadkill to process. If I didn't know a name or a term they used, which was often, I asked what it meant. I was honest about the fact that I had never climbed into a dumpster in my life and had no idea what anarchism actually meant. I wore gloves when I helped process black walnuts because I worked at a children's clothing boutique and couldn't have stained fingers while handling the expensive onesies. Around this time a new friend told me, with obvious admiration, that I was one of the least cool people she'd ever met. To this day, it is still one of the best compliments I've ever received. In a world where coolness was as ubiquitous as knuckle tattoos, I let my dorky naivete and enthusiasm bloom like weeds. Sometimes, I think everyone in this world is just waiting for everyone else to be themselves, so they can finally let their hair down too. By the end of the year, nearly everyone in that house had become my closest friends.

The camping spot where I had set up my tarp was a secret among the community, only passed down to those in the inner circle. Somehow, despite being a total normie with a painfully straight-edged haircut and a deep love for Hallmark channel movies, I had become a part of this network of radically cool punk kids. The map to the spot in my pocket was proof of my belonging. Years later I found this quote by Brené Brown in *Daring Greatly*—"True belonging only happens when we present our authentic, imperfect selves to the world, our sense of belonging can never be greater than our level of self-acceptance."[3] As the years wore on, the community house eventually ended but, to this day, some of those original housemates are still my most beloved friends. In time, I would find out that these friends weren't nearly as cool as I once thought, which just made them all the more interesting, and spectacularly lovable, to me.

Searching the duff around my campsite, I found an old cooking grate a friend must have left behind. I chuckled to myself about those early memories as I began my dinner. It was rough going. The rice was undercooked and nearly inedible. I couldn't keep a fire going long enough to get warm. But when I went to bed that night, curling myself around the most tender part of me, I felt proud.

Vernal Springs

"Head down the trail and turn off to the right before you hit the pedicularis flower patch. Walk toward the ridge for ten minutes through the woods and you'll see it."

These were the directions my friend Matt Hansen gave me to find the spring for drinking water near my campsite. Having woken up the next morning, refreshed and ready for an adventure, I set off to find the spring. Locating the point on the trail he mentioned, I tip-toed over a thicket of white anemone flowers in what I prayed was the right direction. There was no trail to the small watering hole, just a series of forking animal paths and blind hope. I had brought extra water just in case, but it would be an uncomfortably thirsty few days if I didn't find the spring. I climbed over downed trees, careful not to disturb the moss, and tried to make my footfall as light as possible so I wouldn't crush any mayapple stalks. Finally, I knew I must be getting close because I spied the distinctive sprinkle of mottled trout lily leaves. When giving me his bare-bones directions, Matt had reassured me, "you'll know you've found the spring because the forest there is covered in trout lilies."

Trout lilies are named for the patterns on their leaves, marbled like the markings of a trout glimpsed under water. In comparison to our common garden lilies, trout lilies are diminutive. No taller than a hand, the flowers rise as a single yellow bell from the thicket of their maroon-flecked leaves. Face turned downward, petals curling toward the canopy, trout lilies look like tiny faeries, gazing closely at the moss around their feet. Often found in moist areas, these spring ephemerals love to colonize the banks of creeks and small seeps. When you find them, you must step carefully because they are easy to crush underfoot. Though trout lilies may be delicate aboveground, they have amazing longevity. While the flowers themselves may only bloom for the short breath of early spring, their colonies can flourish for decades. Some trout lily communities are so old they predate the surrounding trees.

As I got closer to the spring, I gasped. Trout lilies speckled the ground as far as the eye could see. I had never encountered so many of these sun-colored flowers in one place. I followed their small yellow lights through the woods until the earth dropped away into a moss-lined pool between the trees—I had found the spring.

Sitting down among the lilies, I used two cupped hands to drink directly from the earth. I had been warned that this was a vernal spring, liable to disappear once summer began, but today it was full of clear water, sweet to the taste. After I filled my belly, I lay down, curled like a fawn in the sunshine, and gazed up into the pinwheels of a trout lily close by. Soaked in contentment, I couldn't help but appreciate the ephemeral within me. Eager, tender, sensitive—and yet so much more resilient than I gave myself credit for. Just like these flowers, beneath the outward softness and fragility, there was a profound strength in me.

Walking back to my campsite I remembered, with a smile, that the word *vernal*, which means "of spring," is also a synonym for tender and youthful. I, the spring, and the trout lilies were all vernal creatures— and it was a beautiful thing.

That evening, ensconced back at camp with a gallon of fresh spring water, I set to cooking dinner. Before starting the fire, I wandered bare-foot into the woods, looking to see what I could gather. There was early wood nettle, mountain chickweed, and a spattering of heart-shaped violet greens. Most of the trees were just starting to unfurl, but a basswood had already set out its soft leaves. The size of small plates, the leaves would make perfect wraps for my freshly cooked rice. As I collected a few for dinner, I noticed I wasn't the first one to munch these new leaves. Spring is the most vulnerable time to be a deciduous tree. Soft and tasty, a tree's new leaves are a boon to deer with winter-hungry bellies, emerging insects, and humans such as myself. Tenderness nearly always means risk, but that same vulnerability is what literally feeds the world. As Brené Brown so powerfully captures, "Vulnerability is the birthplace of love, belonging, joy, courage, empathy, and creativity. It is the source of hope, empathy, accountability, and authenticity. If we want greater clarity in our purpose or deeper and more meaningful spiritual lives, vulnerability is the path."[4]

I thought about this as the sun began to fade between the trees, and the embers of my fire picked up the colors of the sunset, glowing brighter. My rice bubbled away happily. I moved a branch to make the flame steady and singed the tip of my finger. I abandoned my pot for a moment to plunge my hand in the cold drift of the creek. I couldn't help but chuckle. Every experience was teaching me something new, and I was grateful.

We spend so much time on Earth trying to protect ourselves from the unknown, thinking that if we only insulate ourselves with thick-enough padding, we can avoid the pitfalls of being human. But we didn't come here to be foolproof. If we wanted to experience that, we would have stayed in the place we were in before we came—whether you think of that place as heaven, source, higher realms, or a safe dispersion of molecules. Vulnerability is not the bad card in the bargain of humanity; it is the gift we came here to receive. To be here is to experience the tenderness of being in form, the blessed vulnerability of having a body that ages, loved ones that are born and then die, and hopes that rise and fall like hot air balloons. Our spirit came in on the wings of our immense curiosity to experience having a heart that can be broken open

by both disaster and beauty. We came here to forget, and then redis-
cover, the most fragile and essential tendril of all—how cherished we
are. We came so we could go on the journey of rediscovering this goodness and to experience the revelation of being our fully miraculous, and
entirely fallible, selves. We are here to remember that, just like a sprig
of chickweed in spring, the earnestness of our being is both an earthly
refreshment and a truly nourishing offering.

New Lambs

For the rest of my week in the woods, the days and nights flowed as
seamlessly into one another as songbirds winging from tree to tree.
During the day I explored the neighboring coves, wildflower ID books
in hand, sometimes getting lost but always finding my way back again.
By night I cooked up my rice and ate while gazing up into the blanket of
the sky, the light from beyond shining through the pinpricks of the canopy's weave to find my expanding eyes. One night I woke up, sure that
I had heard a bear scratching around my tarp. I lay for a while, looking
at the quicksilver of the moving creek, until I fell back into dreams. I
slept differently out there. I woke up more easily, and more frequently,
to the startle of sounds or the shock of stars overhead—and yet every
day I felt even more deeply rested. On the last morning of my sojourn, I
undid the sturdy knots holding my tarp in place and felt a warm flame
of pride leap in the center of my chest. I had completed my first solo
camping trip.

I stopped by the spring one last time to fill up my canteen, then
started on the trail, my pack lighter now for all the food I had eaten.
As I made my way up the now-familiar path, I bid goodbye to all the
various ephemerals I had come here to meet. The trout lilies with their
happy yellow bells and trilliums with their dappled toadstool leaves.
The small fingernail-sized spring beauties tipped with their impossible
dots of pink. Shooting stars exploding like tiny orange-ringed rockets

from the ground. The pink lady's slipper orchids, stunning and familiar, an entrance into the softest parts of my own being.

As I walked, I reflected on all the worries I had brought with me into this camping trip—the inadequacy I felt in my business, the way the shadow of imposter syndrome perpetually followed me, the fear that I somehow wasn't enough. After a week of living among the flowers, of letting myself be as brave and vulnerable as spring itself, all these worries seemed as far away as the clouds. I didn't have to worry about being perfect or inviolable. I just had to be myself.

When I got back to the parking lot and saw my car waiting for me at the trailhead, I was surprised. Everything looked the same, and yet I felt as if I were a new person. My foal legs had strengthened over the days away. I both felt both more tender and more confident. More innocent and even more sure of myself. I sat in the parking lot again before I drove away, this time lingering out of pure enjoyment. When I was ready, I started the car for the long drive home.

At the time of this trip I lived at the end of a rural valley road, dotted by homesteads and farms. In early spring, the miles of pasture and hillsides came alive. Driving along that road never failed to make my heart soar. I adored seeing the return of the green fields and the great blankets of streamside flowers, but my favorite were all the wee creatures that begin to make their appearance in the frocked hillsides. The new calves swishing their tails in uncoordinated excitement as they drank milk from their mother's bellies. The little rabbits darting with bouncy ears between the stones of the farm walls. And the lambs—tiny and fleece covered, their tender silliness melting the most ice-hardened heart. In early spring one of my greatest delights was spotting them prancing across the field, flicking their soft ears and flopping down on legs askew.

I wanted to delay my return home a bit longer, so once I got to the valley, I pulled my car over to the side of the rural road to visit the newly arrived lambs. Standing on the other side of the fence, the lambs were all curiosity and open wonder. They cocked their ears at me and danced sideways; each new experience seemed to delight their whole bodies. So trusting and precious, the lambs broke my chest right open. A series of questions, just as curious as the lamb's gaze, began to form in my mind.

If we are willing to be open, to let ourselves be vulnerable and unsure, could we possibly hold ourselves with as much holy joy as we do the newly arrived lamb? If we can value our own tenderness, could we start to see the angels within everything again?

There is something wholly angelic about early spring. Every time I connect with the vernal newness of the flowers, the lambs, the new leaves on the trees, I can't help but think about heavenly beings. Sometimes relegated to the realms of antiquity, angels have continued to survive across many different religious and spiritual divides. Amazingly, in one 2011 poll, eight out of ten Americans said they believed in these higher guides.[5] Angels, whether seen as metaphor, mythology, or actual guidance from the unseen, have remained in our psyche as a symbol of unconditional love for millennia. As a culture, we have continued to believe in angels because there is a part of us that still trusts in the veracity of that which is vernal, eternal, tender, and optimistic. Angel energy is pure warmth, acceptance, and understanding. It is complete nonjudgmental care, benevolence, and optimism. To me, the Earth herself is an angel. Every spring, I remember how lucky I am to have her as my guardian.

In her luminous book *Lessons from the Twelve Archangels*, Belinda Womack describes angels as the ultimate parents. In her words, "Each person's true desire is 'Please, take care of me.' . . . Angels are parents who are available at all times and in all situations."[6] Regardless of whether a belief in literal angels sustains you, there is something deeply moving about acknowledging an energy that loves and cherishes you unconditionally. It is healing to embrace the possibility of an energy that celebrates and nurtures your newness and sensitivity. One that is, in essence, the great warm encouragement of the Earth in spring. No matter our belief system, we need only open our heart to the tender reality of a spring flower to feel this current of angelic energy running through all things—including our own ephemeral beings.

Do not be afraid to embrace what is tender and naive about you—to love what is innocent. Do not be ashamed of the part of you that doesn't know, the part that isn't sure it's going to work, because that is the same part of you that is willing to bloom. Within you is the lamb in the field. The ephemeral in the forest. The leaf with its newborn green. When we cherish our vulnerable naivete, we protect our ability to build new dreams of hope for this planet. Just like the white halo of a bloodroot flower, you become an angel in this world every time you are brave enough to bloom.

EXERCISE:

Valuing Vulnerability

Take your time to answer the following reflection questions to embrace the wisdom inherent to your own courageous vulnerability.

1. What is one of the bravest things you've ever done? How did you feel right before you did it? How did you feel after?

2. What is the one thing about you that others might judge as naive? How might this quality actually be a source of strength for you?

3. Who is an emblem of courage to you? What about them do you admire?

4. What is one brave thing you did today?

5. If a child asked you, how would you define the word *bravery*?

6. If no one told you it was unrealistic, what future would you dream for the Earth and all human beings?

6

DROP DOSAGES

THE MUD SQUELCHED beneath my boots. It was a warm day on the empty lake bottom, and the silt was soft as pudding underfoot. More than once, my rubbers stayed stuck as my stockinged foot popped out of my boot to make the next step, hanging comically in the cold air instead. In winter, when the dam that creates this reservoir is opened to create room for storm runoff, the lake disappears, becoming a mud-hollowed bowl. Throughout the summer the lake is a mirrored paradise of green and blue, but in January the land transforms into a soggy moonscape. Docks from vacation houses stretch down the long hillsides into nothing. A small creek trickles over the flats, its snake-quiet flow all that remains of the expanse.

Despite this emptiness, winter is my favorite time to visit the lake. I come with civic pride to pick up the plastic flotsam that has settled to the bottom and with curiosity to see the alien contours of a land exposed. But mostly, I come because there are diamonds in the dirt.

Tiny quartz crystals, perfectly pointed, clear as air, live in the silt here. Formed millions of years ago, these "diamonds" are a local treasure, and winter is a rare opportunity to find them. Rockhounding typically requires two things—mud-worthy clothes and the slow shifting of one's perception. At first, you can't see the crystals at all. Like tiger stripes in the jungle that made them, the diamonds blend in expertly with the mud and the twinkle of discarded glass. Once you know how to see them, however, you'll start finding them everywhere.

The first time I visited the lake to look for diamonds, I was told to go on a sunny day in midwinter and follow the glitter. For half an hour, all I found were pieces of old broken bottles until I began to recognize the subtle flash of quartz. It didn't take me long to figure out that the smallest ones gave off the greatest glint. Whenever I saw an extravagant wink, a lighthouse beacon that seemed to promise a boulder, inevitably, my shining goliath turned out to be the size of an ant's abdomen. At first I was disappointed. But I soon learned that these little diamonds are the most perfect specimens at the lake. While the larger ones are often muddled, broken, or half-formed, the tiny ones are always the clearest, with two symmetrical points at their poles. It turns out that the smallest ones are the greatest treasures of all.

At the end of my day traversing the muddy lake bottom, I could gather all the crystals I had found in a single hand. A galaxy swirled across my palm. Once home, I arranged the diamonds in a starry cluster on my bedside table. When I fell asleep that night I saw a kaleidoscope behind my eyes—tiny pinpricks that shimmered like the surface of the water before I slipped under. Each diamond felt like a little seed, bringing me into my dreams.

A Little Fish in a Big Pond

I used to think smallness meant unimportance. When I was a child and was told I was "little," I'd puff out my chest indignantly and say, "I'm big!" The way I understood it, bigness meant you got to sit at the grownups table and go on rollercoasters and make decisions for your-self. For a long time, I thought all I wanted was to be "big." What I didn't know was that the race for bigness doesn't end when you become adult-sized; it only spreads into further corners of your life—finances, houses, friend circles. In our culture, bigness isn't a singular accomplishment, it's an ever-growing goal; how hard we're willing to run after it often defines our perceived success.

Over time, I centered this chase in my own life. When I did well in school, I wanted to do better. When I finished one project, I imme-diately began planning another. When I accomplished an import-ant goal, I didn't stop to relish the moment but pushed myself to set my sights even higher. Like most people who grew up in similar environs, I caught the bigness virus, unconsciously letting it repli-cate within me because I believed that I needed to be big in order to be worthy. I still remember the moment, however, when I real-ized bigness wouldn't buy me the one thing I sought through all this success—self-acceptance.

I was a few years into running my business and had finally bal-anced my books in the black. I had begun making enough money sell-ing my wares at farmers markets to pay my bills, and my local classes had developed a bit of a following. I maintained a newsletter that I sent out four times a year and a quiet Facebook presence, but mostly I hadn't ventured into the world of social media.

Then I found out about a new platform called Instagram. It was being touted as the best way to reach people, so I made an account and started posting. One of the first things I noticed was how much this pressure to be *big* made me feel small. My audience grew very slowly at first. I was so proud when it finally hit one hundred people. But as soon as I compared myself to my friends with thousands of follow-ers, I'd feel bad about my littleness. In those moments of self-doubt, the pressure to discard my account was strong—what did it matter if I was only talking to a comparatively small handful of people? In a world where bigness is synonymous with success, what was the point if I was so very small?

One day I made a decision. No matter how small my audience was, I would keep speaking to them. In fact, *because* my audience was so small, it felt easier to envision who I was speaking to. So, I began sharing as if I were talking directly to each individual person; I stopped worrying if the message had carrying power for the hoards. I still struggled with self-doubt—I wondered if what I had to share was truly valuable and often felt like a tiny fish in an intimidatingly big pond—but a few months after I began posting, I got a message. It was a brief note that has stayed with me to this day. It said, "Everything you write feels as if you are speaking directly to me. Sometimes I feel so small in my life, but every time I read something you post, I feel seen." It was one of the first pieces of fan mail I'd ever received. It was tiny, just a few lines, but it completely changed the way I thought—about my business and myself.

I didn't have to make it big to make a difference. I didn't have to *be* big. I could just be me, a person speaking to other people, letting them know that our littleness was as precious, and powerful, as any diamond. I came to see that smallness was a gift and, over time, my willingness to pay attention to the little things, like tucking love notes into each outgoing package, would become the building block of my "big success."

As the years rolled on, my audience grew much larger than I ever could have anticipated, but it was all rooted in my commitment to relishing the glimmers in the lake bottom, the small beacons of belief that shone through the mud of my self-doubt. As my business grew, I got to see firsthand that getting bigger does not mean the worries, doubts, or struggles with self-worth disappear. In fact, bigness itself often acts as a microscope, asking us to focus, with even more attentiveness, on the details of who we are, what we believe, and what truly matters. But when we are willing to cherish these fine details, we find diamonds. The deeper you look into the microscopic realms, the more you will notice that the littlest things are the most powerful of all. The smallest elements of our world are giants that call our attention back to what is so vastly important.

The Blessing of Being Small

This world was once a big place, full of oceans that stretched into the Otherworld, old-growth giants six feet around, wooly mammoths and dinosaurs—and in the midst of all the bigness, we had the privilege of being blessedly small. For many millennia, human beings were a little presence upon this Earth. For most of our history, we have lived in close bands, our species surviving, in large part, off the generosity of the land's smallest gifts—berries, nuts, spruce tips and, yes, even grubs. Some archeologists hypothesize that this long stretch of preagricultural smallness was a golden age for humanity, a time marked by egalitarianism, sustainability, and peace between us and the world.[1] Sometime after the advent of agriculture, however, came the rise of the large.

In some corners of the world, vast monocrops of grains led to bigger populations, the advent of city-states, and cycles of inequality and exploitation. Along the way, the measure for success became defined by quantity instead of quality, largess instead of expertise or finesse. Western culture today is the great-grandchild of this shift. The further we moved away from valuing the tiny workings of the world, the more we became obsessed with becoming as large as the Earth itself. We built skyscrapers as tall as the trees, colonization became as far reaching as dandelion seeds, and the wide native prairie lands of North America disappeared under fields of soybeans.

The problem with this admiration for the larger-than life is that it disconnects us from our ability to *be* a part of life itself. When we dam a river to provide electricity, we forget that true power is the fertileness of free-flowing waterways. In the end, our obsession with largeness inevitably obscures the blessing of being human—the ability to be devotees of the small. Our hands, and expert opposable thumbs, were made to do such intricate things as cradle thimble berries, knot rugs, and find crystals in the mud. Our eyes were designed to notice the subtly of emotion in an animal track, to see patterns in the shoreline. Our hearts were created to be moved by understated majesty.

For all the bigness we've historically enshrined, we also live in a time when we are beginning to question the primacy of such large living. Tiny houses, slow fashion, local food—the promise of the small is returning like a glimmer underfoot. Just like searching for diamonds in the silt, it may take a moment until we can see the way forward, but each small glimmer acts like a breadcrumb through the forest. Today, science acknowledges that all the most important things in life are spun from the smallest material—like DNA, algae, and the elements that make up our soil, the same minerals that get washed away with the inattention of large-scale agriculture. These miniature things are the building blocks of life itself, and we are waking up to the realization that, if we want a future in this big world, we will need to learn how to cherish what is so preciously little. A new era is underway, and it starts with the medicine of the small.

What Holds You Back from Flowering?

I put four drops of the sweet water directly onto my tongue. Twisting the dropper back into its tiny blue bottle, I felt an immediate shift inside of me—as subtle, yet unmistakable, as the sun coming out from behind a cloud. I put the bottle back down next to the sink and looked into the bathroom mirror—did my eyes just get brighter? I smiled at myself in the reflection. I often don't realize how fogged I'm feeling until I take a few drops of a flower essence and the glass clears.

Before I ever learned about how to make tinctures, wildcraft, or camp in the wilderness, I fell in love with flower essences. I had just moved to New York City and was unpacking my suitcase when a book about Bach flower remedies fell out of the zippered compartment. Stashed there by my mother, the book had been a gift from one of her clients. Aware of my growing obsession with plants, she thought I might be interested and passed it along. For the first few months in New York I was busy, commuting every day to Manhattan for my job watering office plants in skyscrapers and tending our backyard garden. For months, the book sat on my shelf unopened. I was intrigued, but also skeptical about this subtle realm of plant medicine.

I'm not sure what finally drew me to pick it up, but one day I was curious enough to crack the book open. I began reading, my incredulousness perched like spectacles between me and the page. Before I reached the end of the first chapter, however, I had tears gathering in my eyes. To this day, I can still remember the texture and feeling of that moment—it was one of the most shockingly reorienting and wonderous experiences of my life. I put the book down and began to cry, not because I was sad, but because what I had just read felt so deeply true inside.

Physically speaking, flower essences are made by floating blooms in water underneath the sun's light. Through the process, the water becomes the carrier of that particular flower's vibration. This infusion is then preserved (typically with brandy) and further diluted to be taken in drop dosages. The theory of flower essences is founded on the idea that a flower's inherent energy can help us to heal the deepest emotional wounds, shifting the seemingly unchangeable internal patterns that are holding us back from flowering.

When I opened that book, a whole new, and yet profoundly familiar, world unfolded before me—a world where the healing we most need is as subtle as flower water and as potent as allowing yourself to bloom. Sitting in my windowless room in Brooklyn, I surrendered to the gravity of the moment as tears rolled down my face. In time, I would start making my own essences, eventually teaching thousands of people around the world the process, but in that moment, all I knew was that some small part of me was forever changed.

The contemporary practice of flower essences was first developed by Edward Bach in the early part of the twentieth century. An English bacteriologist and pathologist by trade, Bach's earlier career was defined by vaccine research and development.[2] In 1917, he collapsed from a tumor and was diagnosed with only three months to live. Like many healing crises, this ended up being a moment of sacred reorientation in his life.

After hearing his prognosis, Bach accepted a position at the Royal London Homeopathic Hospital. There, he began to notice similarities between homeopathy and vaccines. In his quest for healing, he soon gave up the position and moved out of the city altogether. In the countryside, Bach began experimenting with creating highly dilute flower remedies as a way to heal the emotional undercurrents of illness. He started by collecting the morning dew off blossoms—a process that was exquisite, yet labor intensive. Eventually, he developed a more sustainable practice of making essences by floating flowers in spring water, allowing them to infuse through the natural alchemies of sunshine and time. We still use this same process to make flower essences today.

Flowers have their own special energy in the lifecycle of a flowering plant. They are the penultimate expression of a plant reaching its full potential, a symbol of its growth and its inherent gifts. When a plant flowers, it has realized one of its primary life purposes—to give its pollen, seed, and fruit to the world, giving birth to the next generation and essentially feeding creation itself. Flower essences, made from this energy of blooming and fruition, help people connect into the blueprint of what is possible for them in this lifetime so they can begin to give their gifts to the world.

Much like a single acorn contains all the information needed to become the mighty oak, each one of us is born with a blueprint that holds all the magnificent possibilities of our lives. Flower essences work by dismantling whatever is inside of us that is blocking this natural unfurling. In flower essence theory, these inner blockages come from our negative self-beliefs, the programs of maladaptive thinking that limit our growth and disconnect us from experiencing the true reality of our being. Flower essences help us become aware of these beliefs as the unproductive protection mechanisms that they are, releasing them from their unnecessary service. In the midst of life's hardships, it's normal to calcify or constrict our views of ourselves, or what is possible. Flower essences help to dilate the spirit once again and open our eyes to all the ways in which we are meant to blossom.

In the years after Bach debuted this new form of therapy, it proved so effective, people came from all over Europe to experience healing at the Bach center. Twenty years after his original prognosis, Bach developed the thirty-eight remedies known as the Bach compendium, creating a subtle healing modality that would become a worldwide phenomenon. Today, the practice of making flower essences continues to bloom among herbalists, acupuncturists, veterinarians, and medicine makers across the globe.

Going through the Keyhole

For those of us who are used to dwelling in the scientific world of observable phenomenon, flower essences can be hard to wrap our heads around—doing so requires us to move our gaze away from the obvious and into the realms of the subtle. After over a decade of working with flower essences in my practice, I've experienced healing that could be called miraculous. I've seen people with tricky conditions who never seemed to respond to conventional medicine have their ailments evaporate after finding just the right flower essence. I've witnessed people stuck in a decade-long holding pattern suddenly break free and begin a new chapter. I've watched as my own self-limiting beliefs, patterns I thought were simply going to be constants in my life, fade so completely that I forget whatever held me back in the first place. Every step of the way in my journey of becoming an herbalist, spiritual teacher, healer, and writer has been supported by these subtle, powerful medicines. I have seen myself born, and reborn, through the gentle angels of these essences.

Sometimes, when I teach about flower essences, students are curious how something so dilute can be so potent. In response, I nearly always mention the efficacy of vaccines, or the devastation of something as minute as a virus. Small, clearly, does not mean inconsequential. In the end, however, flower essences don't work by convincing the mind; they are most effective when they go all the way to the heart of a matter. So most of the time, to answer this question, I explain with a single metaphor—the keyhole.

Some things have been buried so deep inside of us, it is as if they are under lock and key. Traumas, belief systems, wounds, memories. Like a chest buried in the sea, we keep the hardest things hidden within the deep. Trying to reach these places with big medicines like pharmaceuticals or even more potent herbal preparations is like attempting to open a jewelry box with a beach ball. Approaching what we've locked away straight-on doesn't seem to work either—all our inner alarm bells go off the moment we sense an approach and we curl into ourselves like clams. In order to reach what has been most profoundly locked within our beings, we need something that is small enough to go through the keyhole. We need a subtle medicine, one that can drift past our defenses and deliver healing to the part of us that needs it the most. Flower essences can help heal the deepest parts of us because they are small enough to move through the keyhole.

Big things are obvious, easy to point to, and hard to avoid. Big things need big landings and cause big repercussions when they are deployed—meteorites, tsunami waves, fireworks. Big medicine is similar. Pharmaceuticals, surgery, and chemotherapy are all powerhouses with an important place in the realm of healing, but as devotees of the big guns, we forget that, by relishing and caring for the small, we can sometimes avoid the need for such grand artillery after all. When we tend the subtle, we can sometimes head off the overt. When we eat an apple a day, we no longer need the root canal. When we take care of our inner emotional terrain, landslides don't happen as often. Flower essences, daily multivitamins, an acupuncture needle. The small is a quiet revolution, able to shift things on a cellular and spiritual level.

The bigger things get the more we unconsciously crave the subtle. I remember hearing once that an overwhelming sugar tooth is often an ancestral craving for small bits of bitter, which can help stimulate digestion. You'll notice, if you ever make a batch of too-sweet cookies, that sugar eaten in excess begins to become bitter. Sometimes we can curb a sugar binge simply by taking a few drops of a bitter elixir. Our craving for the subtle is similar. We may think that we are hungering for a big change in our life, but what we're really wanting is a subtle shift in thinking, feeling, and experiencing—a shift that begins in the smallest places of our being.

We live in a time and culture that often scoffs at the small. Whether it's the size of your social media following, the number of books you've read this year, or the amount of dollars in your bank account. As a society, we can be so hyper-focused on the big that we miss all of the healing that the subtle has to offer. Yet even the most tightly sealed door has some sort of opening, no matter how small. The gates of an outmoded cultural structure also have a keyhole.

I often remind my students as they leave to go back home that they are just like flower essences. They may live in families or communities where the idea of a flower essence would seem as foreign as the ocean's bottom—but just by returning to those communities and being willing to bloom where they are they help shift the tide. All you need is a few drops of a flower essence in a cup of water and the water itself changes. Each of us carries our own medicine—minute and amazingly powerful. You are the drop that can shift the whole aquifer of our culture. You are a flower essence for our Earth. When you can appreciate the tiniest building blocks of yourself, you make a quantum leap that can change the world.

Making a Quantum Leap

In recent years, the field of quantum physics has been creating big waves in science, changing the way we perceive reality. Often overlapping with the long-held wisdom of Indigenous cultures, quantum physics' research into the smallest particles of matter has found mathematical evidence for things like the flexibility of time, the idea that the world we see around us is a reflection of a much wider reality, and the basic concept that everything is made up of invisible energy.

In pop culture we often use the term *quantum leap* to signify a monumental shift in thinking or being. We use the phrase so often, most of us have forgotten where the term actually came from. In physics, a quantum leap isn't a large thing—it's microscopic. A change that happens within an atom, a quantum leap is when an electron jumps from one energy level to another. Physically speaking, it's a tiny shift, but one that can instantaneously change the whole nature of the atom, and therefore matter itself. First theorized in 1913 by Niels Bohr, quantum leaps (then called quantum jumps) shocked the scientific establishment.

When we take a quantum leap, we have the ability to change on a dime, to go from Point A to Point Z, bypassing the laborious steps in-between. On a physical level, a quantum leap is infinitesimal, but when the leap is made, reality changes instantly.

Looking at the state of our world—including the health of our oceans, our soil, and our own psyches—no one would deny that a change is needed. But perhaps the shift that we are seeking is not an obvious overhaul, but something much more subtle, something each of us can initiate by focusing on the minutia of our own healing. Microscopic shifts within can cause profound changes without.

By giving ourselves permission to tend to the humblest details of our own journey, monumental sea-changes can happen in the world at large. When we discard the idea that any self-focus is selfish, we recognize that the journey of seeking self-compassion is actually how we empower the smallest units of our beings, giving ourselves the energy needed to make a quantum shift here on Earth. The jumps we make in our own thinking can create a leap in the overall consciousness of our planet. From the perspective of the quantum, the next step in humanity's evolution is not to grow larger, but to reclaim the transformational power of the small.

Becoming Swamp Angels

A place of miracles in miniature, Florida is rich in a vast array of habitats and cultures. Before the arrival of the Spanish, Florida supported over 350,000 people in a multitude of distinct populations, with as many dialects as there were microhabitats.[3] Florida was home to several vastly powerful civilizations, including the Apalachee, the Timucua, and the most legendary of all—the Calusa. The *Calusa*, a word that is purported to have meant "fierce ones" in their language, were unique among the world's large civilizations. Though similar in vastness and complexity to other cultures, the Calusa civilization was built on the sheer bounty of the ocean.[4] For a long time, Western scholars assumed that all politically and socially complex societies must practice large-scale agriculture, but the Calusa rewrote history, showing that highly powerful, influential, artistic, and culturally rich societies can flourish by relying on the small gifts of food offered by a lush land. Because their waters teemed with such abundance, there was no need to focus on cultivating large fields of sunflowers, corn, or squash. Instead, like the mountainous middens along their beaches, they built a whole civilization from the gifts of the sea.

Like many Indigenous peoples around the world, the Calusa believed in reincarnation, but their hue of rebirth looked very different from how we conceive of it today. Like the Darwinian theory of evolution, we normally assume the purpose of reincarnation is to get "bigger," graduating from smaller or less complex lifeforms so we can eventually ascend to the apex of evolution—the ranks of humanity. For the Calusa, however, reincarnation *began* with being human.[5] Instead of getting larger or more complex with each go-around, we got smaller. Once you shed the shell of being human you could become an alligator or a deer. From there you might pick through the marsh as a heron, run under the waves as a pinfish, and finally, alight upon the world as a mosquito. Over time, the Calusa believed, you would evolve into smaller and smaller packages until, one day, you became so little you simply disappeared into the vast light. For the Calusa, the smaller you became, the closer you drew to the divine.

This humble perception of evolution sustained one of the most impressive civilizations on Earth—and remained an unchanging piece of the Calusa faith. Though they faced terrible pressure and military might, the Calusa are legendary for having resisted all attempts at missionization. Like the many heartbreaking stories of colonization, however, Spanish disease, enslavement, and genocide eventually fragmented the mighty Calusa civilization. Surviving populations fled to Cuba or integrated into newly arriving groups of Native peoples, including the current-day Seminole and Miccosukee.[6] Though the Calusa empire fell, their legacy still lives on today within the tribes of Florida and the earth itself, embedded like diamonds within the landscape.

I look forward to two things each winter—hunting for diamonds at the lake and heading down to Florida for a week of canoe camping. Every year I go to these abundant, subtropical shores to warm my bones and remember my smallness. At home, embroiled in To-Do lists, I have a tendency to heap too many responsibilities on my plate, as if it were up to me to shoulder the whole world. When I go to the forests of Florida's dwarf pines, I remember the beauty of being my tiny, wondrously fallible self. Among the forests of live oaks, I can strip off the costume of the teacher or the healer and just be a devotee, someone who is perpetually at the beginning of my evolution.

In the wilderness, I surrender to the bliss of stripping my thoughts down to simple, light-filled things—like how far I want to paddle for the day or when to feed the fire with palmetto fronds. I eat wild clementines on the shore and I feel, with blessed relief, just how refreshing it is to be little. I listen to the distant lilt of the whip-poor-will and remember that true inner-evolution isn't about getting bigger, but about letting go of that inner critic who is always pushing me to become more. Peering up at the sky to find the north star, so much closer to the horizon in these southern climes, I become a speck of light in the darkness and am reborn. It is a kind of coziness, to remember how small we truly are—and it is a blessing that could save our world. In Florida I allow myself to become so wonderfully little that I return to the heaven that is possible here on Earth.

I normally try to make it down south before the mosquitos awake from their wintertime lull, but it doesn't always happen that way. Sometimes, sitting in my canoe at dusk, watching the migratory mergansers swim among their nebula of kin, I catch a mosquito alighting on my bare skin. Before I wave it away, I greet this little one with the name still used by Florida's old-timers—swamp angel. Every time I see one of these slim, sentient beings, I try to find a space of gratitude within me, even as I encourage them to search elsewhere for their dinner. Later at night, when I inevitably find a few rogue bites on my arms, I remind myself that, in the Calusa's way of thinking, I have just been visited by an elder soul. The next wave of our evolution is not to grow bigger, but to return to the heaven of being small.

The Tiny Gift of Everything

The world about you is vast and wide, but the world you live in is actually very small. The more you live in that smaller world, the happier and healthier you will become. You will experience safety there and love. Your work in that world will be plain and easy to accomplish, and your place in it will be easy to recognize. Birds don't make their nests in the sky.

—OUR LADY OF WOODSTOCK A MARIAN APPARITION,
VIA CLARK STRAND AND PERDITA FINN

I once had the opportunity to attend a Japanese tea ceremony. Robed in plain cotton yukatas, we sat in the bare room with a master ceremonialist perched on the tatami mat before us. The ritual was deceptively simple. If you weren't paying attention, it would seem like barely anything was happening at all. A whisk is picked up. A whisk is put back down. Water steams. A bowl is turned, and then turned again. The ceremony itself is an intricate artwork of the subtle, like lacquer-work glowing in a dark room. Every motion has a purpose. Each small gesture is infused with elegant intent. In a Japanese tea ceremony, the simple motions are imbued with such profundity, by the time you finally bring the tea to your lips it tastes like nothing you've ever experienced.

Floating on my back in the Florida springs, gazing up into the blue-white sky, I can feel another way of being in the world. The best things in my life happen, not when I'm pushing for excess, but when I move from a place of minutely elegant intent—when I act as if I were a tea master and life itself was the ceremony. Sometimes, I picture a world where every small motion was given that much thought. A world that was defined by unending presence and attention, a love for the subtle, a reverence for what is small. Floating there, with the tiny bubbles of the water gathering around me, I imagine a world like that would truly feel like heaven on Earth—and then I remember that this world is already here now. When we are willing to appreciate the smallness of our own selves, we become a flower essence in the well, ancient crystals arising from the lake's bottom. When we embrace ourselves in all our glorious limitations and precious littleness, we slow down enough to recognize the gorgeous niche we get to fulfill in this world. When we release the need for every gesture to be grand, our life becomes as elegant, meaningful, and essential as a tea-steeped ritual on a quiet afternoon. When we let go of pushing ourselves to be more, we can relish all the little things that make our lives possible and bless their existence in return.

In *Braiding Sweetgrass*, Robin Wall Kimmerer talks about the benediction of strawberries and how their ripening illustrates the true nature of Earth's economy. Little blessings given feely from the soil, strawberries are reminders that the wider world practices an ever-cycling gift economy. Each time the gift changes hands, its life-giving qualities are amplified. Kimmerer writes—

> Strawberries first shaped my view of a world full of gifts simply scattered at your feet. A gift comes to you through no action of your own, free, having moved towards you without your beckoning.

It is not a reward; you cannot earn it, or call it to you, or even deserve it. And yet it appears. Your only role is to be open-eyed and present. Gifts exist in a realm of humility and mystery—as with random acts of kindness, we do not know their source.[7]

It is humbling to be the recipient of such goodness, and yet, for every gift that we receive, we naturally give back in return. After the bears fill their bellies with wild berries, they carry those seeds in their digestive tract, inevitably bringing the gift of new berry patches wherever they go. We are no different. When we embrace the tiny gifts we've been handed, we carry their seeds within us, naturally paying them forward.

Often, when people reflect on the acts of spontaneous kindness that changed their lives, the moments recalled usually did not involve gigantic demonstrations of charity. They were smiles given at just the right moment, a dinner bill paid when someone was on their last dollar, a card sent in the midst of unspeakable loss. Though small, it was these gestures that ultimately changed the shape of someone's life.

The world, as it turns out, is made up of tiny blessings. We receive them but we are also *one of them*. To be a human being, gathering strawberries in a basket or finding seashells on the shore, is to be a part of a gift economy based on the smallest and most life-giving exchanges. We, through these little gestures, can help the generosity of the Earth to endure.

Perhaps this was why the Calusa believed in their particular brand of soulful evolution. When we embrace the small, we do not lose our power; we can simply *give more of it* to the world. By taking on a smaller form, we free our spirit to gift its boundless essence to the Earth. When we simplify our motions, the simple whisking of tea can become monumental. When we slow down enough to plant seeds, we become attuned to the smallest needs of the soil. We have been trying to become better by upgrading, but the human spirit can grow as wide as a mountainside when we embrace the gift of humility.

At its heart, humility isn't about the downgrading of one's self; it is about recognizing your specialness through the lens of all the blessings you've been bestowed. Humility is gazing up into the sky, remembering there are more stars in the universe than grains of sand on all the beaches in the world, and feeling exhilarated because you *get to be* a part of it all. It is knowing that you are as small as a quantum with the power to change the world.

We keep waiting for a catastrophe to wake us up or a worldwide moratorium on war. Meanwhile, we each have been given everything we need to dissolve the locked doors before us, slipping through the keyhole to open the door. It begins with recognizing that who you are in this moment is powerful and perfect. Your smallness is your power.

Reseeding the World

May I be the tiniest nail in the house of the universe, tiny but useful.

—MARY OLIVER

I believe deeply that the Earth is fed by our gift giving—whether we are donating our talents through charity work, raising a family, or leaving a literal offering in the soil. Wherever I go now, I take a small pouch of lake diamonds. After years of hounding for these quartz crystals, I realized that what I truly desired was to give them all away. So every time I visit somewhere special—like the Florida springs—or I am brought to my knees by the gift of a handful of berries, I leave a crystal behind. As I push that tiny perfect light into the earth, the feeling of completeness and contentment is nearly indescribable. Watching my small bag of diamonds dwindle over the years, I've realized that I'm excited for the day when I've given away the whole collection and created, in its place, a constellation of gratitude. When we love ourselves in our smallness, we become the perennial recipients of the gift of being on this planet—and are able to recognize the gifts we have to share in return.

Each of us, in our own way, is invited to be a part of that world I glimpsed in the Florida springs and found buried in the lake's mud. A world where people exclaim with joy over the first berry that is ready on the vine. A world where it's normal for humans to get lost in the beauty of a single quartz crystal. A world where we take time to wonder at the whole constellation of seeds in a single wild tangerine or notice the small bits of Spanish moss the cormorants carry, beak by beak, back to their collective rookeries.

Every time we stop to notice the moment and cherish ourselves for who we are, we have the opportunity to feed this world. You call this world into being through the smallest gestures, something as simple as holding your morning egg in your hands before you crack it into the cast iron, giving thanks for the gift of this tiny nourishment. Every small motion of recognition and gratitude is like a seed, helping us bloom anew. All it takes is for each of us to tend to the smallest things of life with the utmost care, and a revolution will be born—that tidal wave in perception we've all been waiting for.

EXERCISE:

Making a Flower Essence

What You'll Need

Glass bowl	Funnel
Water (preferably spring or well water)	Coffee filter or cloth
	Jar or bottle
Scissors or pruners (if needed)	Alcohol or vinegar to preserve

The Process

1. Let the flower call you in. It could be that you dreamt about a particular flower or had a bloom catch your eye. If a certain flower seems very beautiful, prevalent, or stands out in some way, it's probably because its medicine is pertinent to you at this moment.

2. Once you decide on the flower (or it decides on you), bring a bowl with water (and a pair of scissors if you need them). Sit with the bloom and ask permission to make an essence. This would be a good time to make an offering, say a prayer, or connect in meditation to the plant. Wait until you feel an affirmation of consent. This may be the way the breeze changes, how a bee lands on the bloom, an audible sound, or the rise of an emotion. Be open to the diversity of communication, and trust your own inner knowing.

3. Use your scissors or hands to drop one or several blooms into the bowl of water, and then set the essence out under the sun. There is no specific number of blooms that you should pick. One single flower can make a powerful essence. Use your intuition and ask each blossom for permission to be picked.

4. Let the bowl of water and flowers sit for as long as feels right. Your essence may only need a couple hours in the sun, or perhaps you'll want to let your bowl sit under the moonlight. The right amount of time is a feeling-sense more than anything else, but when the essence is complete, the blooms will often look physically wilted or spent.

5. When the essence feels done, siphon the water through a funnel lined with a coffee filter into another jar or bottle. Take the leftover blooms to a special place outside, and give them back to the earth in gratitude.

6. Preserve your original essence water, now called the *mother essence*, by adding an equal amount of alcohol to the essence water. Brandy is traditional. (*For an alcohol-free version, see the following note about preserving with vinegar.*) Label your essence with the flower name, location, date, any special details, and the fact that it is the mother essence.

7. According to the following instructions, dilute your mother essence down further into a stock or dosage bottle. Stock bottles are typically what you find and purchase from the store. Stock bottles are usually indicated for more overt conditions like acute anxiety, illness, or pain, while dosage bottles (which are more dilute) are thought to be more effective for long-term emotional states or chronic illness.

Mother essence: Original flower essence water preserved with equal parts alcohol (50/50) or apple cider vinegar. (*See the following note.*)

Stock bottle: One to seven drops of the mother essence in a new solution of equal parts water and alcohol (50/50) or 100 percent vinegar.

Dosage bottle: One to seven drops of the stock essence in water. To be taken as drop dosage immediately (within two to three weeks of bottling). If you want to preserve long term, add up to 50 percent alcohol or 100 percent vinegar.

General dosage: Two to four drops (from stock or dosage bottle) up to four times per day in water or directly on the tongue. You can also massage the essence directly onto your skin. (The wrists, heart center, and temples are lovely places to try.)

Preserving with Vinegar: If you are avoiding alcohol, you can preserve your essence with vinegar. Because vinegar is less shelf stable than alcohol, I recommend keeping any vinegar-preserved flower essences in the fridge. Mother essences stored with 50 percent vinegar may last as long as three to six months in the fridge. I recommend making stock and dosage bottles with 100 percent vinegar (plus the drops of your essence). At this ratio, your vinegar-preserved stock and dosage bottles can last many years when refrigerated.

Note on toxicity and scarcity: If diluted properly, all flowers are theoretically safe to make and take as an essence. But please use caution when working with flowers that have known toxicity. Please also exercise thoughtfulness and restraint with any flowers that are rare or endangered.

7

THE WORLD SEES YOU

WE ALL GO through times in life when we feel invisible. Like the mist that leaves the hillside, periods of invisibility come and go throughout our lives. You don't realize that you are in the cloudbank until you look down and can no longer see the ground of yourself.

It was an invisible type of winter. After moving out of my first house in the mountains, my little blue cottage, I decided to live alone for the first time in my life. In a strange limbo between relationships and jobs, I rented a little wooden trailer covered in freshly hewn pine in the thick of the mountains, as far out as I could go before hitting the Tennessee state line. To get there, I had to drive up and over a pass called Lonesome Mountain, and down a curl of winding country road so inaccessible that the area it led to didn't have electricity until the 1960s.

I chose this part of the country, in part, because it was notorious for its isolation. The Scots-Irish and English settlers who arrived here centuries earlier entered through the river valleys and didn't leave again. Remaining virtually unknown to the outside world until the 1920s, this craggy part of the mountains came into global awareness when Cecil Sharp, a musicologist and the founder of the folk-song revival in England, journeyed with his recorder into the inaccessible coves and found an entire repertoire of traditional ballads still being sung by the community there.[1] The remote nature of this part of the mountains meant that these songs, some of which had disappeared from memory on the other side of the pond, had been kept alive by mountain folk. Listen to one of these ballads, as full of feeling as the creek water singing in the veins of the hills, and chills will spread through you. By the very nature of their isolation and poverty, the folks who carried these songs were virtually unseen by the wider world—until their voices, immortalized by those early recordings, lifted from the hollers like birdsong. Looking back, I don't know if it was sheer geographic isolation or the songs that first made me fall in love with Sodom.

According to the albums made by those first song collectors, this area of the mountains is known as Laurel or Revere, but ask a local what this particular community is called, and they'll say, without hesitation, Sodom. The name, as the story is told, comes from the Civil War. Mountain women, just concerned with getting by, started following both the Confederate and the Union troops around as "laundresses." An itinerant preacher with Confederate leanings saw these women trailing the Union army with as much enterprise as they followed their Confederate brethren and deemed the whole community from which they came "Sodom." Never without a sense of humor, locals adopted the name.

It can be hard to find a place to live out in Sodom. It's steep, windy, preeminently out-of-the-way, and historically everyone is family. Most people who settle in this part of the county do so because they know someone, or there is an old parcel of land still in their lineage. I had no such connections, but I still somehow found myself in a little wood-covered trailer, perched on a bare pine-dotted hill at the start of the winter.

In the newly born quiet of November, I began to unpack. The inside of the trailer was covered in fresh white pine. My first week there I put a nail into the wall, and sap actually oozed out. That winter, I would spend hours in my small bedroom finding faces in the swirls and burls. The house was just off the "main" road, where an hour or more might pass before a car drove by. To leave the house and get anywhere, I had to drive up and over the treacherous lonesome mountain pass. In times that were unexpectedly icy, snowy, or blustery, there was simply no way out.

For weeks at a time I saw no one else but the angels and wolves looking down at me from the animated burls on the ceiling—and Billy the postman, of course. Most days my only real social engagements were with the cows that pastured above the property on a slope of land that rose neatly into the round sky. In secret, I snipped the lowest line of the barbed wire between my land and the pasture so I could climb in on my belly and go walking among the herd and their gentleness. During one of the first thaw days in February, I caught an off-smell and followed it to find one of the cows had died at the lip of a steep ravine down to the creek. I tied grass in a knot and left it on her swollen belly with reverence, wondering if she had a calf somewhere who was grieving her death. Later that year, I went back to find the bulk of her bones pushed by scavengers all down the embankment; they looked like runes where they had landed. The skull had been picked clean and set on its side among a patch of chickweed. I took it home, telling myself it was to honor her, knowing that I was also tending a part of me that had felt similarly scattered and stripped by that long, lonely winter.

Someone Tapping at the Window

Sometimes the greatest healing comes not from finding the antidote to your pain but in stumbling across the perfect corollary, a mirror that shows you *this is how it is*. We need sad songs when we are sad not because they change how we're feeling but because with them, we are seen. I went out to Sodom seeking solitude because it so neatly echoed the loneliness already inside of me. That fall, my housemate at the cottage, my beloved friend Owen who had been brave enough to move down to these mountains with me four years prior, moved back up to New York State. Shortly thereafter, my most recent sweetheart and I snapped our relationship in two, and I was suddenly single again. Around the same time, I decided to take the leap to leave my job and work on One Willow Apothecaries full time. Partner-less, anchorless, and drifting through my savings, it seemed the perfect time to disappear into the hills. Cecil Sharp once called Sodom a "nest of singing birds." In my heart I hoped that by moving to Sodom, I'd find the tune I was meant to sing, but it would still be many months until the return of the songbirds that spring.

All winter I woke up alone to watch the late morning dust motes move in itinerant swirls across my bed. Feeling as invisible as snow against a white sky, and with ample time on my hands, I found myself flashing back to all the moments of invisibility in my life. The hours spent, quiet and unsure, observing from the back of the classroom. That one birthday party where none of my friends would come up from the basement to sing to me. The abusive relationship that no one knew about. The years I spent dealing with chronic pain in the most hidden part of me. In comic books, invisibility is linked with inviolability, but in the human world, where being seen and accepted by one's community is how we literally ensure our survival, invisibility can feel like the furthest thing from safety.

There is something distinctly soul-endangering about feeling invisible—as if you could lose your grip on the earth and keep on floating upward, with no one to tug you back. Being invisible means having a song that you are burning to sing, but no one is there to hear it. It is knowing that you have just exposed the very center of yourself and that it went entirely unnoticed. Despite its insubstantiality, invisibility might just be the most weighty experience on Earth.

Invisibility often begins with something we want to hide—our shyness, our wounds, our differences, our failures—but eventually it becomes something that hides us. In order to protect ourselves, we create our invisibility, even as it uncreates us. To be human means to rely on our clans to survive, so when we feel unseen by our partners, friends, family, or community, it can seem like we've been cut off from the very stream of energy that keeps us alive—but we only become invisible when we look in the wrong places to be seen.

No matter how insubstantial you feel, there is a vibrant community that never ceased to see your worthiness, that flame of goodness at the center of your being. Nature is our wider family, and it always recognizes us as kin. As blind as we've become to the natural world surrounding us, the denizens of this world never stopped seeing us. The trees around your home recognize you; the squirrels watch as you go past. The cardinals fly to get a closer look at the color of your shirt, and the deer in the woods know the moment you step foot on the path. We have felt alone for so long because we have been distanced from this wider family, but we need only step outside to recognize how deeply we are seen.

Spring came softly that year out in Sodom, surprising me with a secret patch of ginseng planted in the pines and a raucous profusion of chickweed sprouting from the cow patties. For all the glory of the season's lushness, I still woke up most days feelings strangely insubstantial—like I was waiting for an invitation to come back to life. Then, one sunlit morning, much earlier than I normally awoke, I was roused by a tap at my window. Tangled in the covers and still partially underneath the surface of sleep, I assumed the tapping must be a branch brushing the glass. Then it happened again. *Tap.* My mind illogically skipped to the image of a small child crouched outside my window. *Tap.* I quickly shelved that idea as a phantasm of sleep. But who, then, was tapping at my window?

I sat up in bed and looked out the glass. There, perched at eye level, was a saffron-colored goldfinch. Bright as new butter in the morning light, he looked at me, directly into me, and then tapped the glass once more. He didn't fly away as I gazed back at him but softly knocked again, like a fingertip tapping on the door of a loved one who is expecting you.

As I was held in his gaze, something shifted inside of me. The fortress within dissolved. I was disheveled and sad, aimless and alone—and yet despite it all, I had been seen. I gazed back in wonder at the impossible neon of this goldfinch in the full finery of spring. I put one hand over my heart and said out loud, with salt-brimmed eyes, *Thank you*. He tapped once more and flew like sunlight into the pines.

All winter, I had hidden myself away in invisibility, but on that sunlit morning, all it took was the glance of a goldfinch to realize that I had been seen all along. With one tap, and a glimpse of the fathomless kindness of those onyx-dark eyes, I realized that my goodness had never been in question. I was seen. No matter how dim I had felt myself to be, the wider world was simply waiting for me to realize my light again—to come join them in the natural radiance of everything. I saw that not once had the Earth ever judged me. For all the heart-aching walks I had taken in my PJs, or the days when I ate chips for dinner, not one inch of my "failures" was reflected back to me from the wider world. All the trees had seen, all the birds had sung, all the cows had communicated to me was that I was human—that I was colorful and moving and worthy of belonging. No matter how much I thought I was separate, to them, I was never something apart. I was a member of the family; I was a part of everything.

Later that day, I walked up into the pines and noticed, with hope-cleared ears, that the forest was alive with the music of migrating songbirds. The wood thrushes had returned and the warblers were singing like flutes from the eaves of the trees. I hiked among a symphony all the way up to the top of the ridge, where I paused to look down into the cove beyond. Rumor had it, just on the other side of that steep slope was the old cabin where some of the most legendary recordings of Sodom's singers took place. I realized, in a rush that rippled through me like wind in the new grass of spring, that these old songs had never been hidden from the wider world. Long before the musicologists came with their recording devices, the trees had been listening. The crickets joined in chorus during those late-night ballads with whole families spread across the front porch. The birds must have known every tune, hearing them as the people worked in the same fields that gave the winged ones safe haven and seeds to eat. Research shows that we share genes with songbirds, that the birds listen when we sing, sometimes even picking up our melodies.[2] The ballads carried by the people of these hills had never been "undiscovered" or invisible. They had been heard all along, perhaps even echoed by the songbirds themselves, passed in tiny arias all up and down the hills.

We are never truly invisible. We can only feel as unseen as we are blind to the entire living world around us. I found myself whistling as I crested the hill that day to look out over the green curves of this place I called home. The cows glanced up at me as I passed and then went back to their munching. A rabbit bounded out in front of my feet and then crouched behind a patch of clover to watch. A hawk sailed overhead, and the same wind that lifted her from the ground moved me too, my hair skipping in the sidelong breeze. The day was bright as birdsong, and I was ready to sing.

The Birds Are Singing about You

When I first moved to Southern Appalachia I was eager to find community. For most of my life I never felt a part of any group. Throughout childhood, college, and my years in New York City, I always saw myself as orbiting on the edge, outside of things. Arriving in the mountains, I was eager to have a true friend network and an experience of belonging. In herbal school I made my first new friends, including my buddies at the punk house. Because they had lived in the mountains for years, many of these people were deeply connected into the social scene. These early friends were the ones who first introduced me to the world of earth skills and the unique community that practiced them.

Sometimes called *primitive skills*—a term that is a deep misnomer, as anyone who has tried to learn these skills can attest to the incredible complexity and artistry involved in mastering them—these traditional techniques, which include hide tanning, basket weaving, blacksmith-ing, and wildcrafting, attracted a wide array of beautifully feral souls. I fell in love with the earth skills community immediately. A few months after I first moved to the mountains, our local earth skills gathering was scheduled to take place. I decided to use the last bit of money in my savings to buy a weekend pass and packed up all my shiny new camp-ing gear.

Arriving at the Firefly gathering for the first time felt like stepping into another world. People were camped out in tents, yurts, and hand-stitched tarps all across the hillsides. In the mornings, families cooked over open fires, and every other person seemed to be clad in impossibly soft buckskin. A four-day event where people came to learn traditional skills, Firefly felt like a clan gathering from ancient times. People came every year, bringing their children as they grew and also their parents, silver-haired septuagenarians who were welcomed as elders. Every night there were several generations gathered around the fire, singing together as the lamps of the fireflies flickered on and off.

Each skill had its own camp. There was the blacksmithing tent where you could hear the dings and happy sighs of metal settling into form. And the hide tanners camp, with students laboring over their deer skins, discards from local hunters. After several intensive days of scraping, stretching, and softening, the stiff buckskin was as supple as an embrace. There was the herbal tent with its multicolored jars of violet and green elixirs, the tarps where people learned how to use drop spindles, and the singing circles that spilled, like their voices, out from the natural amphitheater of the woods.

On my first day at the gathering I signed up for a birding class that was meeting early the next morning at the edge of the forest. I woke up the next day in darkness and dressed, putting my shirt on inside out, before hastily zipping up my tent to try to find a cup of coffee. Meeting in a small clearing, the group gathered haphazardly around the instructors, two men with calm smiles, crinkled clothes, impossibly bright morning eyes, and well-loved binoculars. Considering how early it was, there was quite a large turnout. Waving their clipboards, the instructors got everyone's attention.

Before we began, they oriented us to what birds we might be hearing at this time of the year and to the special guest stars they were hoping we'd glimpse. Their excitement was contagious. The crowd began to simmer with anticipation. Just as everyone was picking up their backpacks to venture into the forest, the instructor with sand colored hair and thick eyeglasses shared one last thing. "People assume that the forest is alive with loud calls at all times of the day. But often what you hear when you walk into the woods is the birds talking about *you!* Birds are like the town criers of the forest; they will alert other birds to the fact that humans are in their midst. Those same calls are then picked up and spread from one end of the forest to another, traveling from bird to fox to deer. The message will travel faster than you do, so by the time you reach the middle of the forest, most likely, all the creatures there already know you're coming." He paused to smile good naturedly at us, "This is why, if you want to hear the really good stuff, it's best to learn how to walk quietly or, even better, sit still for a long time."

With that, everyone giggled and tried their best to step softly as they gathered up their things. But I stood stock still. Rooted to the spot and utterly grounded by wonder, my brain tried to catch up to this revelation. The bird calls I've heard in the forest my whole life aren't just the random background sounds of the world going about its business; they have, at times, been *songs about me*. The birds talked about me. They used their voices to speak about my presence and, when they did, the whole web of the world woke up to the knowing that I was there. All the times I had gone out walking in the woods alone, all the times I had thought myself to be utterly invisible, were a fantasy. All along, it was, in fact, *I* who had been blind. Even during my loneliest days, the world was literally singing about me. It shocked me, like the smile of a stranger knocks you when you already feel on the edge of tears. All this time I felt invisible, I had been seen. I hurried into the woods belatedly, following the group with my inevitably rustling footfall, shaking with emotion.

The Green Wall

Seeing is something we take for granted, and yet we do not each experience it the same. We see based on what we've *learned* to see. Inside our brains are neurons called *sensory gateways*. Depending on what we've been taught is important to pay attention to, we will selectively let in certain sensory experiences and gate, or block, others. This is why a child on a farm might be able to point out twenty different plants in the world around them, while a kid raised in the city might only see one or two distinguishable plants. It is not that this latter child can't learn them but that they literally haven't been taught to see them.

There's a video that goes around on the internet from time-to-time showing a team of teenagers, in black and white shirts, passing a basketball to each other. Based on the research of Daniel Simons and Christopher Chabris, the video starts by asking the viewer to count how many passes the team members in white make. At the end, they let you know how many occurred so you can test your counting. Then they ask, with a jokester-like nod, " . . . but did you see the gorilla?"[3] Watching the video rewind before your eyes, you see what had been totally invisible to you before. While you were counting passes, a person in a gorilla costume walked right into the middle of the screen, thumped on their chest, and then exited out the other side. You never saw it, of course, because you were too focused on counting each pass. In so many ways, this is how we interact with the world around us today. We are taught to count things like monetary value or the number of likes we get on a post, which means we miss the rich reality of what is really going on around us. But there is a whole world, invisible to us, that comes alive when we learn how to look.

Depending on how we were raised, most of us grew up without ever being taught to see the natural world. The late, and legendary, herbalist Frank Cook called this hazy, nondescript view of nature *the green wall*. From a young age many of us inherited the implicit cultural belief that nature is simply not as important as the human world. Before we learn to pick out the denizens of the green world, to know their shape and call them by name, it is literally as if we cannot see them.

I still remember the first time the green wall dissolved before my eyes. I was in college and had stumbled across the website of Steve Brill, an ecologist and wild foods gatherer who lived in New York City. Because I was going to school in the Hudson Valley, just a short train ride away from the Big Apple, I read through his website and deduced that similar plants were growing on our campus. Using his guides, I identified my first plant—jewelweed. On campus that fall, the jewelweed was just transitioning from its tangelo-colored, trumpet-shaped flowers to seed pods that, upon touch, would spring open in a burst. I still remember the moment I realized that a particular footbridge I had crossed every day for the past few years was lined with jewelweed . . . and its edible seeds! It was as if my eyes suddenly grew new cones. All along I had been surrounded by these warm-hearted characters who had waved to me, day-in and day-out, but only now could I see them. I rerouted my path to class just to cross this bridge, letting the seeds spring into my hands so I could eat half and scatter the other half into the rich soil of the creek-bed. I was often lonely in college. Dealing with chronic pain, I spent a lot of afternoons wandering by myself in the woods. Looking back at this moment, however, I realized I was never alone. I had been with jewelweed. I saw these plants, and, wonder of all wonders, I realized that all along *they had been seeing me.*

So often we go about our human-centric life thinking that we are invisible, irredeemable, or simply alone—meanwhile the living world recognizes us as a part of the whole. We walk into nature and assume that what we are hearing is the ongoing hubbub of a world that doesn't notice us, yet the Earth is continually responding to our presence. Whether it is the bird call that announces our steps in the forest, the squirrel that is watching us to see whether we might leave a scrap of sandwich behind, or the seeds of the jewelweed springing out like rain the moment we brush past them—no matter how invisible we think we are, we are seen. No matter how low we feel, we're always being held by the world around us.

In Indigenous cultures, this understanding, that the Earth is constantly watching over us like a mother observes her children, is nothing new—it is a knowing as native and elemental as a baby's instinct to meet their parents' gaze. A friend of mine once made a pilgrimage with a group to Peru to study with a Paqo, a traditional medicine person of the Andes. She told me later that on their first outing, the group spent hours waiting at the foot of a mountain before they were able to ascend. According to their Andean guide, the mountain needed, first, to see them.

For those of us who weren't raised in a culture that is in intimate relationship with the living world, the realization that the whole of the Earth is responding to our presence with perpetual recognition and nonjudgement tends to cause a cascade of deep feeling. Science is still an infant in terms of recognizing the larger reality of this interconnection, but even in this most empirical of fields, the acknowledgment of communication and exchange between humans and nature is growing. For example, while it makes sense that animals might be reacting to us, new studies show that plants not only feel when they are being touched by humans, but respond to the subtleties of how we touch them.[4] We have insulated ourselves so entirely from the world around us that we have forgotten the entire world feels our touch. When we come home to this realization, we open our hearts to the deeply touching reality that we have always belonged.

Whether or not we realize it, so many of us feel alone on this planet. We point to social media or our globalized economy, but the loneliness we feel goes so much deeper. Disconnected from the wider family with whom we share this planet—the goldfinches and pines, the creek newts and the gentle bovines—the part of us that is the Earth feels orphaned. We don't need any kind of elaborate ritual to belong. We don't need to do anything special in order to be seen. All we have to do is open our own eyes, and we will recognize that we never left home.

The Brightest Bulbs in the Box

You don't have to do anything sensational for people to love you.

—FRED ROGERS

When I was in second grade we got a dog. A border terrier with wiry hair, a loud bark, and a sturdy muscular build, we named him Griffin. I still remember the day he became a part of our family. He was mostly black then, with big floppy ears and boundless energy. He fell asleep in my lap on the way home, and I thought he was the softest, sweetest creature in all the world. From the get-go, this was a dog who was deeply loved. As time wore on, Griffin continued to be an unreservedly cherished part of our family—even after we realized, as my parents humorously put it, that he wasn't "the brightest bulb in the box." It took years before he comprehended commands, and he never seemed to be able to understand that if he ran after a squirrel, his lead, which was attached to the deck, would snap him back like an airborne yo-yo as soon as he hit the end of his tether. He never stopped thinking he could bound through the glass of the front door to attack a cat, and he ate the same exact food every day for sixteen years as if it was the most delicious thing God had ever created.

He wasn't particularly extraordinary—he wasn't going to sniff out a bomb or save a child from a burning building—but he was beloved. Sometimes, when my sister or I were feeling down on ourselves, my mom would hold us in her arms and call Griffin to come sit. His gentle, goofy demeanor would release the ache in our hearts and make us giggle. With a smile on our faces, my mom would hold us tightly and say, "Look at Griffin; he'll remind you that you don't need to do anything special in order to be loved."

I think about this as an adult more than I ever did as a child. As a kid, I was lucky to experience acceptance as a given. As an adult, however, such love feels like a benediction. I ruminate on this often as I go for my walk in the woods. In a culture where we feel like we need to do something stupendous to even get noticed, it is a kind of medicine to recognize that however I am that day—doubting, hurting, lonely, or low—every time I step outside, I'm being seen by the living world.

Years ago, a college student reposted a meme about how an elephant's brain lights up in similar ways when they see humans as our brain reacts when we see puppies. The conclusion: elephants think we're cute. The meme, shared by millions, took off like wildfire, with biologists confusedly running behind. It turns out that the meme wasn't based on any scientific study but likely came from observing the uniquely tender relationship elephants can have with their human caregivers in wildlife rehabilitation centers. Nevertheless, the popularity of the post speaks volumes. The humans who read and reposted it did so because they felt its truth. It touched the part of them that aches to be seen by the wider world. It spoke to the place within us that remembers that we don't have to do anything special in order to be loved.

Science is one language; feeling is another. I don't have any scientific facts that prove that I loved my dog Griffin. I don't have any studies to show that the trees around my home not only recognize me, but embrace me as kin. I don't have proof, but I still feel it nearly every time I step outside my door. When I slow down enough to see the world, I am often brought to my knees with how heartbreakingly precious each individual truly is—the gray squirrel scratching her hind, the birch rustling in autumn sunshine, the quartz-white bolder wet with creek water. When I stay present with this awe, a chill of recognition will eventually run up my back, the same shiver you get when you realize that you are being looked at.

The more I open my heart to loving the world, the more I understand that the world has never stopped loving me back. Some Indigenous peoples call humans the "younger brothers and sisters" of existence—evolutionarily speaking, we are very new on the scene. As Chickasaw poet and novelist Linda Hogan reminds us, "In most indigenous creation stories, humans were the last ones created. Around us are many teachers."[5] Nearly every creature on Earth is our elder. Just like our human big brothers and sisters, our aunties and caretakers, the family of the natural world is not impartial to our existence. They are looking at us, not just with familiarity, but with forgiveness. Humans may not be the brightest bulbs in the box, but we are loved regardless.

As I write, my cat Tula is curled up in my lap. When I make a sudden move in my chair, she lifts her head to look at me, blinking her green-yellow eyes slowly before resting her head back down to sleep. Almost every day I tell her, in earnest, "I love you with all my heart." I didn't choose to start saying this; it just poured out of my mouth one day. But

I mean it, with every ounce of my being. It shocks me sometimes to feel the intensity of this entirely unconditional love. She doesn't have to do anything special to deserve it, and she could never lose it. On the hardest days of my existence, I take myself outside and curl up like a kitten in the sunlit leaves. I do nothing but let the world hold me, allowing the soft voice of the forest to speak—*there is nothing you need to do to deserve this, and you will never lose it. You are loved unconditionally.*

The Hawk's Shadow

A few weeks after my first birding class I stuffed my journal and a satchel of snacks into my backpack and headed to the woods. I was curious about who I might spot, now that I knew a handful of birds by sight and sound—but I was even more interested in how my experience of the forest might have changed now that I knew I was part of the song.

There was a trail I loved, just a short jaunt up the road. For all the years I had walked there, I had never encountered another human on my rambles. I saw wild anemones and a bear, a stack of boulders with a hidden geo cache—a plastic Tupperware with a notebook dated to several years earlier—but never any hikers. At the entrance to the path there was a spring that locals had tapped. I paused before I entered the woods to drink from my hands, splashing the cold water over the crown of my head and dipping two fingers to anoint my heart. Normally my head is crowded with thoughts when I enter the woods, my worries so loud they drown out any other sounds. But today, I stood at the threshold of the path and purposefully cleared all the inner interference. I wanted to hear the forest's song for myself.

It felt like an initiation to take that first step onto the path and pause to listen. Sure enough, I heard the long loop of a bird call, and then another one further down. The arias hopscotched back and forth into the forest and past my range of hearing. I kept my ears perked as I walked up the steep slope and began to pick out the clear instrumental notes of specific birds. The fiddle step of the goldfinches and the seed-filled rattle of the chickadees. Everyone sounded happy to me.

I imagined they were chatting about sweet, sun-filled things like where to bathe in the clearest water or which fruit has the roundest seeds. Or perhaps they were simply calling to each other from the trees, like lovers touching toes in the coziness of morning, murmuring sweetly—"I'm here, I'm here, you are here with me." It warmed my heart to think that amid the gentle symphony there might be a few notes, whole and uncomplicated, being sung about me.

I don't have a great voice by any account, but as I walked, I felt inspired to sing too. I made up sweet little ditties about the birds. Every one that winged past me was woven into the melody. I sung, not because it felt like an even exchange, but because the immenseness of what the world offered me was so sweet, it felt right to proffer a bit of honeyed melody, even if it was slightly off-key.

Nobody knows when humans began singing, only that the practice is so old we have likely been humming since the beginning. Perhaps, even before words, there were songs. Some scientists theorize that it was the birds that first taught us language.[6] As we learned their melodies, their music became the bedrock of our own speech. Ancient humans would have been listening intimately to the avian world. After all, as denizen of the forest, the messages the birds passed on would have been valuable information—the first language we likely spoke was bird song. In human culture singing eventually became an important skill, one that was intricately woven into the most essential aspects of life, including passing on creation stories, remembering the lineages, and memorizing information about migration routes and resources. Included in this litany of vital importance were the first and most important songs—those that contained praise for the world around them.

At some point in my walk, I took a purposeful turn off the path to go softly into the woods and disappear for a time under the trees. I wanted to find a spot to sit and listen so the constant rustling of my footfall didn't distract the songbirds around me. At the edge of a small opening in the woods, I found a nook of an oak's roots and took off my pack to lean against the tree. As I closed my eyes to feel the beams of sun on my face, I began to get sleepy. I found myself sliding down the tree trunk to make a bed in the forest leaves, curling into myself like a fox making a circle with her body.

Napping outdoors is a unique experience. Normally, when I go to bed, it takes a while for me to fall asleep—so many thoughts are twittering through my head. Once I'm asleep, however, I might as well have left the world entirely for how deeply I depart from reality. Napping outside is completely different. Like the sunlight dappling through the canopy, I drift in and out of sleep. The boundary between the dream world and the waking world becomes blurry, the sounds of the forest incorporated into my dreams. Instead of leaving my body, I come more fully into presence, as if I'm seeping into the earth like spring water. I have never felt as cozy in myself, or inside the arms of the world, as I do when I fall asleep on the earth.

Dozing in and out like this, one part of my brain kept track of the lullabies of the birds around me, while the other part dissolved happily into sleep. I rode the trickle of my consciousness like a spring, rising from beneath the stones of the earth to touch the surface, and then dipping back under again. I don't know how long I rested beneath the tree, but I remember clearly the moment I awakened. The part of my brain that was still listening to the birds heard something unusual. A sharp call, then utter silence. The animal of my body awoke immediately, responding to a message that my conscious mind didn't understand at all. All I knew was that my attention was needed now. My eyes flipped open, and I had just enough time to register the silent, strange tension running through the forest before a winged shadow swept over me. I looked up, expecting to see a cloud, and instead spied the source of my awakening—a hawk drifting with sharp eyes above me.

I gazed with wonder at this silent hunter and at the world around me. The birds had called out to let everyone in the vicinity know that a hawk was in their midst, and I had heard. In the depths of my slumbering mind, I understood exactly what was being spoken. It was a true awakening. All the beliefs I still had about how I was always on the fringe of things, never fully a part of any real community, dissolved. I was here, in the middle of the woods, and I was a part of a wider song.

This was a language I could speak, and no matter how illiterate I sometimes felt when reconnecting with the natural world, a part of me never stopped being fluent in my native tongue. The Earth had recognized me as a singer, and I was invited to harmonize with everything again.

The Flower Seen by the Bee

What would happen if you could walk through the world and know that you were being seen—by the trees, the creeks, the hawks circling quietly? What if you knew for certain that you weren't alone, that the part of you that aches to rejoin the wider world is being called back to the fold? When we are seen, everything changes. When we are seen, we become free to be ourselves in our precious entirety.

The disconnect we feel between ourselves and the community of the wider world is a sorrow at the center of our being. It is the wound unseen that we are constantly trying to feed. But the wound isn't bottomless, and the balm is all around us. The world not only sees us, but wants us to *know* that we are seen.

The need to be seen isn't a frivolity of the ego; it's a natural part of learning how to become the people we were meant to be. Without being seen, how will the flower attract the bee? Without being recognized by those that surround you, how can you give your gifts to the wider community?

When you let yourself be seen for who you are, you become a flower for this world—a being who carries the seeds of a new beginning. There is no part of you that the Earth does not know, and so there is no piece of you, no matter how hidden, that is unworthy of being seen. We must only let in the possibly that we are worthy of such belonging.

Everywhere, at every moment, we are being seen by the wider world. Go for a walk down the street—the trees there do not begrudge your existence; they accept you as fully as their leaves embrace the wind. Watch the spider respin her web in the corner of your bedroom; to her, you are as natural as the sun. Open the door and watch your dog come bounding up to meet you; let their exuberant welcome flow straight into your bones. This is how happy the world is when you return to the fold. This is how *loved* you have always been, and this is how profoundly you are home.

EXERCISE:
Let a Tree See You

This exercise is simple yet powerful. To start, find a tree to sit with. Once settled, speak out loud all of the things you judge yourself for. Tell this tree all the things you've ever done or thought about that bring up shame. As Brené Brown says, shame is like a gremlin: we must only expose it to the light to loosen its grip on our insides.[7] Tell this tree everything. Say anything that comes to you, then note how you feel now that you've spoken the unspeakable aloud.

You will find there is no judgement here, only acceptance.

In the absorbing silence, be open to the ways in which the tree, and the world, might be responding to you. You might notice a particular sensation drifting on the breeze or a sense of grounded immovability within the roots of the tree. That sensation is non-judgement, and it is the very stuff that makes up the lifeforce of this world.

Let the gentle acceptance of the Earth in completely—cry, sigh, laugh, sing. You are seen and loved unconditionally.

8

YOUNG FORESTS

ONE OF THE first things I noticed about my house was its height. Perched on tall stilts twenty-five feet up into the canopy and nestled among lanky tulip poplars, my house looks out into a thicket of green. Perhaps the technical term for this would be an elevated home, or a structure built on piers, but really, it's a treehouse. Throughout fall the deck is covered in a thick frosting of fallen leaves, and in early spring I get a bird's-eye view as the greenery sprouts from floor to ceiling. A few of the trees around my home are grand, but my house also faces a tumble of thin saplings in the more recently cut corners of the land. Peering out from the back deck into the tangle of undergrowth, I see the same kind of forest I've known my whole life—dense, crowded, young. To me, the close trees and profusion of leaves is simply what defines the woodlands, but look back a century, and this land was a different place entirely.

Before the 1900s, these hills, like many large swathes of the Eastern woodlands, were covered in old growth. Back then, the forest was a kind of cathedral with massive bark buttresses—limbs like ornately carved beams and an impossibly open forest floor. Around the turn of the century, however, practically every last corner of the woods was logged, including the hills of Appalachia. The legacy of these years can still be found everywhere.

The path I walk from my house up to the ridgeline was once an old logging road. In our forests today, these old roads are some of the only walking outlets still accessible, as the regenerating woodlands are often crowded with a cacophony of multiflora rose, poison ivy, newly sprouted trees, and blackberries. Every once in a while, walking the thin passes, you might stumble upon an old homestead obscured by saplings. Marked by the remains of their locust posts or broken chestnut siding, many of these cabins are over a hundred years old, remnants of a time when vast tracks of the mountains were turned into pasture for livestock or fields for tobacco in the wake of the first great loggings.

As sporadic as these old wood-built homesteads are, stumbling upon their living predecessors is even more rare. Sometimes left as boundary markers between properties, every once in a while, you can find a true old-growth tree. There is one such oak at the top of the ridgeline above my house. It's as wide as four people holding hands, with bark swirled like eyes. Bent into fantastical shapes, it appears to be moving in an invisible wind.

Every day since this land with its overgrown gardens and tall tree-house became my permanent home, I have made the puffing hike up the logging road to visit this old oak. Gazing at the ancient eddies of its bark, I often close my eyes to imagine what this land looked like when *all* the trees were this big. It is awe-inspiring to envision; a wonderfully remembered dream. No matter how long I linger in that reverie, however, I always open my eyes so I can return to the woods around me.

The path to and from the oak is cut through white pines and scrawny young beeches, buckeyes that shoot up like weeds and yellow birches that fall periodically whenever we get a hard soak. It is an undoubtedly skinny forest, new-looking even to those who do not know the history—and yet it is beautiful. I always do my best thinking on these walks. Though my destination is the mighty oak at the top of the cove, this young upstart of a forest is my home. Stretching my legs through this country of newness, I have a distinct sense of encountering my own self.

Like many who love this Earth, I often long for what is lost—old-growth forests, spreading estuaries, and pristine rivers. I think back on what was and ache for the depth and diversity of such ecosystems. Even though this longing is a natural response to the dramatic change of the past few centuries, I notice that when I focus on what is gone, I forget to open my eyes to the value of what is growing in now. When I was younger I made pilgrimages to National Parks but seldom walked into the brush outside my home. I enshrined ancient groves set far into the forest and was blind to the scruffy patch of pines next to the supermarket. A yowling coyote-like cry is coming from these newly grown and less-than-glamorous places—the waysides, the weed fields, the young forests. These spaces are speaking directly to us, and what they have to share is important. In the past, I ignored these common, newly sprouted places because I thought they had less to teach me than the old growth. But it turns out that these young forests are the exact teachers we need—and they are carrying some of the most precious medicine for our times.

The cement lot overgrown with volunteer buckeyes reminds us of the worthiness of beginning again. The blackberry vine in the clear-cut shows us what regeneration looks like. The skinny forest of the ridge-line teaches us to see the beauty in our own growing selves. As humans, we aren't that different from these recovering places. The new forests that cover so much of our Earth today aren't here to remind us of our loss—or to be seen as a less-admirable version of what was—they are the pioneers who have come to help our Earth heal. Embracing these forests in all their young magnificence will help us to see the inaugural gifts that we, as saplings of this world, are also here to bring.

It's no easy feat to be on Earth. It takes untold bravery to root here, and yet, each and every one of us does. Every day when we wake up, we agree anew to be a part of this great experiment of what it looks like to return to wholeness. We are sacred volunteers, and those of us who are being born at this time have been given the exact skills needed to help our Earth heal—we must only trust our leggy newness and pioneering souls.

The Sacred Volunteers

I desperately wanted a vegetable garden at the treehouse that John and I would come to call the Highly Sensitive Sanctuary, but first I had to contend with the tangle of blackberry vines that had become the yard. The south-facing hillside across from our house had once been a neatly maintained set of terraced beds, but after they had lain fallow for several years, they had grown in with volunteer brambles.

One day in early spring, I put on my thickest pair of overalls and got to work. It wasn't easy—blackberry vines are designed to stop you in your path—but I slowly cleared my way through the first bed. Pausing to wipe my brow, I looked out over the yard. The bed I had been working in was full of freshly turned soil, while the others were still a tangle of purple vines and prickles. Although I had planned to clear the whole garden, I now wondered if I might not leave one bed to the brambles. The birds loved to hide among them, and a handful of blackberries in midsummer was always a delight. If I left them, sooner or later, the forest would grow back into that bed as well. Blackberries are classic pioneer species—one of the first forerunners to reclaim the land so the trees can return. I looked at the forest behind me, and at the brambles ahead, and shrugged. For today, I'd leave them. After all, these were some of the toughest plants on the planet. Who wouldn't want to give them a little space to flourish?

Pioneer species are the sacred volunteers of the plant world. As the first trailblazers to move into a shocked or comprised ecosystem, these plants are experts at weathering hard times and bringing life back after devastation. Make no mistake, these volunteers are a hardy crowd. Land that has been disturbed, whether by human activity or natural forces, is often left with very thin or poor-quality soil, which lacks the nutrients needed to sustain many forms of life. When the ancient forests of Appalachia were logged, we lost thousands of years of accumulated topsoil. While old-growth forests need this kind of rich soil to survive, pioneer species are able to thrive on very little. With adaptations, like long earth-stabilizing root systems, the ability to fix nitrogen, and the capacity to reproduce asexually or through wind pollination, pioneer plants are angels that can bring barren places back to life. By reducing runoff, anchoring the earth, and increasing biomass, over time, these species completely refurbish the soil, literally rebuilding the ecosystem from the ground up.

In scientific terminology, this process of returning to a stable ecosystem, or climax community, is called *succession*. Succession is nature's capacity to respond to trauma with resiliency, to call upon its inner resources to find center after upset. In psychotherapeutic circles, *resiliency*, or the ability to feel distinctly grounded, settled, and supported in the present moment, is the key to healing from trauma. Pioneer species are nature's inborn agents of resiliency. They are emblems of the powerful healing, and regrowth, that can happen when we become present with what is.

In the past six hundred years of capitalism and colonization, the trauma that nature, including our own species, has endured is immense. It's no wonder that those who care deeply for the natural world often find themselves looping back to the past with pain or anxiously projecting into the future of our planet. And yet, having the ability to stay present with the process of inner and outer succession we are now experiencing is a kind of medicine, both for ourselves and the larger nervous system of our planet. Trauma, as something that continually pitches us out of the present moment and into the past or future, begins to heal the moment we ground in the present. Becoming present with reverence—to the new forests and to what is healing within the soil of our own psyche—is perhaps the most profound gift we can give our Earth today. This presence is what will allow us to take up our role as pioneer species in the Earth's healing.

Pioneer plants are normally divided into two categories—primary and secondary succession species. Primary succession species are the very first plants that arrive onto the scene where there has been a total decimation, or phase shift, of the land. These species root in sand dunes, cooled lava flows, exposed rocks, as well as areas made barren by human overuse. From an ecological perspective, primary succession species arrive to a blank slate, with very little to build on nutritionally. These enterprising species are experts at transforming barrenness into life. Lichens are a prime example of primary succession species.

Growing directly into the tiny niches of still air and moisture found within pockets of stone, lichens slowly break down the rocks upon which they perch to create an entire microhabitat of nutrients, making it possible for the forests to one day return.

Secondary succession species, by contrast, are the plants that move into areas that have been deeply disturbed but still retain some of the vital elements needed for growth. Woodlands that have resprouted after logging are an example of secondary succession forests. Though a massive amount of fertile topsoil was lost when the forest around my house was logged, the woods around me certainly are not beginning from scratch. Secondary succession species build on what is there, even if the foundations might be a bit shaky.

Some of us will feel like primary succession people. The backgrounds we came from might well have been bare rock for all the support or nourishment they gave us. For many, what we were handed might have felt as devoid of nutrients as a lava field. Others might identify as secondary succession folks, people who were blessed with a thin top-layer of soil to work with—whether that's because we grew up with ancestral traditions of Earth reverence, had a stable childhood home, or experienced freedom from poverty or bigotry. No matter who we are and where we come from, the gifts we bring to this world are vital. Just like a dandelion sprouting from the cracks in the concrete, we give these gifts innately every time we grow. Our Earth is healing successionally, and as she does so, she will need all of us—primary and secondary volunteers alike—to bring our inborn abilities to help restore wholeness. You, in your fumbling newness, your leggy beginnings, your trying and sometimes failing, are here to help the succession of healing—and all you need to do is be your most natural self.

Secessional healing takes time. But it takes more than time; for us humans, it takes understanding. It takes being willing to dismantle the thought patterns that prevent us from seeing ourselves so we can dissolve the cultural stories of damaged versus whole that we've internalized and recognize how worthy we are. It means embracing everything about ourselves, even that which seems most challenging to love.

Untying the Knots

My feet are growing numb from the cold water, but my hands keep up the rhythm. I'm standing in the creek bed just outside my house, but it looks as though I'm in the middle of the rainforest. On all sides of me, stretching over head and crunching underfoot, are the branching bamboo-like stalks of Japanese knotweed. The foliage is so dense that even in the middle of the creek it feels like I'm walking through jungle undergrowth. Digging knife in hand, I pry any roots I can from the water, tossing them into a nearby bucket. The older plants, settled like melted wax between the stones, won't budge. The best I can do is scythe them down at the base and wait for them to spring back, which they will, in only a handful of days. This is my yearly act of service for the native plants in my cove. I clip back the knotweed to give those plants a chance to thrive. In the process, I come into contact with the parts of myself that are just as tenacious as these weeds. The parts that are hardest to love and yet brilliant in their strategy.

No matter where you are in the world, weeds exist. Finding their way into every nook and cranny, weedy plants are usually the first ones to show up in a recently disturbed place—and are often the last ones to leave. If you've ever tried to get rid of a weed, you know this intimately. Weedy plants that are not native, but have a tendency to spread rapidly and overwhelm the local population, are called *invasives*. In the mountains where I live, Japanese knotweed has become one of the most notorious invasive species. In April they shoot up like alien asparagus, and by May nearly every creek is covered. Japanese knotweed first arrived in the US in the late-1800s as an ornamental, but by the 1930s it was already becoming a problem.[1] According to folks around these parts, it takes seven years of continuously cutting knotweed back before the root will die. Even when dug up, the whole plant can regenerate from the smallest fragment. If I leave pieces of the root out on the driveway after harvesting, I will come back a few days later to find a brand-new sprout. In a globally connected world, invasive species are a fact of life.

The question we ask each invasive plant that comes into our landscape is this: *Who are* you *to be growing here?* Every time we direct this question out into the world, however, we mirror our own inquiring psyches, the part of us that is continuously, unconsciously, pointing a finger within to ask ourselves the same question—*who am* I *to be growing here?* Many of us who struggle with self-worth can feel guilt for the space we take up in this world. For those who are intimately connected to the Earth, this sense of unworthy belonging can even extend to our whole tenure as humans on this planet. When it comes to invasive species, humans are undoubtedly at the apex of the list. In fact, we are the reason why most invasive plants have been able to enter into nonnative habitats in the first place. In light of this, many of us can't help but ask ourselves—*who are* we *to be here?* Normally, the tangle of these self-beliefs stays buried beneath our awareness, until the knotted roots rise to the surface to be untied.

If we simply shift the wording, it's easy to see how our repulsion to invasive species can act like a mirror, reflecting back to us the stories we unconsciously tell ourselves about our own essential being and sense of belonging. Just like I chastise and ostracize the parts of me that I deem unworthy, I often slip blindly into demonizing this plant that has grown into the creek. But then I remember something that stops my thoughts in their tracks, something I can't believe I ever forgot—this invasive plant once helped me heal from one of the most profound health challenges of my life.

When I was in the midst of dealing with Lyme disease, Japanese knotweed was integral in helping me to heal. Because it is one of the few plants with antibacterial compounds that specifically combat spirochetes, the ancient bacterium that cause Lyme disease, Japanese knotweed, the same plant that is vilified by nearly all local nature lovers, has helped countless people heal from the depths of this insidious chronic illness. Amazingly, the spread of this plant across the country has been nearly lock-step with the spread of Lyme, a disease that, once it becomes chronic, is extremely difficult to treat by conventional means.

Whenever I remember this, the gateways of recognition, both inner and outer, flood open. Before we know anything different, invasive species are often our most beloved plants. For those of us who grew up eating honeysuckle or blowing dandelion seeds, these herbs are at the center of our most precious childhood memories and healthful connections to the Earth. As an herbalist, these invasive species are the first medicines I turn to, as they are both prolific and effective. I am always amazed, in the midst of my battleground in the creek, to realize that I can hold such contradictory admiration and judgement for these plants—as well for my own self. Coming face to face with my own cognitive dissonance, I recognize with awe that the very things I resist, within and without, always have their own medicine.

When I reground in this gratitude, it helps me to see that the power of my dislike is an uncomfortable reflection of my complicated relationship with my own self, someone who is also of settler descent, living in a country far away from the land of my ancestors. Someone who still sometimes doubts my goodness and belonging on this Earth. When I feel these thoughts take root inside me, I step into the creek and pause my ceaseless clipping to feel the water run over my feet. I watch the wind move through the flute-like stalks of the knotweed, each one speckled with purple dots and nodes like knees. I become present in the moment, and when I do, I can recognize, with gratitude, how these invasives are teaching me to love what is hardest to uproot in my psyche.

Acceptance, Gratitude, Grace

At our hearts, all of us know that we are essentially good—but throughout our lives we inevitably develop invasive belief systems, thought patterns that aren't reflective of our native selves that begin to affect our indigenous ecology of self-esteem. Just as invasive species function as successional plants, typically moving into places that have been disturbed, our most self-defeating thoughts often take root in the wake of trauma. How many of us are plagued by the belief that we aren't enough? Or maybe that we are *too* much? Like a space opened up in the canopy, these beliefs rush into the craters caused by the disruptions of our life. As invasive as they feel, however, they are here to help us heal.

For humans, acceptance in a community is vital for our survival. Early in life we develop beliefs about ourselves that we think will help us fit in better with our family and peers, ensuring acceptance by our caretakers. These beliefs are borne out of an instinct for self-preservation, but they can become counterproductive and distinctly self-negating. In Bill Plotkin's book *Soulcraft: Crossing into the Mysteries of Nature and Psyche,* he calls these belief systems "Loyal Soldiers."[2]

During WWII a group of Japanese soldiers were stationed, and then stranded, on an island in the Philippines. When news of the war's end reached them, they concluded it was propaganda and went deeper into hiding. Thirty years later, the last of these soldiers was found alive, still clothed in his intact military uniform.[3] Believing that the war was ongoing, the solider, Hiroo Onoda, had kept himself ready for battle all those years. At that time, WWII was a distinct pain point for the Japanese, and yet they welcomed Onoda home with deep celebration. They deemed him, and his companions, the "loyal soldiers" and gently began helping him to integrate what he had been unable to accept during those long years—the war was over.

Our earliest belief systems are our loyal soldiers, holding on even after the challenge of childhood has ended. No matter how frustratingly stubborn they might feel when we encounter them, our goal is not to berate these warriors, but to celebrate them so they can feel safe enough to start laying down their weapons. Japanese knotweed is the loyal soldier of an ecosystem. Challenging though these weeds are, originally, they came in to fill a destabilized void. They came to protect disturbed places and secure whatever soil was left. They bring the medicine we need so that, one day, when the disruption is over, we can return to a healthier ecosystem.

The way we decommission the soldiers of these invasive beliefs is the same way the Earth is asking us to approach invasive species—not to fight them, but to work *with* them.

The only invasive species more maligned than Japanese knotweed in our mountains are the great blankets of kudzu leaves. Originally brought to the US as a shade plant for porches and a solution for erosion, eventually kudzu became so invasive it was known as the vine that ate the south. Its tenacity matches the profundity of its medicine. Kudzu vines can be harvested for baskets, and its leaves make yummy fodder for goat farms. Kudzu roots are an important herb in Chinese medicine and are used to help treat, among other things, one of the most prevalent diseases of our time—alcoholism. Nearly all our most invasive plants, and beliefs, contain medicine; we must simply be willing to engage with them.

There is an old Daoist saying: Acceptance leads to gratitude, and gratitude leads to grace. We are trained to struggle against what is—the isness of our thoughts, our bodies, our lives, or the state of the Earth. But when we can accept the beauty of the present, and all the resiliency this brings, we find a way in our hearts to be grateful. This gratitude naturally leads us, and the world we inhabit, to the place we've been striving to get to all along—grace.

It's easy, when I'm ankle deep in the creek fighting a seemingly losing battle, to feel resentful. It's normal to grieve for the loss of the old growth that once covered this cove. It's natural to look at the depth of the world's problems, including mass extinction and oppression, and feel entirely too young, ill-equipped, and out of place to be of service. But inevitably, if I sit long enough with *what is*, finding acceptance of my experience in this present moment, grace arrives.

Back in the creek, I continue cutting down knotweed, but something has changed. I am wielding my clippers now with reverence instead of resistance. I begin to enter into a Zen-like zone of concentration. *Bend, clip, swish.* I stop fighting the fact that the knotweed is here and acknowledge the medicine of this moment. I accept my role as someone who can use my human agency to help native plants regain their niches, and I also accept myself as someone who is unwittingly a part of creating habitat disruption in the first place. *Bend, clip, swish.* I accept myself for not always knowing how to be a part of the healing. I accept myself as someone who is also a non-native and yet cares so deeply for this place. *Bend, clip, swish.* I recognize that all the ways that I tell myself I'm not enough is just another reaction to the challenges I've been handed.

Bend, clip, swish. Quietly, eventually, the gratitude settles in. For the tenacity of this plant. For the jam I will be making from its stalks, which tastes so similar to rhubarb. For the medicine I'll siphon from the roots, medicine that will help countless people heal from Lyme disease. For the ability to stay present with myself as I grow, for my willingness to continually show up with my pruners, and my understanding, when my own negative thought patterns crop up again. *Bend, clip, swish.* Somewhere within this motion, the resistance finally drops away. Like a shaft of light reaching through the new space I've opened up in the canopy, grace comes streaming in.

Looking around at the thin poplars and arcing stalks of Japanese knotweed, I think to myself—*this* is what a young forest looks like, and I'm a part of it. When we accept that there is medicine in the weeds and wayside places, the invasives and the young brush, we can embrace the beauty of our own becoming.

We Are the Young Forests

Many of us were born into what I call *successional cultures,* societies whose earth-based roots were lost in a great logging, communities whose ways of connecting and belonging were disturbed by the wholescale tilling of their soil. The truth is, we are all trying to regrow what was lost, whether or not we are conscious of what has been fueling our search. Today, when I see the scraggly tulip poplars that grow up on the hillside around my house, I recognize them as myself, the one who is slowly regrowing the wisdom of old. The one who is learning how to be a part of healing by doing the hardest work of all—accepting my own self.

The regeneration of any culture begins with those who are willing to become pioneers in their own self-work, those who are willing to thoughtfully reroot in self-compassion and a heartfelt connection to the living world. When I can embrace myself, including recognizing all the loyal soldiers inside of me that are ready to come back home, I heal not only myself, but the Earth as a whole. It might be awkward at first, this medicine that pops up in brambles and starts. It might not be glamourous, but it is as tenacious as a dandelion, as adaptable as the willow.

Collectively, we are the young forests of this era. We are those who are growing up in disturbed ecosystems, places where the old-growth wisdom has been felled. We are the ones that are coming in now with our pluck, our trust, and our skills of regeneration. We might seem disordered and chaotic. We might get snagged on our own selves, but we are here to help the hillsides within which we live to heal. We are the young forests, coming to reinfuse this world with hope.

Beginner's Mind, Beginning of the World

Sometimes we are the wisest right at the start. Beginner's mind, or *shoshin*, is a concept from Zen Buddhism that has come to be cherished throughout many disciplines. Described as the ability to hold a fresh openness, to release preconceptions and embrace possibility, shoshin is the goal of Zen meditation.

In a world in which we are told that we must become experts at everything we do, beginner's mind is a refreshing gift, one that can help redraw the rigid perspectives of our culture. Like a grapevine trained along a fence, when we are deeply developed on a path, we have certain ways of moving that become habituated, wooden, and stiff. Beginner's mind gives us the gift of being able to bend the tendrils of our thoughts in new directions and to find fresh inspiration. As renowned Zen teacher Shunryū Suzuki says in his book *Zen Mind, Beginner's Mind*, "In the beginner's mind there are many possibilities, in the expert's mind there are few."[4]

179

As young forests in a world that desperately needs a fresh perspective, one of the most essential gifts we can bring is our beginner's mind. If we wish to see a change in this world—a renewal of our sacred contract with the Earth as well as the rejuvenation of our forests, communities, and kinships—the most powerful thing we can do is accept the fact that we are just getting started. There is a reason why we use the term *green* for newness. One of the most potent things you can do to feed the world is to cultivate and cherish your own greenness. Our willingness to be beginners is how the world will be reseeded.

Doing novel things is essential for the continued freshness of our minds. Contrary to what science previously assumed, our brain doesn't become fixed in adolescence but remains malleable throughout our lives. No matter our age, we can rewire our brains for the better. Research shows that trying new things, like starting a hobby, or educating yourself on a new topic, literally keeps your brain young.[5] In Western culture, we are taught that you pick a job, become skilled at it, and do it for the rest of your life. We are now seeing this narrative break down as more people find different ways of making a living, one that includes space and time for multiple interests and hobbies—which, as it turns out, only makes us more effective. New studies show that hobbies actually increase productivity levels, not to mention our general happiness.[6] Being willing to start something new is a kind of medicine. The inner work of learning self-compassion is an endeavor that will keep our minds flexible as we move into this new era of healing.

So, let yourself be a beginner. Let yourself start something and not be particularly skilled at it. Allow yourself to not know where you're going, or where it's all leading—just follow the thread of your own curiosity. Begin, fumble, make mistakes. There is no beginning without a few flubs. Allow the falls, slips, and snags; they are a sign that you are growing and helping to start a new beginning for us all.

Whether it's a meditation practice, therapy, a book, a business, an art project, or a family, start today and see how the world will meet you in that beginning. The first sprouts of a forest are not less important than an old-growth woodland—in the same way that children are no less precious than grown adults. With every new thing you allow yourself to explore, you are helping to seed a new worldview—one that will be essential in the time to come.

When we embrace the young forests that we are, we create a new culture, one that is as diverse as wildflower seeds. Borne from our commitment to cultivating ways of being that are earth-honoring, self-accepting, and growth-centered, these seeds will see us through the big changes to come. Your willingness to be brave as a sapling is the medicine that will help, one day, bring back the majestic groves. What you decide to cultivate now within the soil of your mind will be the blooms that take root, stabilizing the ground of our future, when all the untenable structures and thought patterns begin to crumble.

One day, whether it's because of a pathogen or the rising seas or something else entirely, we will have to return to living with the Earth as our primary partner, mirror, mother, and source. A lot of people move to the mountains where I live just to prep for this day—one that could be close at hand, or still many generations away. Rather than stocking our basements with canned goods, I believe the best way we can prepare for what's coming is to start incrementally shifting the roots of our culture. To be sacred volunteers, thought leaders, messengers, and pioneers who are here to help turn our awareness back toward a more compassionate and balanced way of being—so that when the change *does* come, we can be like the brambles or the knotweed, ready to begin again.

Acorns, Oaks, and Blueprints

The creation of a thousand forests is in one acorn.

—RALPH WALDO EMERSON

The blueprint for healing our Earth exists within us, a seed that is its own perfect outline for what is possible in our lives and in this world.

Within it are the original instructions for how to grow, and give, our gifts to this planet. When we release the overbearing expectations that we place on ourselves, the pressure of needing to be complete in our formation, we give this seed inside us a chance to unfurl.

In his seminal book *The Soul's Code*, psychologist James Hillman calls this in-dwelling possibility the "acorn" of ourselves.[7] Each acorn that falls to earth may be small, but within it are all of the instructions it needs to learn how to unfurl into a mighty oak. Each of us has a seed within us that knows what will help the world grow. We don't need to do anything elaborate to let it sprout; we just have to come home to ourselves—like the beaver, who naturally creates a whole new habitat by building their dens, or the prairie dog who aerates compacted soil with aquifers as they dig their tunnels. In finding a way to feel at home with yourself and with this Earth, you will naturally bring forth the gifts within you. It may feel challenging to sprout in the climate of the world today, but the seed inside of you was specifically designed to be ignited by the fire of this time.

At the western edge of our country, every year great tracks of land go up in flames, devastating the human and more-than-human populations. Each fire seems like an apocalypse, and yet fire is essential. California is known for its ancient, majestic, and long-lived groves of Sequoia trees, and the seeds of these trees are only released from their cones in the presence of fire. This is why the Indigenous peoples of what is now called California have maintained controlled burnings of these areas since time immemorial, and why today, on land that was taken away from their careful management, fires have gotten so out of control. In Western culture, we try to suppress the fire in order to encourage growth, whereas Indigenous cultures have always understood that some seeds simply need fire in order to open. We are like these fire-born seeds, ready-made to meet the apocalypse by replanting a whole new forest of being. We may be young, but we are so much stronger than we think.

Last winter the road above my garden washed out in a landslide. Tons of gravel ground down into rivulets over the hill and into the garden beds. I figured all but the tallest trees or heartiest saplings were gone or buried irrevocably, but, to my surprise and delight, the following spring, poking out from underneath a foot of gravel, a whole stand of daffodils arose. Pushing up from between the sharp stones, they were a miracle. The resilience of this world is astounding. Even more astonishing is remembering that we too are forged from such enduring, fire-tested, gravel-ready resilience.

We think we are too fallible for these times, but the reality is the exact opposite. Within your DNA, the inherited wisdom and essential code of your being, is the fresh capacity for reinvention. You are here because your ancestors knew what it meant to be resilient, to begin again. You are the progeny of people who, despite all odds, survived. When we can connect to that seed wisdom, we inevitably realize that the insight, the strength, the knowledge of *how* to move forward has been within us all along. When we can allow ourselves to be the acorn, the sapling in the wood, the "weed tree," the beginner, and the young forest itself, we come home to our ability to help heal the world.

There is an old Chinese proverb, "The best time to plant a tree was twenty years ago. The second-best time is now." So often we become stuck in our progression because we think we should have begun already. We admonish ourselves for not having started our careers, families, or healing earlier in life. Meanwhile, the seed is here and ready to be planted. Meanwhile, the acorns that we are today will be the oaks of the next generation. The old-growth forests we are rebuilding now will not be full-grown in our lifetimes. They will be the inheritance of our descendants, those who will have the gifts to create even more wholeness than we can currently imagine.

Planting a whole forest seems like a tall order, but it doesn't feel so big when you realize that all you need to do is nurture the seed of what is already unfurling within you now. The world is always in the process of moving toward healing. You, beautiful, honest, young-hearted, and eager, are an essential part of that medicine. Your life, exactly as it naturally unfolds, is a successional medicine for the Earth. So place the acorn of yourself here, in the patch of soil that is your life, and let the growing begin.

EXERCISE:

Place-Based Divination
for Seeing Your Gifts

For this exercise go to a place in your environment that has been, in your mind, disturbed, diminished, or otherwise altered negatively by human interaction. Bring a journal to this spot and find a place where you can sit comfortably, preferably somewhere where you won't be disturbed. By noticing the beauty here, you can start to find and value under-cherished parts of yourself and perhaps even glimpse the blueprint that you carry for this world. Try taking a few deep breaths, feeling yourself settle into the earth. When you are ready to begin, respond to the following prompts.

1. *What do you notice?*

   Look all around you, swiveling your head to peer behind you, above you, and at your feet. Feel the ground beneath you. Notice where the air touches your skin. Write down any immediate impressions of the place where you are sitting. Colors, sounds, textures, patterns. Plants, animals, weather, stones. Taking up to five minutes, let yourself list everything that feels prominent. If it comes into your mind, write it down. Each one of these details is important for you at this time. It is its own tiny mirror. You'll notice that every time you do this activity you will record something a bit different. The land reflects back to us exactly what we need to see in that moment.

2. *How do you feel?*

Now turn that same gaze inward to become a witness to your inner landscape. How do you feel in this moment? Record any sensations in your body. Notice what thoughts cross your mind. What emotions are you feeling? Perhaps you are still carrying impressions from earlier in your day, or maybe you have the bourgeoning sensation of something new within? It is all valid. By turning our gaze inward, we connect the outer and inner landscapes, creating a bridge of meaning through which further relationship and guidance can be heard.

3. *Free draw.*

Sit down with the pure impressions of your outer and inner landscapes and let yourself do a free drawing of exactly "where you are" now. You do not have to be an artist to do this, and it does not have to be an accurate landscape or botanical drawing. In fact, I invite you to step into your more abstract mind. Some of my favorite drawings were made with my nondominant hand and lots of squiggles. This exercise is more about capturing a moment in time. Don't think, just draw. Try to clear your mind to let the lines and shapes come through. I often find such free drawing to be one of the best divination oracles.

4. *Record the message from the land.*

Now that you have created a relationship of reflection between the inner and outer worlds, you are ready to receive the message for this time. The world is always communicating with us.

If this place could say anything to you in this moment, what would it be? Imagine the land wants to give you a specific gem of wisdom to take with you—what is it? In what ways is this place showing you something about the role you are here to play in the healing? Allow yourself to enter a soft space of receptivity, a kind of channeling state where you let go and simply write down whatever comes. Don't edit as you write; just let it flow. Read what you wrote afterward, or come back to it later in the day. Let the emotional transmission of this exercise touch you, and recognize the perfection of these words.

After you complete the exercise, take as long as you'd like to rest here in this place. If you have a biodegradable gift to offer, such as a bit of hair for a local bird's nest, some water, or a stone, you can give it to the land now. Stay here for as long as feels good and then move into the rest of your day knowing that you have received a seed of insight that will continue to grow and make itself known.

PART THREE
THE GLOW

Giving Yourself to the World

9

WILLOW WATER

I WALKED SWIFTLY DOWN the steep trail to the river, the path slick with early summer rain. The firs were exhaling a fresh, deep breath, and the ground was slippery as I turned each corner. After a few minutes of switchbacks, I hit the sharp decline to the river's edge. Because this precipice had been eroded by foot traffic, the only steps in sight were the mud-exposed roots of the trees, holding the embankment together. I placed each foot carefully as I climbed down the slippery rope-ladder of roots. Body tensed, eyes focused on the descent, I couldn't see any further than my next step—and so it was that I smelled them before I saw them.

Scent is a funny thing. It unfurls in our mind before we have a chance to find names or places or times, and yet the feeling of all three rushes in unbidden as soon as we are touched by the perfume. In the moments before our memory gets ahold of what is rising, we are moor-less in the waves of our sensing.

With limbs tangled into the loops of tree roots, the animal of my body was suddenly soothed. It felt as if I had been wrapped up into some unseen arms. The scent, and its feeling, were maternal, comfortable, and yet distinctly emotional. Tears came to my eyes—but I had no idea what for.

Another moment and I dropped down onto the riverside, both feet finally on level ground. My eyes skipped from the gray stones beneath me to the fringe of dusty green at the water's edge and *there they were*— growing straight from tumbled serpentine rocks and beams of sunlight was a wickered shoreline of saplings. Waving in thickets of silver and olive, they greeted me with long, ballet-like gestures. I watched their leaves turn like the glint of a thousand lighthouses in the river's wind, and I finally found the source of the perfume that had stirred me to unexpected tears. It was the scent of willows.

Willows have been a part of my life since the beginning. In the weeks following my birth, my dad bought a weeping willow tree at a local nursery, driving home slowly through the July heat while the thin slip of tree waved out our hatchback. My grandfather, a born and raised Brooklynite and avid horticulturist, was visiting us that summer. As my dad dug a hole for the roots, my grandfather warned that the tree probably wouldn't live past thirty. My dad just shrugged. After all, who could even see that far into the future? So they planted the willow together, and one of my earliest companions took root in my life.

Back before developments became a profitable, and possible, way to expand the community, the common area beyond our tiny suburban lawns had been a swamp. Backfilled with dirt and sod, the area was still prone to flooding. From time-to-time our entire backyard would turn into a lagoon. It endangered our basement, causing our tired sump pump to give out more than once, but the weeping willow loved it.

The willow grew as quickly as I did. By the time I was eight the branches stretched tall enough to walk under, and long enough that they formed a kind of curtain around the heart of the tree. Parting the slender leaves and slipping between their green was like entering a whole other world. I used to practice stepping in and out of the velvet drapery to see if I could sense the difference between these two realms of existence. The willow was the first plant I ever remember speaking to. When I was older and longer-limbed, I'd climb into the tree with a journal and a small snack, write poetry, and lean against her heartwood. On hard days, I'd bring my face close into the furrows of her bark and whisper things I couldn't tell anyone else. When I brought my ear in for a response I swore I could feel a wave, like the ripple of wind in long branches, move from her to me. I never doubted that we were having a conversation.

Our ability to converse with plants is ancient. It is a fluency that was basic to our ancestors—and yet, the words for how exactly this conversation happens are hard to come by, perhaps because the communication itself isn't rooted in words, but in feelings that are as whole and subtle as scent.

Later, when I began to throw myself into school and achievement in the academic world, I spent less and less time with the willow. Even though she was right outside the window where my desk was parked, my nose was so buried in textbooks I'd forgotten she was there at all. As a teenager, I stopped climbing into her arms. For a spell, I forgot that I ever thought I could hear her respond to my pleas for help. But one day, not too far in the future, I would remember.

Reaching the willow-lined shore, I paused on the warm stones at the river's edge. In the distance, I could hear a crowd singing—or perhaps it was just the voice of the water. The sound brought an immediate pang of guilt to my stomach. Twenty minutes prior, I had decided, against official recommendation, to skip opening circle of the conference and head to the river. I was there to teach at a large earth skills gathering set back into the forests of Oregon, on the lands of the Takelma people. At this point in my career I was well versed in the rigors of teaching on the road, but four days camping out with five hundred people was still overwhelming for my sensitive nervous system and introverted soul.

Over the years, I had learned that I would need extra time to decompress on the first day of teaching, especially in a new place. I knew this about myself, and yet I was still frustrated at my inability to cope. I was overwhelmed by the crowd and beset by guilt for skipping the morning's activities. While the rest of my colleagues had streamed with linked arms toward the opening circle, I had literally run off in the opposite direction, scurrying down the path until I was out of view. As I walked the rain-slick trail to the river, my inner critic raging like a storm, the jammed circuits of my nervous system turned into a full-on blackout. Unable to forgive myself for feeling so overwhelmed and challenged, I slipped into a familiar, sharp-edged loop of judgment.

We all have days when, no matter how much self-love we've learned, being ourselves seems like no real redemption at all. Times when we feel like we need to apologize for our own existence. Those days that run you ragged and then drive you down a steep path to the river, filled with a heaviness you can only hope to bear. It is always in the midst of these moments that grace comes wafting in on an unexpected breeze.

The willow trees along the riverbank were in full bloom, dotted with the tiny thumbs of their soft catkins. Made to be born on the slightest winds, the willow's seeds drifted like snow flurries on the perfumed breeze. As I took a deep breath, the scent of the willows moved into me. An entire country away from my childhood house in Pennsylvania, I felt as if I were home, safe inside the curtained circle of my beloved weeping willow.

Swaying with overwhelmed fatigue, I finally let go. My nervous system softened. Drifting in on the breeze came a realization as subtle as perfume—something that we were all born understanding and yet forget along the way. The willows were a choir surrounding me with gentle music, and this was their refrain—*No matter how hard you are on yourself, or how harsh life becomes, you are already forgiven for anything you could have ever done.* I was shocked by the out-of-the-blue clarity of this message but soothed beyond belief.

I was forgiven. I was forgiven for my faults and mistakes. Forgiven for my self-doubt. Forgiven for all the ways in which I continued to encounter that inner critic, even as I did the good work of putting myself out into the world. No matter what poison-tipped self-admonishment I slung at myself, it didn't matter. Because the world had already forgiven me for who I was, and the Earth loved me regardless.

Without knowing it, I had brought the heaviness of my heart and given it up to the world, like a child carrying her woes into the arms of a willow. I had asked the Earth, unconsciously, if I could be excused for my faults, and I had been given a unanimous answer—*You are already forgiven.*

I didn't grow up in a world of confessionals or hail Marys, so I had never experienced this moment of baring everything and then having a thumb of holy water pressed upon my forehead. A moment of pure, loving absolution. A wider, wiser power showing up to comfort me when I couldn't bare it anymore. It was the definition of a miracle.

I stood there, breathing deeply as tears streamed down my face, dropping onto the river stones. The willow's seeds moved like tiny angels in the currents of the air as the warm breeze lifted my own scent to dance with the green incense of the wind. I felt like I was in the middle of a snow globe, a benevolent whirlwind of sensation. I held out my arms, as if to be embraced, and closed my eyes. The air was filled with willow seeds and scent, a sense of the whirling preciousness of life and the knowledge that everything would be alright.

Born from Breakage

I grew up thinking of willows as elegant landscape plants and gentle childhood companions, but the truth is that willows are some of the toughest trees on the planet. Taking root in the most challenging landscapes, these pioneer trees have adapted to live among unexpected tides—including water-logged places and riversides. If you break off the flexible wand of a willow's branch, it has the ability to reroot almost anywhere. With this intricate strategy, evolved over many millennia of living beside river currents and stormy tides, willow branches simply allow themselves to be carried downstream where they can grow anew. Born from breakage, willows embrace the turbulence that comes with perching yourself on the bank of a moving world, and they are able to use that tumult to thrive. Part of their ability to reroot almost anywhere is due to their high content of indolebutyric acid (IBA). A plant hormone that stimulates growth, IBA is so good at encouraging regeneration that some gardeners use willow-infused waters to help their seedlings get a head start.

Delicate though they may seem, willows were designed to be able to move into the most extreme environments. In the harsh landscape of the high artic, after even the heartiest conifers cease to grow, you will find whole fields of humble dwarf willows. Seeking water in the desert, you'd be wise to search for their familiar green fringe signaling hidden channels of water. Willows are also especially adapted to move into disturbed ecosystems, helping them to heal.

In more populated areas of the world, willow trees are often grown as riparian buffers, forming natural barriers that can prevent chemical tides from entering into larger waterways. Willows are so adept at cleaning toxins they are even used in wastewater treatment systems and land reclamation efforts. Like angels with wings big enough to embrace a whole ecosystem, willow trees literally hold the land together with their earth-stabilizing roots, shelterbelts, and windbreaks. If you coppice a willow (a process where you cut a plant back to ground level), it will sprout forth with an abundance of new branches. Amazingly, even if a branch is planted upside down, it will still sprout.

As a child, I knew nothing about this elegant tree's resiliency—until our weeping willow began to die. By the time I was in my early twenties, the willow tree began dropping large limbs to the earth. It was sad, at first, to come home from college for a visit and find my beloved tree had lost another perch. But as the crown disintegrated, a profusion of new, whip-like branches bloomed from the tree's heartwood. As the willow slowly poured her lifeforce back into the earth, those lustrous branches grew longer, falling like a fountain of silver-green water. Any one of them, gently broken and carried somewhere else, could have become a new tree. For years, my dad carefully mowed around the tall fountain, sometimes taking cuttings inside to put on the windowsill. Though I didn't carry a literal willow start with me to the mountains, I still ended up transporting the memory of that willow to reroot in new soil. After I graduated herbal school and began creating my own products to sell, I decided to call my new business One Willow Apothecaries.

In a world of breakage and unexpected currents, willows are emblems of adaptability and elegance. Bearers of the reality that even the hardest places have much more *give* than we could ever imagine, willows find flexibility within heartbreak, the forgiveness at the center of every transgression. To stumble upon a copse of river willows is to stand in the presence of a kingdom created from something destroyed. To discover a healthy thicket of these trees is to see the single truth of the world unfurl—the only rule this Earth lives by is growth.

As humans, with brains trained to see a world colored by "right" and "wrong," we easily get trapped into black-and-white thinking. We self-police in order to be good and paint thick rules of conduct over our experience of ourselves and the Earth. But beyond the human assignments of good and bad, favorable growth conditions or difficult situations, miracle or disaster, is the truth that our Earth views *everything* as an opportunity for growth. Even in the wake of something seemingly disastrous, the only question the Earth ever asks is *How can this help the growing?* The falling of one tree in a forest makes way for a myriad of new lives to reach the canopy. The breakage of a single branch means a whole bank of willows further downstream. Our planet only sees in shades of becoming. There is no judgment—there never has been—there is only the invitation to shed what inhibits our natural flourishing.

Growth is the truth that drives lichen to stretch slow as millennia across stone and kudzu to edge over the highway in the course of one hot summer's day. It is the force that makes mushrooms swell from the bodies of dead giants, and the benediction that will eventually birth soil from stone and bones and the refuse of the living world. Growth is the field "out beyond ideas of rightdoing and wrongdoing"—as Rumi so elegantly puts it—and we are simply learning how to get there again.

Going down to the river that day, my sense of being damaged or irredeemable had blocked me from seeing the forest from the trees. The willows reminded me, however, that no matter how many disasters I encountered along my path, everything is always an invitation to grow. The world wants to welcome us back into this ongoing stream of regeneration. But in order to become a part of the healing, we have to be able to do the one thing that opens us to growth again—forgive ourselves.

Allelopathic Roots: Self-Punishment and What Will Not Grow

While willows, and the water made from soaking their cuttings, are known for their ability to help nurture new life, there are plants that lurk at the opposite end of the spectrum, trees whose compounds innately inhibit the growth of others. Known in the ecological world as *negative allelopaths*, a small handful of plants possess a biochemistry that enacts the opposite effect of willow water, emitting compounds that suppress the germination of plants in their vicinity.

Arcing over our two-story barn is a magnificent black walnut tree. In the fall its tennis-ball-size husks drop onto the tin roof like gunshot. If the squirrels don't get to them before we do, by November the hard-shelled walnuts are stored by the bucket load in our pantry. The husks, used for dye, turn your hands a dark brown. Their familiar henna can be spotted around the nailbeds of mountain folks every autumn. Over the years, I've learned the hard way that it's not worth trying to plant anything around the edge of this tree. Black walnuts contain allelopathic compounds, so very few plants thrive at their feet. In a garden, there's not much you can do but respect the circle this tree draws around itself.

Every day we hear examples of how humans can be allelopathic inhibitors of growth. Forests continue to be felled, oil spills into our waterways, and in the middle of the Pacific Ocean there is an island of plastic larger than the state of Texas. The story that humans are negatively allelopathic creatures is one we are all familiar with. Just like the walnut tree's natural adaptation, this story serves a purpose. Harsh and necessary as cold water to the face, this perspective wakes us up from the sleep of obliviousness. Over time, however, this belief can become a kind of poison unto itself.

Some people believe humans have wreaked havoc on the Earth because we have some central defect to our being—but the damage we've caused is not due to an unsolvable problem with our brains, but the *belief* that there is something innately wrong with us in the first place. We harm the world, not because we are innately harmful, but because of how deeply we've been wounded by a culture steeped in the toxicity of self-hatred. The suffering that is caused by the belief that something is intrinsically wrong, or sinful, about you is immense. The resulting damage of believing that we are unforgivable has been powerful enough to touch the whole world. Research shows an unmistakable correlation between self-esteem and the dysfunctional behavior necessary to allow ecological degradation to happen in the first place—including the tendency to make destructive decisions, the readiness to tolerate mistreatment, and the willingness to harm others.[1]

The word *allelopathy* comes from the Greek *allelo* "mutual" and *pathy* "suffering." In this particular state of mutual harm, we have clear cut whole forests so we can be seen as affluent or powerful—and, therefore, worthy of respect and love. We have taken over stolen land, exploited the heart of mountains, dragged dangerous pipelines across some of the most fragile ecosystems on Earth, all simply because—at our hearts—we ache to know that we are good, that we are seen, that we are safe, valued, and cared for. The truth is exposed with every dig of the excavator. Our inability to see our own innate worth outside of money, fame, or the false alcaldes of a culture that is so shallowly rooted is a force that has inhibited life all over the world. Every space on Earth damaged by the human hand was touched by that mutual suffering of someone trying to relocate their own worthiness. As the old adage goes, "hurt people, hurt people." Inevitably, wounded people wound the Earth—but *both* can heal when we heal ourselves. If self-judgement has become a negative allelopathic element for our Earth, then the solution to encourage regrowth is as simple as willow-soaked waters.

Forgiveness is innate to the Earth. It is as natural as water running until it is clear again. As humans, it is incredibly important for our own development that we learn how to forgive. Studies show that the ability to forgive is correlated with higher self-esteem, better mental and physical health, and happier relationships.[2] Learning how to grow on the banks of our current world isn't easy. Like the storm-ravaged places where the willows grow, our collective culture deeply needs regeneration. Forgiveness—beginning with self-forgiveness—is how we will heal the hurt.

Standing on that perfumed shoreline of willows, I wondered: In what ways is self-judgement inhibiting my ability to become a part of the growing once more? How does the weight of my self-resentment impede my capacity to be like the floating angels of the willow's seeds, someone who innately blesses this world? If I forgave myself for my individual "flaws," as well as the errors of my species as a whole, is it possible that I could tap into more potential than I currently realize? I could feel the existence of that reality, bright as the willow branches swaying beside me, just on other side of the veil. If I forgave myself, I could once again access all the living energy within me to become a part of the Earth's dream—to help in the cocreation and to regrow the world.

Clear as Water

Along the walk from my campsite in the woods to the riverbed was a maze of tents, people, and coolers. There were mason jars filled with flowers perched in the curves of trees, lanterns hanging from branches, and small cairns of stones left as offerings. It was heart-warming to see humans living so naturally, in a village dwarfed by cedars and dotted by wild roses, but it was also slightly disconcerting. A part of me couldn't help but worry—how was our footfall affecting the land? What trash would we leave behind? Was our presence here truly welcomed by the forest, or were we just another group of humans trespassing? The schedule of classes at the gathering included seminars about the deepening crisis of species extinction and habitat loss. These classes were packed, often ending with a distinct sense of hopeless, the audience in tears.

There is a real, tangible sorrow for the environmental damage that has been done. Witnessing the world's hurt, many of us worry that we have violated, irrevocably, our contract of reciprocity with the Earth. Knowing how the living world has suffered can deepen the feeling of being irredeemable—but this self-condemnation, if left unchecked, ultimately undermines our ability to be a part of the germination of a new world.

Grudge-holding inhibits growth wherever it takes root. The inability to forgive prevents instead of promotes—in a partnership, in a community, and in our relationship to our own selves. In one study, the inability to forgive was linked to a whole cornucopia of negative mental and physical health issues—including higher levels of cortisol, elevated blood pressure, and increased heartrate.[3] It can be deeply illuminating to dwell for a time in the bitterness of being unforgiven—or unforgiving. That bite can teach us so much about ourselves, shedding light on the constricted places that need a willow's flexibility to feel safe enough to move on. But no matter how far we go down the rabbit hole of self-punishment, everything eventually comes back around to the inalienable, and unstoppable, truth of growth.

Unconsciously, we sensitive humans count every transgression we've enacted against the Earth, one another, and ourselves. We move about the world as if these hurts are unhealable, even though the evidence to the contrary is growing along the banks of every river we come across. We self-punish by keeping ourselves away from the world, and yet the world wants nothing more than to feel its children come home.

The biggest benediction that we can give to this Earth—the task that is at the heart of our quest to become a part of the growing once more—will be our ability to forgive ourselves. As Nelson Mandela famously said after twenty-seven years of imprisonment, "As I walked out the door toward the gate that would lead to my freedom, I knew if I didn't leave my bitterness and hatred behind, I'd still be in prison." Forgiveness is how we get free; it is how we release our energy so it can rejoin the liberatory healing of the world. Standing on the edge of that willow-lined river in the midmorning light, the deep importance of finding forgiveness for my own self was clear as water.

Soothing the Pain

When I was in college I took aspirin nearly every day. Riddled with undiagnosed food allergies that caused wicked headaches, and living with chronic pelvic pain, the relief of aspirin became my safe space. It was normal for me to wake up and pop an aspirin before I made coffee in my tiny two-cup pot. That little pill became my lifeline, a safe harbor in a world heavy with mysterious aches and the growing pains of learning who I was. I felt bad about my daily dependence on this drug. It wasn't until I was in herbal school years later that I learned aspirin is made from a plant that has always been a source of healing in my life.

Beyond its luscious growth-promoting hormones, willow is known for producing one other chemical—salicin. An anti-inflammatory and pain-reliever, salicin is the compound from which our current-day aspirin is derived. Salicin, found naturally in willow bark, has healing benefits that have been used for millennia by cultures around the globe.

This compound makes willow a potent medicine for easing headaches, osteoarthritis, inflammatory conditions like tendonitis, and other persistent aches. The use of willow bark as a pain remedy can be traced back to Hippocrates's writing in 400 BCE—but it has likely been in humanity's medicine cabinet since the beginning.[4]

I still remember my amazement when I learned that this familiar plant from my childhood was such a historically powerful, and contemporarily indispensable, medicine. When I started my herbal practice, I began using willow bark as a go-to for persistent headaches, nagging back pain, and general muscular discomfort. Before I gathered them, I learned to break the twigs of willows and sniff. The more vibrantly wintergreen the scent, the more potent the medicine would be. If I was out for a walk and felt a headache coming on, I'd take a small twig of willow to chew as I strolled. It is nothing less than a revelation to remember—nature is the first pharmacy. Everything we need to feel better is right outside our door. My beloved willow was a plant that could take the pain away, no matter how deep it went.

We are in a time in which willow medicine is much needed. Tucked underneath the ache of our collective disconnection is a painful worry—does this pristine sentience we call nature resent us for all we've done? Does this planet begrudge our existence? Is humanity itself a pain point for the Earth?

Back at the Oregonian riverside, I used my hand to part the thick wicker of the willow's shoots. Ducking between their long branches, I climbed into the thicket of willows and hid myself among them. There, nestled into the basket of their arms, I gave a strand of my hair and, in turn, took a small twig to munch on. The moment I started to chew, something inside of me softened completely, like a headache giving way to the natural relief of being back in your own skin. All the painful worries disappeared.

How could I be beyond redemption if all this goodness was here to greet me? How could the world possibly resent me if all this beauty is still being offered to me? I let the ache in my heart dissolve so I could truly hear the message those willows kept repeating. *I am already forgiven.*

Weaving a New Way

The moment the willow was lifted from the creek, we could smell it—the scent had been intensified by its time in the water. In order to be pliable enough to weave into baskets, willow needs to be soaked beforehand. These particular bundles had been in the creek for two days. A group of us was sitting in a circle, ready to begin weaving. The willow's scent hung in the air like garlands.

Earlier that month, my friend Zac had arrived to the mountains, traveling down from Minnesota with his three-legged dog Bea and a truck full of multicolored willow cuttings. As someone who makes a regular circuit around the country to teach traditional earth skills, he's nearly always toting around the makings of several different craft projects. With his light buckskin pants, bronze vest, and blond hair, Zac is often honey-colored from head-to-toe, with a truly sweet heart to match.

One afternoon a small group of us gathered to weave berry baskets. Zac had submerged several willow bundles in the nearby creek so the slender wands would be soft enough to be woven. When he lifted them, dripping, from the water, their perfume could be smelled across the clearing. Zac laid the willow branches on the picnic tables and began by showing us the basics. You start these types of baskets by lashing together the two branches that will become the rim and the handles using a centerpiece of weaving called a *God's eye*. With overlapping diamonds placed at both junctions, a God's eye is what keeps the basket together so the rest of the weaving can begin. Watching the berry basket come into form beneath Zac's hands felt like witnessing Creation itself. Once he finished demonstrating, each of us got a small pile of willow to work with. I was amazed by the variety of colors—chestnut, ash grey, and lilac. Zac told us that the hues would fade a bit once the basket dried, but we would still be able to see the amazing variance.

Willow is a traditional material for basket making around the world because its branches are flexible enough to bend and yet strong enough to hold a shape. As I began to work with the silky lengths, I fell into a trance. Heady and familiar as mother's milk, soothing to some inner sense of memory, the scent of the willows moved off my hands as I wove. As the hours ticked by, I forgot everything but the rhythm of under-over, under-over. In the repetitive weaving, I forgave myself for all faults, let go of all the things I couldn't fix—about myself or the world—and simply focused on the form that was coming into being beneath my gaze. I slipped loose of the weight I had been carrying and became an empty vessel again. It took most of us a full day to weave our baskets; by the end we were all like kids, grinning at our new creations.

From the beginning, we humans have been weavers, tasked with the ability to be a part of the co-creation. Today, many of the old weaving practices are being resurrected. Besides Zac, I have at least three friends who make their living as basket weavers. Every time I see them flourish, I think *another way is possible*. Right now on Earth we are being asked to learn how to reweave ourselves into the wider basket of the world. To become a strand again in the overall weft, to use our agency to shape a better future for us all.

Today my willow basket sits beside my desk. Instead of berries, I keep cards and other precious mementos in it. It is lopsided, with gaps in the weave and a tilt that sets it slightly askew, but I adore it. Every time I look at this willow basket it reminds me of the world we are attempting to remake with our hands. It reminds me that the old ways aren't dead but are resprouting from coppiced roots. It reminds me that no matter how many programs of harm we learn throughout our lives, much greater patterns of healing are at work, re-creating the wholeness again.

A few years ago the willow tree of my birth finally fell. To the chagrin of their neighbors, my parents had allowed the willow to complete its full lifecycle. By the end, the willow had become a true giving tree—a lookout for hawks, a sounding board for woodpeckers, a playground for squirrels, and fodder for the beetles. After all the limbs fell, my parents kept the biggest branch up on the deck where it became a perch for the robins. One day a few autumns ago, my Dad paused while mowing the lawn to touch the heart of the empty tree and it simply fell over. Light as a corn husk it broke into pieces on the waiting soil. The era of this willow was done—and a new one was just beginning. My own days of self-judgment were not over forever, but the era of forgiving myself, of letting the world see my goodness, and of learning how to use my gifts to truly help the co-creation, were just getting started.

There will always be times when I'll need to hike down to the river to let the emotions of the day wash through me. When I ache to curl up on the warm river stones and remember how to be held. When a part of me wants to just break into the current and let go. As humans, we will always have times when we will doubt that we are loveable. Meanwhile, a stand of willows on a river bend will embrace you no matter what you have ever done. Meanwhile the whole world continues to reach out to touch you. The benevolent benediction of the Earth will find you as easily, and as sweetly, as a scent on the breeze.

Each of us has felt the way the forgiveness of the world can touch us—in the way a rose shares its perfume or in how the water pours forth from the spigots in our gardens. This world, like the whirling dervishes of the willow seeds in the upturn of a river's breeze, is asking you to forgive yourself. Because it wouldn't have made any sense for this Earth to have held onto a grudge in the first place. Resentment has no place within the folds of growth.

Forgiveness is the energy that encourages a mined land to grow once again, strong with blackberries and fireweed. It is the force that causes the trees to breathe deeper, recycling the extra carbon dioxide we've created in the atmosphere. It is the way the Earth will caress you with each step. Every time you take off your shoes, you are kissed.

Forgiveness is like willow-infused water. Whatever it is poured upon will grow. So here, in this moment, tuck yourself into the arms of a riverbank woven from such forgiveness. Drink deep from this cup of broth, love-warmed and willow-soaked, and know that you—as a human, as a person, as a being—are forgiven.

You are forgiven by the Earth. By the river. By the water. You are forgiven by the higher power of the wind. You are forgiven by the gods of the whales and the deities of the willows, dipping their long arms into the water.

Come rinse yourself, they say. Baptize yourself in the knowing. Drink deep and allow yourself this forgiveness. For your growth is the very thing that will feed this world.

EXERCISE
Ask the Earth for Forgiveness

Asking for forgiveness is a powerful prayer of healing, for oneself and the world. When we ask for forgiveness, we loosen shame from its shackles and allow it out into the sunlight where it can evaporate into the love of the world. The Earth already forgives us for anything we could have ever done, but knowing you are forgiven and *feeling* that you are forgiven are two different things entirely. In this exercise, you're invited to ask the Earth for forgiveness so you can dissolve any shame you have around being yourself, or being human, and you can embrace the growth you were meant to bring to this world.

1. To start, gather something biodegradable that you'd like to use as an offering. A flower, a stone, holy water—choose whatever feels right to you.

2. Get out into a quiet place of nature, somewhere you won't be disturbed. Preferably find a place with soft soil or sand where you can dig.

3. If possible, set the space by making a circle around the area from leaves, branches, shells, or stones. Sit in the center of the circle and bring your attention deep into your body.

   Ask yourself *What are the things I've done that feel unforgivable? In what ways do I struggle to forgive myself?*

4. Now dig a small hole in the earth. Lie down on the ground next to it and whisper all those unforgivable things into this hole.

Notice as you say each one that the energy is going into the earth and is being absorbed and transformed. Let anything else that wants to come out have permission to be released. Maybe you want to spit or scream or cry. Let it go.

5. When you've said everything you need to, place the gift you brought into the hole. Lying close to the earth, offer a prayer of forgiveness in your tradition, or try saying the following four mantras. Inspired by the tradition of the Hawaiian Ho'opono-pono prayer, these mantras, developed by Ihaleakala Hew Len, are meant to be repeated to your own self. From Hew Len's perspective, when you can forgive the parts of you that hold responsibility for any kind of hurt, pain itself begins to disappear from the world.

> **I'm sorry**
> **Please forgive me**
> **Thank you**
> **I love you.**

6. Linger on each phrase until you feel you've gotten a response. Tune into the subtlety of your body, notice any feelings of groundedness, and release. When you are done, fill back in the hole and spend a few moments in gratitude with your head upon the earth.

10

THE SUGAR BEES

I STEPPED OFF THE plane into the midsummer heat. After a few months of making the rounds to teach out west, I was ready to be home. When I left the mountains, the trees had just begun budding out, but now the hills were in full flush. The green breathing of the land was so thick, it felt as if I was parting a wave when I stepped onto the tarmac. Coming home to these hills always has a particular feeling—a softening, a melting, a rush, like surrendering to a giant hug. Leg cramped and jet lagged from a red eye, I drove home in a happy daze, eager to see what had begun to bloom in the garden.

At the time, I was living on the top floor of a purple-painted Victorian, a house that, according to legend, once belonged to an old-time mountain healer. A man who was the seventh son of a seventh son, the healer was renowned for the miracles he could work with his faith and the laying-on of hands. Now, it was home to a kind and energetic retired couple who were slowly shaping the land into a permaculture paradise, replete with greenhouses, terraced gardens, and a pizza oven. I was renting the top floor of the house, which had its own entrance set into a hill overlooking the garden.

Lugging my giant suitcase up the grass-rubbed path to my back door, I immediately saw that, in my absence, somebody else had moved into my apartment—a whole group of them. As I got to the porch, a troop of tiny black winged bodies, lit by lines of yellow, zoomed past me. Flying like notes in a sheet of symphony music between the house and the air, a colony of wasps was streaming out of their new residence beside my front door. I saw the dried lava where my landlords had tried unsuccessfully to caulk the door's casing to block their entrance. The wasps had carved the caulk away like it was a soft clay bowl and were flying swiftly in and out of the newly dug hole.

Ducking my head, I walked through their flightpaths and into the house to unpack. It seemed only fair that while I was gone, others had come to inhabit the space I had left. As I dumped the contents of my suitcase into the laundry, I ruminated on whether I should do something about the wasps, but I put the thought away into the cabinets with my toothpaste and hairbrush.

As days turned into weeks, and the weeks turned into months, I found myself simply cohabitating with my new housemates. Every day I would walk out of my home through the crossbars of their music, moving hurriedly, as if passing a cellist in the subway. Though it was skillful and beautiful, I never lingered long to watch the symphony. I was normally in too much of a hurry to slow down for the music happening all around me.

In the back of my head I worried about the wasps' presence—should I remove them? How? Would they be dangerous? Were they destructive to the house? But not once in those weeks, and then months, of passing through their music did I ever get stung. So I left them alone to coexist with me.

Broken Teacups and a Bowl of Bees

One morning in early September there was a knock at the front door. I was in my bathroom, in a long-flowered robe and still linen-creased from sleep. I swung open the sagging screen door to find my downstairs landlady standing there. Bespeckled, friendly, and a bit worry-worn, she was holding a bouquet of garden flowers and smiling hesitatingly. I stepped out into the porch to chat with her about the fall garden crops and coordinating the end of my lease. I had just put in a bid on what would be my future treehouse home and was hoping to move out by the end of year. As we spoke, the day gradually warmed, raising the volume on the symphony of wings above our heads.

The wasps came and went in gradually thickening lines until, finally, one went off path like a rogue note and bumped straight into my land-lady's cheek. "These sugar bees!" she exclaimed, "we have to do some-thing about them." I gestured feebly toward the caulking.

"It's time we sprayed them," she stated, matter-of-factly, already several steps down the yard and making a beeline for the shed. I slipped back inside to finish brushing my teeth. When I emerged again she was looming over the casing of the door, aerosol bottle in hand, already having sprayed the opening to their hive.

"I'm going to close the door!" I threw out at her, "just in case it drifts in!" I shut the door and stood for a moment, not knowing how to feel. The part of me that had already given my notice and was beginning the process of packing up the house was willing to put these sugar bees, as she had called them, into a box with every-thing else. Something that was no longer my problem, like the pile of dull kitchenware destined for Goodwill. I already had one foot out the door and, really, what could I even do when this wasn't my own home? So I made tea and breakfast and took a tray back into my bedroom to write, shutting the door as a barrier between me and the die-off happening outside.

As I worked, I kept finding my mind drifting to eerie thoughts of gas chambers and pesticides. What was it like inside the hive right now? What were those wasps experiencing? Whenever my thoughts wandered into the catacombed darkness, I couldn't help but wonder, with a strange-feeling curiosity—why was the life of a whole hive worth so much less than my own? When was that decided? And why?

I didn't emerge until hours later. Computer fatigued and stretching my bare feet on the hardwood floor, I began padding down the familiar path to the kitchen. When I got to the end of the hallway, I stopped in my tracks. The hive, those that had found a back exit out of their gassed labyrinth and into my house, was now crowded around the insides of my windows and doorframes. Some wasps were stumbling, as if drunk on sour wine. Others were lying still as seeds, eerily empty of life. They were everywhere. On the kitchen floor, perched on lamp shades, moving across the window screens in slow sluggish crawls. Now they were less like music notes, and more like the slow bubble of methane released from the bottom of a lake. There were so many of them, it was as if they were seeping up from the floorboards. With them came a wellspring of grief.

A few days earlier, I had woken up to a text to let me know that a dear friend of mine had ended their life. This friend had been one of the first true heart-connections I had made after moving down to the mountains. I met Aven on a camping trip in a blueberry-rich part of the wilderness; I still remember the moment I first saw them, standing on the trail, smiling shyly behind black-rimmed eyeglasses, exuding gentleness and warmth. After that we would get together from time-to-time to talk about things like plant medicine, spirit guides, our belief in magic, and our challenges as empaths navigating a world that sometimes felt too heavy to bear. Aven was sensitive and spiritual, caring to a fault, and had been struggling deeply for a long time. Unable to process the news in the text message, part of me sealed the information into a vault, unable to feel the fullness of the fact that my friend was no longer in this world. But looking at these little creatures dying in waves across my floor, the tiny pond that had frozen in the center of my chest cracked. The layer I had put up between myself and the world, myself and the sadness, shattered. Sudden as a teacup dropped on a hardwood floor, the sorrow of it all broke open.

Over the next few days, the wasps and I all lived together as companions. They became intimate with me, and I with them. They had become my sugar bees. Climbing across my toothbrush, perched on the kettle, moving toward me across the couch. All the ways in which I had shielded myself, kept myself apart, came down. Though I had been living with them for months, never once had I really stopped to *see* them. Now, I realized each one was an individual, intricate, with wings as small as fairy needles. Their faces held a sweetness, looking up into the world from where they crawled on the floor. In our closeness, I could recognize them now as paper wasps—beings with delicately striped bodies, orange antennae, and small onyx-round faces. Once, I went to pull a shawl down from the coat rack and yelped. One of them had nipped me at the neck, just once and very lightly. I accepted this single sting for the medicine that it was.

In their last days on Earth, and my last days in the house, I tiptoed through the halls, watching my feet so I wouldn't step on my companions that were still resting, dying, or both. My routine moved to the rhythm of their last days. My life became about their death—and how I both tended to and was broken by it.

As they passed, I felt compelled to begin collecting the wasps so I could give them some kind of memorial. Honoring each one of their wondrous bodies seemed like the only offering I could give that could come close to their own inherent exquisiteness. Every day I picked up the dead and placed them in a small white porcelain bowl. It's hard to put into words the tenderness you can feel for a single winged being, tiny as your thumbnail, resting wearily by your napkin on the dinner table and passing away before your eyes. In a seawater swell of grief and feeling, I enacted this small ritual because it was something, perhaps the only thing, I *could* do.

I placed the bowl in the center of a small mandala of rose quartz and flower petals I had made when I heard about Aven's passing. Stretching across the floor in front of the south facing windows of my bedroom, the small monument became a place where I could sit and cry and remember. Now, they were all together—Aven and the sugar bees—on this sunlit stretch of floor, in this perfectly small bowl. For the first time, I felt like I could hold it all.

Cradling a Single Hive

I have, at times in my life, felt crushed by the weight of all the sadness and loss in the world. As a young adult I threw myself into passionate activism, collecting every detail of injustice until I literally couldn't take in anymore. Emotionally, I collapsed. The wrongs felt too great, the grief too big, and I, infinitely too small. I had thought I was meant to respond to what is broken by fixing it. To push for new policy, marching down the greens of the National Mall and protesting in Times Square until things were made right again. But no matter how much I organized, or how hard I fundraised, it never felt like enough. By the end of college I had given up. Emotionally bulldozed, I left New York feeling like I was simply too sensitive to handle all the hurt. In some ways, I was right. I was never meant to single-handedly fix what has been broken. It's not how I was made, and I suspect it's not how most of us are fashioned either. But I was also wrong. I was not too sensitive to make a difference. And I wasn't too small to be able to hold it all—at least not the things I'm here to hold.

The truth is, we weren't meant to bear the weight of the whole world. Human beings simply weren't designed for that. But we *are* big enough to cradle a single hive, to hold space for the small births and deaths around us, to embrace ourselves, our neighbors, those co-inhabitants with whom we share this Earth. We were meant to be stewards, those who look after the well-being of the whole through coming into intimate relationship with one another. We are here to tend the small worlds that surround us—our inner landscape, the wildflowers in the lot next door, the neighbor whose dog needs a walk, the spider making a nest in the corner of our window.

Love emboldens us to grow bigger. When we develop heart-to-heart connections with our innermost selves, as well as the beings who share our small corners of the world, we become available for this moment on Earth. The moment we stop seeing the living individuals that make up our world, we close ourselves off from the magnificent bigness of love that we *can* hold. When we recognize the dignity, preciousness, and personhood of all the beings that share our home with us, we become large enough to hold it all.

Falling in love with the intimate faces of the sugar bees helped me weather more than I ever thought I could—including the loss of my friend and the wider sadness of the news cycle that challenging fall. We may not be able to wrap our arms around the world, but we can hold a porcelain cup of wasps, or the warm shell of a turtle who is trying to cross the road, or the hand of a friend who is grieving. We may feel too small for the tasks at hand in the world, but the reality is that we have always been big enough to hold love for it all. The connections that you tend will only help the shelter of your heart grow larger.

When we learn how to forgive ourselves for being who we are— human, sensitive, fallible—we can come back to the greatness of just how much love we can hold. The grief, the sadness, the loss. The dying bees and the falling trees. We may not be able to fix it—ultimately, only the Earth can do this—but we can hold one another through it all. We can take care of our neighbors, our loved ones, our kin of wing and feet and feather. Because that connection and care, in the end, is all the Earth is really asking of us to remember.

How Much the Heart Can Carry

In the dark times, will there be singing?
Yes, there will be singing. About the dark times.

—BERTOLT BRECHT

No matter what challenges we are moving through, no matter how dark the days or how suddenly an individual symphony is silenced, the music never ends. After the last wasp died, I returned the small porcelain bowl to the makeshift altar I had created for them and Aven. Entirely full now, the bowl felt no heavier than it had when I began. That morning, I sat in the center of my floor-wide memorial, holding the lightness of this impossibly full bowl, and I sang. I sang the notes of each one of their bodies, now in eternal flight. I sang the grief, and the joy, at having known them. I sang to help whatever part of them was still navigating their transition, reaching that home on the other side. I sang because in the darkness, those notes were a light.

A few weeks later a group of us gathered in vigil for Aven. We went around the circle to share stories. When words failed, a mutual friend, who is known for keeping the old ballads of these hills alive, led us all in song. We cried together, sang together, ate together, and even though the pain was so huge, somehow, it was all made bearable. I had thought that I couldn't handle it all, but inside this community, I felt stronger. Here we were, not "holding it together," but simply holding each other. That night I recognized, with amazement, just how much the heart can carry when what it is holding is love.

People say that the depths of our grief match how profoundly we loved. If this is true, then the overwhelming emotion that we feel when we witness all the ecological loss in our world today is a measure of how deeply we love this planet, and, perhaps, how profoundly the Earth loves us in return.

We think we are too fragile for these times, but we are not. As saner cultures begin to sprout, and healthier ways of relating take root again, we are learning the one skill we need to survive it all—how to let the Earth hold us so we can remember how to hold ourselves. Once we know this, no matter how dark it gets, we'll always be able find each other—to join hands with our beloveds in the human and more than-human-world, as we find the songs that will guide us forward. In the end, all that is being asked of us is that we don't freeze over or pack up our belongings without looking around. All that is being asked is that we stay here. That we allow ourselves to feel. That we remain with it all—because *this* is where love dwells.

I once heard a story about a tantric master who came to a thicket of brambles. The onlookers, also spiritual people, had all kinds of recommendations for how to get through—build a bridge, clear a path, take it as a sign to search for an alternate route. But for the tantric master, one who communes with the divine through the embodied experience of being alive, there was only one way through—straight into the arms of the thorns. The deeper I go into the thicket of life, the more I realize how true the old adage is: *The only way out is through.* The deepest healing, for ourselves and for the Earth, comes from simply deciding to stay present with what is. To experience the song from start to finish and wait until the refrain begins again.

Blessedly, the choice is simple. Either you are in—in for the ride of life; in for all the feelings, emotions, heartache, and joy; in for opening your heart to seeing all the tiny lives around you spark, flame, die, and return—or you are out.

On the next full moon, I took the bowl of sugar bees outside and dug a hole. I buried the wasps with a piece of rose quartz from Aven's mandala. A complicated swell of grief and bewilderment rose inside of me but, instead of pushing the hive of emotions away, I embraced them. Like a child who hasn't been hugged in far too long, I held the emotions and accepted them. At the height of my tears, I said out loud, the words ringing like a song in the cold mountain air: "I'm in." I spoke to the angels, the ancestors, the air—to whoever needed to hear it, including my own self—"I'm in." I'm in for the feelings and the sting. I'm in for this precious experience of being alive. I'm in for the love and the grief. If this is what it means to be here, then I'm in.

In that moment, I realized I was choosing. Choosing to feel, choosing to live, choosing to be here despite it all—even as others made a different choice or had that choice disappear. I sat down in the pearl-light, among the dew-tipped grass, and made a promise to every loved one, the bees and the beloveds, who had left—I will stay here. Looking up at the cool bright stars, I promised to stay present with the grief and the exaltation both. To keep following my own journey of self-compassion and forgiveness, of breaking and becoming whole. In the end, I chose the brambles, because I could see now that heartbreak was part of love. "If this is life," I said out loud, "then, I'm in."

Zen masters and social workers alike will tell you that the most helpful thing you can do in times of hardship is simply be present. When we are present, we draw close to the truth of the moment, the heart of our companions, the soul of the Earth. When things get hard, our minds and spirits often stretch at their reins—eager to fight or flee the pain— but one of the most profound gifts we can give this planet is simply to become present with the ache. Sitting in presence, like actively listening to someone who is hurting, might seem like a small offering, but to that person, it is everything. Being present with the Earth as this healing takes place may seem like too little a gesture, but to the more-than-human people of our planet, this presence—a force that has been missing from their relationship with humanity for too long—is everything.

The more present we are, the kinder, gentler, and wiser our world grows. The more we can understand and have compassion for our own selves, the greater our ability to be present becomes. If rushing out of our bodies is part of what has gotten humanity into this tangle, becoming present is the antidote. It is the song we have to offer. It is the only thing the world truly wants of us—to *be here* with the beauty of the forests and the depths of our grief, with the joy of birdsong or the sound of water lapping at the shore. When we are present, we can hear the deepest music of the Earth, the song she has never stopped singing, nor ever will—*Hope never dies. Every ending is a beginning. A new way is growing, even still.*

EXERCISE
A Grief Ritual

When we create a ritual around our grief, we give ourselves space to allow the charge attached to the grief to flow through us. In Chinese medicine, all health imbalances are related to a blockage of Qi, or energy. By ritualizing our grief, we allow the energy behind it to flow, creating health and vitality within ourselves and the world at large. Currently on Earth, we have a backflow of grief that hasn't been given the space to be felt. When we create a container for ourselves to feel and express this grief in a healthy way, we not only free up our own energy, but we help to move the stuck Qi of the Earth, creating renewal for us all.

This grieving ritual is inspired by the Irish keening tradition of my ancestors. The word *keening* comes from the Irish and Scottish Gaelic term *caoineadh*, "to cry, to weep." In Ireland, there is a long-standing tradition of keening over the body before and during the funeral. Often depicted as crying or wailing, keening also includes poetic elements, such as listing the lineage of the deceased and giving praise. Using our voices to grieve is a powerful way to help the energy move.

At the center of our nervous systems is the vagus nerve, a long wandering nerve that goes from our pelvis to our throat. The vagus nerve is our body's center line of communication, and the primary source for our ability to shift from a state of activation into one of rest. If a feeling is too overwhelming to be processed at once, and we freeze in the midst of activation, we create what we call trauma. When we sing, intone, or hum, the tip of the vagus nerve is directly stimulated, enabling us to discharge trapped energy and to help our whole body vibrate with well-being.

To do this ritual, find a private place and time where it feels safe to make noise or where you won't be worried about being overhead. You can choose to follow the guidance of this ritual to the end or stop whenever it feels right to you.

Steps for the Ritual

1. Set the scene by lighting a candle if you are inside, or try taking five deep belly breaths. Begin by noticing the place where your body meets the Earth. Notice the space where your skin meets the air, perhaps on your hands or face. Look around you at the environment you are in, taking note of the quality of light, the colors or textures. You can let your gaze rest on anything that brings you comfort or relaxation.

2. Now, bring your attention back to yourself and begin your keening. Start by saying out loud what you feel sad about today. Begin with something small. Perhaps you are sad that you haven't heard from a friend. Or that you didn't get a chance to have breakfast with your partner before they left for work. Once you find that smallest sadness, from there you can let yourself branch out. Giving yourself as much time as you need, name everything that you feel sad about.

   If you have a hard time starting with sadness, begin with anger. What makes you mad? Say out loud "I'm mad about . . ." and list the things that frustrate you. Often, if we can't access our grief, it's because we need to feel anger first. Let yourself get as big with this sadness or anger as you want to—addressing wider issues of society, culture, ecology, the world.

3. When you come to the end of your list, or you get to a moment in which the emotion feels too big to bear, try vocalizing. Growl

yelp, moan. Engage your throat and allow yourself to make whatever sounds seem natural. If you feel numb, try grabbing a pillow or bringing your face close to the earth and then let out a scream. One of my personal mantras is, "if you can't cry, try screaming." Whenever I feel too dazed to access my feelings, all I have to do is let out one big healthy howl, and suddenly tears are streaming down my face.

Remember when you were a kid and you cried your heart out, screamed, or threw a temper tantrum? This wasn't just theatrics; you were literally discharging energy from your body. In this grief ritual, give yourself full permission to shake, move, and keen as long and as loudly as you like.

4. When you come to the other side of your grief, or it feels as if you are complete with your keening for the day, list at least ten things (including people or beings) that you love. Grief shows us how profoundly we love. Let this ritual illuminate for you how deeply you love, and allow that love to permeate your being.

   Imagine all the energy of your emotions, and this wellspring of love, moving from you into the Earth. See the soil receiving all of these feelings and being fed by their electricity. Your emotions are food for the Earth; when you release them, you nourish the ground beneath you.

5. Rest in this space for as long as you need to, noticing how the energy of grief, love, and aliveness is moving through you now. Thank yourself for this time and space.

11

CHESTNUT GROVES AND THE RESPROUTING OF HOPE

NO ONE TOLD me they were coming. The sun was still hidden behind the ice-blue hills when an entourage of trucks lumbered up the driveway, sounding from a distance like a dragon dragging its belly on gravel. Before I lived in the purple-painted Victorian with its sugar bees, I was blessed to housesit for a winter on the grounds of a hundred-year-old summer camp. Set into a grove of old trees and dotted with cabins from the turn of the century, the camp was a wonderland of pristine woods and streams. That winter, I was living in the first camp owner's home, beautifully restored with shining chestnut walls and a view of the hillside. The new owners of the camp—John's aunt and uncle—were away until April. When I first saw the trucks lumbering up the road that morning I was confused—until I saw the hardhats, chains, and saws. A team of arborists had come to cut down the majestic, ailing hemlocks on the hills.

The word *arborist* always seemed fantastical to me—a noun reminiscent of lithe-footed acrobats. The reality of what arborists do, however, has a bit more gravitas. I watched from the window as they started with the biggest tree—clearly diseased and on its way out. They cut the limbs off first, and a good bit of the crown. Each crashing limb was big enough to be a tree unto itself. It took an hour of *thunking* to pare the hemlock down to a size that would fall with safety to the ground. Even though I knew what was happening, the animal of my body grew frightened. The pound of tree limbs hitting the earth sounded exactly like the electric, overhead thunder of a storm.

Finally, the huge hemlock, eighty-feet high, was ready to be felled. I was afraid—both to watch it fall and of what might happen if I turned my back. The arborists were ready, but I wasn't. The falling was somehow both fast and slow, as I imagine a giant wave must be when yawing overhead. The sound of it blew out everything else when it struck the ground. Louder than any lightning bolt, it blanched the senses like a blizzard of snow. The floor tipped in an earthquake. While my rational mind understood clearly what was happening, my body still let out an incoherent yelp. The brief, yet primal, fear was as obliterating as the sound itself. Then it was done. I was still shaking when the lids to the herb jars settled once more. I put the kettle on and prepared myself for the next quake. There were still two more trees to go.

The eastern hemlock (*Tsuga canadensis*) is a stately evergreen that can live to be over five hundred years old. Once called "The Redwood of the East," hemlocks are some of the most iconic trees of the Blue Ridge mountains. Nestled along creeks, hemlocks create cool, dim microclimates, as well as homes for unique niches of birds and salamanders. Considered a keystone tree, the disappearance of the hemlocks, according to the National Park Service, could reduce the overall variety of species in our mountains by a third or more.[1] Unfortunately, the hemlocks have already been falling in thunder waves. In 1951 a small insect called a hemlock wooly adelgid (*Adelges tsugae*) hopped a ride, likely on an ornamental import, from Asia to the north coast of this continent. It has been nestling into the fringe of hemlock tips ever since, feeding off the plant's sap, and slowly toppling these magnificent trees. Since the adelgid arrived in the southern Appalachians in the late 1980s, as much as 80 percent of our hemlocks have been lost.[2] The giant trees being felled outside my window were some of the last of their kind, but they were not the first of the area's keystone species to be so decimated in these mountains.

Chestnut Ghosts

Today, the hills surrounding most homesteads in Southern Appalachia are burred with a thick tangle of saplings and shrubs, the leggy heights of first succession trees and blackberry thorns, but when the cabins that leaned against the hillsides of this camp were first built, these mountains were defined by two ancient tree communities—the hemlocks and the American chestnuts (*Castanea dentata*).

Magnificent giants that sustained entire communities with their fast-growing wood and bountiful mast of food, chestnuts were as quintessential to Southern Appalachia as the cloud-smoke that moves over its blue ridges. Just over a hundred years ago, one out of every four trees in these forests was an American chestnut. As professor Charlotte Ross of Appalachian State University summarized, "If ever there was a place defined by a tree, it was Appalachia."[3] Considered to be the perfect tree, the chestnut grew quick and straight up to the canopy, producing prolific lightweight wood that was strong and versatile. "By the time the white oak acorn makes a baseball bat," author J. Russel Smith wrote at the turn of the century, "the chestnut stump has made a railroad tie."[4] Chestnuts were also a staple food, not just for humans, but for a whole cornucopia of species, including bear, turkey, racoon, deer, squirrel, grouse, cooper's hawk, and bobcat. Every year chestnut forests produced such a prolific number of nuts that, in some groves, you could walk knee-deep in bounty.[5]

Just a hundred years ago, the forests of Southern Appalachia were still defined by the giant buttresses of these ancient trees. The early Scots-Irish settlers who came here in the eighteenth century must have thought that they had stepped in a wild garden of Eden. There is ample evidence, however, that these chestnut forests, like many "wilderness" spaces across the continent, were not the result of happenstance, but of the prodigious skill of Indigenous peoples. Today, many paleobotanists and ecologists assert that the wildly prolific woods of the East were so expertly managed that the Appalachian forests as we know them are a direct result of the careful tending of Indigenous communities.[6] These woodlands were sculpted, planted, nurtured, and loved by its First People. Of all the keystone species in Appalachia to be devastated by colonialism, causing a riptide of destructive effects throughout the entire ecosystem, the loss of Indigenous communities was undoubtedly one of the most profound. Though the Eastern Band of Cherokee is still strongly rooted in their ancestral mountain lands today, the government's forced removal of over sixteen thousand *Tsalagi* (or DhBⵔⵀⵀ *Aniyunwiya*) people in the mid-1800's Trail of Tears was an ecological and humanitarian holocaust that still reverberates through the land. One generation after Removal, the chestnut forests began to fall.

Once upon a time, it must have seemed incomprehensible to imagine Appalachia without her magnificent columns of chestnuts, the open churches of the woods. It would have been like imagining the ocean without waves. But today, only saplings remain. In 1904 a tiny stowaway arrived from a nursery in Asia. These handful of spores were from a fungus called *Cryphonectria parasitica*, a relatively common parasite of the Chinese chestnut that nevertheless proved fatal to our native *Castanea*. Entering through small wounds in the bark, *C. parasitica* slowly kills the cambium of the tree, effectively girdling it. The fungus, blooming in frightening fire-bright tendrils, causes a cascade of infected cankers up and down the tree before it kills the crown back to the roots.

It took twenty-five years for the fungus, called simply The Blight, to get down to Southern Appalachia. When it did, it came as an unstoppable force. Appearing as ember-colored wildfire on distant hills, the blight caused whole ridgelines to go up in a single season. Thinking the trees were doomed, the government urged folks to topple every chestnut before they died so the wood could be salvaged. It wasn't until decades later that we realized, in felling every tree, we also destroyed the small percentage of the population that might have held the genetic secret to resisting the blight and bringing back this keystone species. At the time, the government saw no other possibilities—so the chestnuts fell.

In a span of forty years, the entire four-billion-strong population of North American chestnuts—two trees for every person on the planet at the time—was decimated. Life in Appalachia was never the same. In her book, *American Chestnut: The Life, Death and Rebirth of a Perfect Tree*, Susan Freinkel captures the lingering profundity of this loss: "As the blight reached Appalachia and the beloved trees began to topple, the region filled with despair, an ecological grief that has dimmed with time but still lingers, vaporlike, in the air."[7] Unlike dogwoods or elms, the chestnut was largely a country tree. Its death most affected the rural poor, those whose stories have been passed down through a largely oral tradition. To this day people still talk about the chestnut groves of old as if recounting the painful loss of a grandmother.

Though the groves are gone, in the mountains today you are never far from a chestnut. Every time I swung open the doors to one of the old summer camp cabins, I'd find their ghosts in the floorboards and walls. Though some of the cabin's wood came from trees harvested before the fungus arrived, others were the grandchildren of the blight itself. Pockmarked and precious, these boards, called wormy chestnut, were often harvested decades after the tree fell. Chestnuts are so resistant to rot they can lie on the forest floor for years, strong and utile, despite the persistent mountain rainfall. Distillers used to say that a plant's scent housed its spirit. If you scratch a chestnut plank and inhale, you will find that the soul of this tree is still alive in Appalachia.

I once heard a fascinating tale about palo santo, the South American tree whose fingers of wood are burned for their aromatic smoke. At a conference with an ethnobotanist from Columbia, I listened with fascination as he explained the long tapestry of lore woven around this sacred tree. It is widely known in the forests there that you cannot cut down palo santo for its scent; you must wait for it to fall before its rich, resinous-citrus aroma arises. According to locals, when the tree is standing, its perfume is slight, almost insubstantial. Its legendary scent only begins to mature once the tree ends its life naturally and is lying on the forest floor. Perhaps, the ethnobotanist wondered, this was only a tale told to prevent the destruction of these trees from encroaching corporate greed, but according to the Indigenous communities who have lived with this tree since the beginning, it is the truth. "If palo santo is a bottle of perfume," the ethnobotanist spoke with a final poetic lilt, "then the stopper is the woods themselves."

Though the chestnuts have fallen in our forest, their vaporous spirits remain. Standing inside the cabin as the next hemlock was prepped to come down, I couldn't help but wonder, even among the devastation of these deaths, if there wasn't some unseen second-life arising. All winter long I had sat by my cabin's woodstove as the coals flickered their sunset colors across the chestnut paneling. In those moments I swore I could smell it, the perfume of some new-old era unfurling. It was as stubborn as pipe smoke—nostalgic, heartbreaking, and transcendent. Whenever I wandered the hillsides of the camp, ducking in and out of the old chestnut-built structures, I could feel the presence of new life within all this loss, sprouting like bittersweet vines from between the floorboards. As I watched the hemlocks come down that day, their earthquakes shook loose something inside me. What if the gift of all this death is that we learn how to believe in the power of beginning again—in the wisdom of possibility?

It's natural to be shaken by the forests that have fallen. To be felled by the sadness of everything that has been lost in the earthquake of the Anthropocene. To take to our beds and not want to come out again. Our grief, surely, is a marker of how deeply we have loved. But there is also another way of seeing, a hope chest that we've forgotten, cedar-bright and enduring at the foot of our bed. There is a perspective that has sustained humankind for millennia. A way of being that acknowledges both the beauty of *what was* and the possibility of *what will be*. One that recognizes each fallen tree and greets the mystery. Inside this hope chest is a way of seeing that can replant the forests of our collective well-being. If you peer into the heart of any ending, what you will see is the enduring magic of *possibility*.

The Granny Witches

When I was seven years old I asked to be a witch for Halloween. "With warts on your chin and frizzy hair?" my older next-door neighbor jibbed with a laugh.

"No!" I said with inflection, a bit defensive, "a beautiful witch with curly hair and sparkles."

He rolled his eyes and went back to playing with his bottle rockets. Having visited the Halloween stores, I knew that witch costumes were often grouped with things that go bump-in-the-night, but that wasn't the kind of witch I wanted to be. I saw witches differently. They were more like fairy godmothers than monsters to me. So that year I was a witch with orange ruffles on my sleeves, sparkly studs in my ears, and a shiny black hat. On Halloween, when I went door to door for candy, I quickly informed each homeowner before they could ask that I was a "good" witch, just in case they were confused. I had big feelings about what it meant to be a witch—I just didn't have the vocabulary to describe it. Now I realize that frustration was a symptom of how deeply buried the ancient meaning of this word has become. I didn't know it then, but the beautifully gnarled roots of the word *witch* stretch so far back in history that to follow it is to find a tap root of a long-buried perspective shift.

Witch is a term as shifting and volatile as mercury. Over time it has been an accusation, a slur, a fear, a fairytale, and a costume. More recently it has become a badge of honor in circles of herbalists, activists, and healers. In the beginning, however, a witch was simply someone who had a direct relationship to the medicine of those things we cannot immediately see, including the lifeforce of all beings. The etymological roots of the word *witch* are mixed, murky, and a bit mysterious, but scholars like Max Dashu of the Suppressed History Archives argue that *witch* can be traced back to the Indo-European root word *weg*, which meant "to live." This root later gave birth to the word *wick*, a word that both referred to the central lifeforce of a thing, like the twist of linen that holds a candle's flame, as well as the winding patterns of vitality that underlie all of nature.[8] A witch was someone who perceived these wider patterns, the life at the center of things, a continuing root of possibility, when others only saw death, endings, or inanimacy.

In many old European traditions, a witch was synonymous with a healer, one who could work with the possibilities of remediation beyond what was immediately perceived. Healers, in a traditional sense, are different from our doctors today. Where contemporary physicians seek to fix, the traditional healer or medicine person seeks to *understand*. The ultimate goal for a healer is not to alleviate a symptom, but to recognize and right the imbalanced lifeforce. To be a healer of any kind is to see possibilities. Where there is pain, there could be relief. Where there is death, regeneration can be leased. When we open our minds to perceive possibility—including the possibility of healing—we open our consciousness to an entirely new way of seeing.

Though witches were revered for their visions throughout ancient history, by the Middle Ages these traditional healers of old Europe were oppressed and demonized for both their abilities and perspectives. As religiously rooted doctrines of domination spread across the continent, the historical covenant of working with the common sanctity of all life—the basis of any witch's magic—became a source of fear. Starting in the 1450s, the mania of the European witchhunts resulted in an estimated 100,000 executions.[9] The witches who were burned were most often women, but also men and nonbinary folks. They were healers, mystics, herbalists, midwives, wisdom keepers—or sometimes just those who owned land or resources that the more powerful elite wished to possess. Each witch held within them another way of seeing, one that was no longer welcome in the traumatized overculture that had come to dominate the European continent. When the witches fell, a central buttress of pre-Christian European traditions went with them. They were the chestnuts of their cultures, those who died with a history changing quake—and yet, here in the mountains, the witch tradition and this ancient way of seeing has survived.

For the past handful of centuries, whole lineages of Appalachian granny witches—also called granny women, granny healers, and granny doctors—have thrived in these coves. In the time before roads and stable pavement, living up in the mountains meant relying on the land and the grace of your neighbors for your well-being. Far from any hospital, it was the granny witches who cared for folks. As healers who were skilled in midwifery, herbalism, divination, spells, and energy work, granny witches, normally the elder women in their community, could heal an ailment, predict the weather, give spiritual guidance, or bring a baby into the world. Though the granny witch culture has roots in the healing arts of old Europe, the tradition today owes its legacy to a rich confluence of sources, including the wisdom traditions of the Cherokee, the African diaspora, and folk Christianity.

Equally as amazing as the survival of this diverse practice is the fact that the terms *witch*, *witchcraft*, *spells*, and *charms* never became taboo in parts of Appalachian culture. As recounted by Ginger Strivelli, a local mountain writer and witch, "Nearly every mountain top and 'holler' community had their local 'Witch' who was openly called such, as a title of honor, not as an insult or a charge of crime, as the term came to be used in other more urban American cultures of the seventeen, eighteen and nineteen hundreds."[10] Like the blight of the chestnut groves, the witch hunts seemed to have been the death knoll for the folk traditions of old Europe—but they weren't. The survival of the granny witch tradition reminds us that even in the midst of what looks like wholescale endings, the seeds of possibility remain, if only we are willing to look for them. Once found, these seeds have the ability to heal the only thing that can truly change our trajectory as a planet—our perspective.

Spellwork

To be a medicine person of any lineage is to understand the direct link between perception and healing. Traditional healers know that our mind and consciousness shape our experience of reality, which is one reason why charms and spells are an integral part of a granny witch's practice. *Spells*, the intentional speaking of words or ritualized actions, shift reality by changing our perception of a given situation. In one example of Appalachian spellwork, granny witches would put an ax under the bed of those in labor to help "cut the pain." In another, coverings were put over a mirror once a person passed to encourage their soul to move toward the wider light awaiting them.[11] Folks in these mountains stayed alive, physically and spiritually, through such charms because they understood that perception changes reality.

In contemporary scientific thinking, this kind of healing is often called "the placebo effect" and written off as a trick of the mind— but this doesn't change the power of perceptual healing. Perception is so adept at creating change that some researchers claim up to 75 percent of the efficacy of antidepressants is due to this so-called placebo effect.[12] In light of this, perhaps it's time we stopped calling such healing *placebo* and simply called it by the name Granny witches use— medicine. Instead of discounting the fact that changing our beliefs can change our reality, what if we saw the efficacy of this kind of spellwork, charms, and medicine as evidence of just how powerful our perceptions can be?

In the perceptually rigid cultures of Europe and colonial America, witches were routinely killed for their life-steeped and distinctly animistic viewpoints and beliefs. If we wish to change our world, to transform the dead end of devastation into the wick of new life, we must first be curious about what we are open to perceiving. To embrace the possibility that the healing we've been waiting for will arise naturally when we shift our way of seeing. The witch hunts ended as European leaders traded the specific rigidity of religious-based thinking for scientific inquiry—and yet, even as the "Age of Reason" wore on, it became clear that these thinkers just swapped one narrow viewpoint for another. In the wake of this shift to a materialism devoid of mysticism, our collective gaze constricted, excluding everything we cannot see with our own eyes or explain with our contemporary technologies as unimportant or even nonexistent. Ironically, this same narrow perspective is how we first failed to recognize things like bacteria and black matter. And it is how we are missing, still, the understanding of how the old medicine, the medicine of witches, shamans, folk healers, and culture shifters, truly works.

For some, *witch* still remains a fearful word, synonymous with someone who has the frightening ability to control reality. At its heart, however, being a witch doesn't mean that you manipulate the world to your liking; it means that you can see and call forth manifold possibilities. It means that your perception of reality goes beyond what has been handed to you, that you can perceive the presence of freedom, and healing, in all things. This is why the word *witch* has remained embedded in our culture until today—and why it is resurging now among those whose work is focused on the liberation of our spirits, our bodies, and our thinking.

The old German word *wikkiyaz*, a possible relative to the root-word *witch*, meant "one who wakes the dead."[13] From the viewpoint of a witch, an ending is just an invitation to look at what is ready to awaken. A chestnut that has fallen to the ground can become the walls of a home that will stand for centuries. The decomposing tree can transform into a nursery for mushrooms, and its absence can provide an open space in the canopy for new flowers or weeds. In the winding wick of an ecology, every wound, every loss, every illness opens new possibility.

I thought about all of this as I watched the arborists begin to stack the fallen hemlocks in our driveway that afternoon. I squinted from the windows as the large trunks were laid on top of one another. A part of me wished I could cast a spell—to heal the trees, to send the adelgids, and the blight, and the pain of trauma, oppression, and colonialism back to where they all came from, to make everything right again. But the granny witch within me recognized that just sitting here, being open to the possibility of the new life that could come from this loss, was where true healing began.

We do not need major initiation rites, long periods of pilgrimages, aestheticism, or trials in order to become witches, magicians, or healers in the world. All we must do is open ourselves to the possibilities. When we can engage with the presence of possibility—that nothing is set in stone, nothing is irreparable, nothing is truly lost—all of life becomes infused with magic because magic is simply the recognition of life's possibilities..

Realists of a Larger Reality

What happens when the thin-bodied forests that cover our hills now are no longer seen as the remnants of what was, but are recognized as a sacred opportunity for cultural reincarnation? What changes when we can gaze at the precious contours of a chestnut-made cabin and recognize the raw and humble blessings of a new beginning?

The spring after the giant hemlocks were cut down from the camp's hillsides, a garden of gladiolas and roses went in. In the opening of what was felled, there was ample sun and space for the folds of peach, burgundy, and pastel, the Coral Knockouts and Queen of Sweden's, the Earth Angels and Ebb Tides. A family wedding was held on the land a few summers later. The wedding, celebrating the union of two women who loved each other deeply, was simple and beautiful. It struck me, as I watched their vows, that this ceremony wouldn't have been legally possible even just a few years ago in North Carolina. When the chapel they were married in was built at the turn of the century, this union would have been a distant and unimaginable dream. That knowledge brought tears to my eyes. Many of the flower arrangements decorating the high, lace-lined tables came directly from that garden planted among the hemlock's roots. Each one felt like a blossom-headed saint —and their doctrine of possibility, a kind of deliverance.

For as much as I worry about the trajectory of our planet, the political and ecological backslidings and reactionary contractions, beneath it all remains a deep truth of rebirth, always arising. Our Earth doesn't know endings. Only change, only possibility. Every time a tree falls in the forest a raucous growth of understory flowers, shrubs, and saplings rises up in its wake. Every time a bird dies, a field floods, a drought strips the leaves from the trees, new life and lifeways are nourished and invented. In nature, there is no good or bad. Simply different, changing. Possibility is the very language our planet speaks.

We are currently in the middle of what ecologists are calling the Anthropocene extinction, a time of mass species loss that humans are both the cause of and witness to. For those paying attention, it is a daily heartbreak, but it is not the first time such seed banks have been lost. The mistake we could make now would be to clear-cut our own hope, to sever our imaginative tendon and be unable to move forward for the grief. Today, the Earth is asking us to both mourn what has been lost and begin to nurture the garden of what might be. For it is this very vision-shifting that will help us dream into a new future.

In a talk at the 2014 National Book awards, the late Ursula Le Guin, a true witch of the word and worlds, gave a speech that urged those who can see such possibility to keep on dreaming. A legendary author across nearly every genre, Le Guin accepted the award on behalf of all those who are usually ignored at such ceremonies, including, "authors of fantasy and science fiction, writers of the imagination, who for 50 years have watched the beautiful rewards go to the so-called realists." Le Guin went on to champion, "[in the hard times to come] we will be wanting the voices of [those] who can see alternatives to how we live now and can see through our fear-stricken society and its obsessive technologies to other ways of being, and even imagine some real grounds for hope. We will need writers who can remember freedom— poets, visionaries; the realists of a larger reality."[14]

In the end, it is not so-called realism that will help a clear-cut heart, or a generation of woodlands, to regenerate—it is that small-boned kaleidoscope called possibility, waiting to stoke our imagination. Fear constricts the imagination—not to mention the very daily functioning of our brains. Sometimes we are in situations that demand we think of our survival but, most of the time, we are being invited to consciously release this coat of stones called fatalism. Hope is to hold the seeds of the future in one's hand, tiny and irreplaceable, and know that a whole forest can fit in the open palm of such possibility.

The world will continue to change around us, but the key that will change the course of the world is our own ability to perceive something different. If you ask the visionaries, sci-fi writers, poets, and witches—those realists of a larger reality—about the vision of fear and endings we are handed every day, I guarantee they will say that for all the spell-words that have the possibility to truly change reality, perhaps the most important of all is *maybe*.

The Magic of Maybe

Magic, the power to influence events by mysterious forces, is no more supernatural than electricity or compassion. Real magic, as any performing magician will tell you, is simply about shifting your perception. In *The Spell of the Sensuous*, sleight-of-hand magician and ecological philosopher David Abram captures this truth effortlessly. "The task of the magician" he whispers, "is to startle our senses and free us from outmoded ways of thinking."[15] In his book, which details his travels to Bali as a researcher, Abram observes how *dukuns*, traditional Balinese shamans, employ very similar techniques to the common stage magician.[16] Using theatrical healing ceremonies, dukuns help shift the perception of the person who is ailing, creating very tangible healing. Unlike the stage magician, however, the dukuns aren't trying to entertain or deceive; they are intentionally working with the very real magic of belief, and all the possibilities of healing it can reveal. Magic begins when we unshackle ourselves from the paradigm of inevitability and open the way for quantum leaps in our imagination. Magic starts when we are able to question our automatic beliefs, the patterns of thinking that we often mistake for natural law. Magic takes root when we can approach a dead end and then continue past it, repeating the mantra of *maybe*.

There is an ancient Daoist story that goes like this . . .

Once, there was an old farmer who had worked his land for many years. One day his horse ran away. When the neighbors heard the news, they cried, "What bad luck!" To which he just replied, "maybe . . ."

The next morning the horse returned with three wild ponies in tow. "What good fortune!" the neighbors exclaimed this time! To which the farmer once again said, "maybe . . ."

The following day the farmer's son tried to ride one of these new ponies and was thrown, breaking his leg. The neighbors once again came to offer sympathy. "What misfortune," they hummed in chorus, but the farmer just reflected, "maybe . . ."

The very next day the military came to the village to conscript all young men into service. Every able-bodied son in the village was drafted into the army, but because his leg was broken, the young son was allowed to remain at home. Everyone in the village, of course, congratulated the farmer on what seemed like a supreme bit of luck. The farmer nodded and just replied with a smile, "maybe."

It was early evening by the time the arborists had left the hemlocks sawed into ship-length pieces, stacked neatly on the lawn. As the sun slipped behind the wall of forest to the west, I went out to visit the fallen trees. Stranded next to the driveway, the trunks looked like beached whales, majestic and eerily out of their element. As the temperature dropped into evening, my gloved hands started to sting. Shaking off the needles of cold, I put my index finger to the outermost layer of the first tree's bark and began counting the rings. A decade, then two, then three. When I got to the center the tip of my finger was numb. I had counted over one hundred and fifty rings. This being was five times older than me, and now it was gone.

I felt a seductive pull to fall into the sad gravity of it all, to build a buffer between me and the moment by retreating into the absorbing blackness, the simplicity, of fatalism. Part of me wanted to be stopped by a dead end because it felt easier then admitting there was still a pathway beyond the bend. But another part of me looked beyond. On the other side of this desolation, I couldn't help but notice that something was glimmering. I could feel it, rising like a thaw in the center of me, a series of questions emanating from the heartwood of these trees—*What would happen in this moment if you could lift your hope as high as the old hemlocks? What if you didn't settle for these obvious endings, but kept climbing the world tree of possibilities? What if you opened your imagination to another way of perceiving? What then could you see?*

The same year I dressed as a witch for Halloween, I became obsessed with whales. I don't remember when I first learned about whales or their plight with extinction, but I do remember the intensity of my passion and grief. At school they called me "whale girl." To this day, one of the far-reaching Google hits for my name is a quote from me in our local newspaper; when interviewed about the expansion of the school library I said I was looking forward to it because I had read every whale book on the shelves. In my free time I researched everything I could, soaking up every detail about all the different whales of the ocean, their habits of living, being, and migrating. I remember, in particular, the moment when I learned that whales were as intelligent as humans. Sitting with the big book in my lap, it felt as if reality was twinkling. This fact confirmed something I had known all along—the Earth is sentient; the world is so much more magical than we have been told. I was in awe, but also horrified. If these exquisite, intelligent beings could be going extinct, what would happen to the magic of the world?

I remember feeling tortured by images of whales beached by sonar or poison. My whale obsession cracked me open; it taught me about ecological grief, but it also began to train me how to use that grief to fuel a different dream. I found that when I dwelled in despair, I only sunk further into sluggish torpor. But when I looked to the hope of possibility, I was suddenly filled with creativity. I could make a slideshow to educate my classmates. I could research organizations that were helping. I could organize a raffle to raise money to support whale protection. So I held the sadness in one hand and my hope in another, and I dreamed into a new future for the whales—and for all of the Earth's beings.

Standing with the great giants of those fallen hemlocks that evening, I took off my gloves and put both palms to the places where they had been cut. I allowed my grief to well up naturally, and in return, I felt a visceral wave move through me from the heartwood of the trees. It was as indecipherable as a whale song, and yet equally as moving, intelligent, and deep. It sounded like the word *maybe,* and it felt like forgiveness. I had come to these cut logs with a fatal sorrow and, in return, they had showed me possibility.

True, they were no longer growing trees, but they would become the walls of a home, tables to eat from, mulch to nourish the garden. They would be a nursery for medicinal reishi mushrooms and mycelium. Their bark would tan hides, become cordage. Most life-giving of all, this ending, like all the endings we are witnessing now, had the ability to change my perception, to help me align myself with the way the Earth views things. Death can transform our hearts. It can show us, not just what is ending, but what is aching to begin. In our most dire moments, the Earth whispers to us—if we can only open to this possibility, life will never cease.

Chestnut Sprouts

Once, sitting in class with my acupuncturist, I learned the secret of immortality. "In Chinese medicine," she said, "it's thought that when a person dies of old age it's because their heart has stopped believing in life's possibilities." From a Chinese medicine perspective, when the possible paths we may have taken in life begin to concretize, our heart loses its elasticity and eventually ceases to beat. In the end, our death is literally caused by our inability to see life's continuing possibilities. Everything changes when we can look at the death of the world around us and see not endings, but beginnings.

The possibilities inherent to colonialism, capitalism, and hierarchical thinking are dying. Where once we surveyed an open field of opportunity, we are now beginning to see that this path, never destined to take us far at all, has reached its peak. This particular cultural paradigm has come to the end of its natural life. As we let this worldview die of old age, we can embrace a new incarnation, one that is steeped in earthly regeneration and the eternal possibilities inherent to a paradigm that honors the lifeforce in all beings. We call this new collective era into being simply by shifting the way we each perceive reality.

A few years ago I was in a hypnotherapy training for health professionals. At the start of the class, the teacher promised to demonstrate the various techniques that we were there to learn. But before he began, he told us that the most powerful sessions wouldn't arise from technique alone. If we truly wanted to help our clients go deep, we would have to first shift our own perception. He told us with a gentle smile that the scripts we would use to help people enter a meditative place were designed to first alter our *own* consciousness. In his work in Bali, David Abram noticed the same thing with the dukuns. "It's only by the magician entering deeply into [the] trance," he reflects, "that the others will be led to experience the trance as richly and as deeply as the magician."[17]

If we want to see the world change, we must first change the way we see the world. If we want to help the Earth in her natural process of outliving all the endings of this era, we must shift our own inner realities by embracing the life-giving power of new possibilities.

There were several efforts, throughout the years of blight, to save the chestnuts. People tried everything, from clear-cutting whole belts of contagion zones to rubbing mud on the tree's open sores, but nothing seemed to work. By the time the blight ran down the ridges of Appalachia, the general populous had given up hope—but not everyone. Ever since the blight was first diagnosed, a ragtag group of scientists, ecologists, botanists, and believers have continued to puzzle out a solution. In the years following the blight's arrival, it became obvious that the infection, though horrific in its decimation of the aboveground trees, does not kill the roots. Underground, the bulk of the chestnuts survive. To this day you can still walk in the woods and find chestnut saplings arising from ancient root systems. Hope truly does spring eternal.

While these saplings normally can't reach maturity before the fungus finds them, a group of researchers have been working on creating a blight-resistant strain of chestnuts that could repopulate our forests—the first fruits of their labor have already been planted in our Appalachian soil. I first heard about The American Chestnut Foundation (TACF) when I moved to the mountains. With their office just down the road from me, I figured the organization was a small enterprise, committed to keeping the memory of the chestnut alive in our local community, but TACF has a much bigger vision than that. With chapters in twenty different states, TACF has been on a multifaceted, single-minded mission for the past thirty years—to restore the iconic American chestnuts to their native habitats.

After decades of genetic backcrossing, breeding American chestnut genes with the heartier Chinese chestnut, in fall 2007, TACF began harvesting its first potentially blight-resistant American chestnuts.[18] Today, these seeds have gone out to TACF chapters around the country. It's possible that, right now, we are witnessing the beginnings of restored chestnut forests across the eastern seaboard. Working with land refor-estation initiatives, TACF has also helped to plant more than 1.8 mil-lion seedlings on previously mined lands. With their high tolerance for certain chemicals and predilection for ridgetops, the hearty American chestnuts can grow in the most unlikely of places, including summits decimated by mountaintop removal. To date, TACF has helped to restore over three thousand acres. They refused to give up on the possibility of the chestnut's survival, and now the chestnuts are helping to bring life back to the most devastated places in these mountains. The chestnut lives, and with it, so does our belief in the possibility of healing.

My tenure as a house sitter at the camp ended just a few months after the hemlocks were felled, but on a later visit, I saw what became of those elders. Claus and Debbie, the generous owners of the camp, showed me where the branches had been chipped and spread as mulch throughout the sunny flower-lit gardens. They'd had trunks milled and used throughout the property to help repair the older cabins, preserving them for the future generations, and a beautiful new dining room table stood in their home. After our walk, I took the winding trail around the property to visit each regenerated structure. The care taken to restore the cabins emanated from every board. Passing under the shade of the still-standing hemlocks mixed among the maples and birches, I strolled up the forested path to the old chapel.

Nestled on a bit of highland in a clearing in the woods, the chapel had always been one of my favorite places at the camp. It is an expan-sive, peaceful place with a small graveyard underneath two huge tulip poplars. As the venue for the previous year's flower-studded wedding, the chapel still held a glow from that happy evening. As I approached the open-air benches of this sanctuary, I stopped to squint at the hillside, my eyes searching for what my memory could see clear as day—two young American chestnuts. As a part of their local TACF chapter, Claus and Debbie had decided to plant the two precious cross-bred saplings as a kind of prayer in front of the chapel. It gave my heart a lift to see that they were bigger now than when I had lived here. Every year they grow and, with them, our hope expands.

The world isn't ending—it is just beginning. The rigid perspectives that led us to this point in history are dissolving, and the Earth-led way of perpetual regeneration is taking ahold again. If we are only willing to let go of what we think we know and embrace the possibilities of what might be coming, we can align ourselves with the New Earth that is arising.

EXERCISE
The Maybe Game

Children have a game that I've come to love—or, to be more honest, I never *stopped* loving from my own childhood. They ask a question and then the question lives on eternally through the help of one simple addendum—why?

In the Maybe Game, we take this similar spirit of inquiry and expand our own concepts of reality by adding *maybe* onto everything we believe to be true. With *maybe* we can begin to see how, just by shifting our perception, we can change our reality.

1. Make a list of all the unavoidably painful things about existence (the hard stuff of your life, humanity, politics, the fate of the world, etc.) *Example: Our environment is on the brink of collapse.*

2. Now, next to each phrase, write, *or maybe . . .* and then add your own positive alternative. Be as fantastical and imaginative as you can. What are all the ways you could shift these painful dead ends into possibility? In your dream of dreams, what could be true? *Example: Our environment is on the brink of collapse . . . or maybe, it is on the cusp of a great rebirth.*

3. Go back and reread each original statement before your maybes. Pause and notice your body. What sensations are you experiencing? Where do you feel it?

4. Now, read each statement again with its positive addendums. Drop back into your body's sensation. What are you feeling now? How is this feeling different than before?

5. We are often told that the most important thing is to be "rational" or "realistic," but rarely do we ever ask ourselves what kind of perception is truly life-giving. Thinking back on each original statement before you added your maybes with their positive alternatives, ask yourself: *Does this first viewpoint feed the creative spark of new beginnings, or does it deplete my own ability to believe in the goodness of things?*

   Inquire with honesty—which statement was more life giving? The original, or the alternative? Think back on a moment of revelation, of profound creativity, or a breakthrough in your life. How did your body feel then? Which most closely matches the sensation you had in your body at the time—the way you feel when you read the original statement, or when you read the addendums? Be curious.

6. Finally, ask yourself, *What beliefs open my heart to feel more possibility?* Try each statement on and see if it's actually a better fit for the life you are here to lead.

12

THE REISHI TREE

I STRIPPED OFF MY hiking shoes and left them in a pile on the side of the trail. The pillowy soil of the forest floor was beckoning for bare feet. My socks and leggings soon followed. I wanted as little as possible between me and that particular softness of the forest after a summer's rain. The earth was as supple as a cheek, and every leaf seemed to glisten with welcome.

Turning off the well-worn path, I began to carefully pick my way down the steep slope to the creek, placing each foot diagonally for purchase. Even from a distance I could tell that the water was rain-swelled, pushing muscularly up over the smooth stones of the bank. It was early summer, and already the leaves of the canopy had grown so close together that inside the forest was dark as a thunderstorm. The air was heavy with water, the scent of the earth close as rain. As I hiked down the slope, I could almost see the forest debris beneath me soften, becoming autumn's rich compost. It was the perfect afternoon for mushroom hunting.

In the thick of the warm season, when the rains come full as sound, the mountains of Appalachia explode at the seams with blossoms. Red fireworks of beebalm and the pale lace of hydrangeas. Rhododendrons lit like candles in dark hollers and azaleas on fire. But not all blooms that grace our summer mountains are flowers; many are not even plants at all. In the midst of the rainiest months, another kind of bloom flushes across the forest. In the bodies of the trees, on wooded paths, nestled into carefully laid mulch—mushrooms arise.

We know very little about mushrooms in the grand scheme of things—to date, only ten percent of the world's mushroom species have even been identified.[1] We know that some mushrooms are food, some are medicine, and some can kill us as swiftly as lightning. We also know that mushrooms breathe oxygen, just like mammals. Even though we often lump herbs and fungi together, mushrooms are more closely related to animals than to the plant kingdom. Evolutionarily speaking, they are more human than plant. In fact, six million years ago, humans and fungi shared a common ancestor.

Deep lore surrounds mushrooms in every corner of the globe. In Ireland a circle of growing mushrooms is called a fairy ring. Believed to be a portal into the Otherworld, one of these rings might transport you to the halls of the wee folk if you accidentally fall asleep inside it. In some Lithuanian folklore, mushrooms are considered to be the long fingers of Velnias, the Lithuanian god of the dead, piercing the veil to bring food to the less fortunate.[2] Mushroom collecting is such a beloved part of Lithuanian culture there is even a word that describes that moment of losing both the thread of a conversation and your bearing in the woods while out mushroom picking—*nugrybauti*.[3] Some people even believe that when mushrooms bloom, they bring music into the world. Contemporary Czech composter Vaclav Halek has composed over six thousand songs based on the symphonies he has overheard from the fungi kingdom.[4]

In everyday speak, we use the words *mushroom* and *fungi* interchangeably, but technically, mushrooms are the fruit bearing bodies (aka the flowers) that arise from the underground fungi. Growing in places where other life is waning, fungi feed on decomposing material and act as angels of the ecosystem, helping ease the transition from life to afterlife. After a deep rain, many mushrooms seem to pop up over-night—a mystery arriving with the dawn. In the Anishinaabe language, there is even a word for the force that pushes mushrooms up out of the ground overnight—*Puhpowee*.[5] As Robin Wall Kimmerer writes, after first hearing this word from Anishinaabe ethnobotanist Keewaydino-quay, "The makers of this word understood a world of being, full of unseen energies that animate everything."[6] Whenever we've forgotten the profound mystery of the Earth's aliveness, mushrooms will be there to remind us.

The vast network of fungi that underlies our soil is called *mycelium*. Pull up any log that's been sitting on the forest floor and you'll find gossamer white strands running like webs through the softly disinte-grating wood. Up until recently mycelium went unresearched in the Western scientific world—but once we started gazing with our micro-scopes, we saw something incredible. These fine white filaments don't just stretch beneath newly fallen trees; they run underneath our entire world. Mycelium is so interwoven with a given ecology that a single cubic inch of topsoil can have enough fungal cells to stretch eight miles. Master mycologist Paul Stamets calculates that every footstep in the forest can impact more than three hundred miles of mycelium. Even more incredible, researchers have found that mycelium forms relation-ships of exchange with nearby plants, creating a web of ecological co-creation and communication that predates the internet by 450 million years. This network, sometimes called the Wood Wide Web, connects fungus and plants in a beneficial relationship that allows trees to trade nutrients and communicate with one another, sending signals of joy or danger, even helping other species of trees in need. Stamets calls myce-lium the neurological network of nature. Just like our own neurological system, research shows that all habitats on Earth rely upon fungi. With-out them, Stamets asserts simply, "the life-support system of the Earth would soon collapse."[7] Not only do mycelial networks literally hold our soil together, but their fungal enzymes, acids, and antibiotics create the soil as we know it. Fungi, these otherworldly angels of death, are the unseen backbone of our world.

Magnificently mysterious and evocative, fungi push at the edges of our understanding, opening up our awareness to the unperceivable. As Stamets writes with wonder, "what is so exciting about mycology is that the depth of undiscovered knowledge laying [sic] before us is more vast than our minds can imagine."[8] The frontier of mushroom science is both thrillingly mysterious and revolutionary in its implications. Today, environmentalists and mycologists are starting to explore the way fungi can help us reverse the damage we've caused to the world, including regenerating soil, rebuilding forests, filtering water, and preventing infectious diseases. Highly adept at breaking complex molecules down into simpler compounds, mushrooms have the potential to help clear pollution, removing many different kinds of toxins from the environment. *Mycoremediation*, a term coined by Stamets, may be used in the future to clean up oil spills, break down heavy metals, and heal contaminated soil.[9] Perhaps this is just as the Earth always intended it. In his book, *Mycelium Running*, Stamets hypothesizes that the mycelial network, as the conscious nervous system of our planet, is here to help make manifest the dreams of a sentient Earth. It is enough to wonder if mushrooms, and our relationship to them, might be the mystery that one day saves our world.

In the first warm stretch of the year, as the days reach their longer peaks and mushroom season unfurls, I am always on a very particular mission. With a sharp knife and gathering bags, I head to the woods to look for one mushroom—reishi. Seen from a distance as daubs of orange-red lacquer, reishi mushrooms gleam like oil paints among the summer-dark woods. In our mountains, the weeks leading up to the summer solstice mark the peak of this mushroom's season. To prepare, I normally try to scope out my reishi spots earlier in the spring, when the mushrooms are just budding out from the bark with their white tips, soft and innocent as snow. By the time they are ready to harvest, each reishi mushroom will have formed a seashell-like shelf sticking out at a ninety-degree angle from the bark. Growing anywhere from palm-sized to chest-wide, reishis are easily identified by their porous creamy underbellies and shiny red tops that fade to an outer rind of yellow and white.

Reishi mushrooms grow all over the world. Our local reishi species, *Ganoderma tsugae*, is named for the genus of the tree on which they flourish, the iconic Eastern hemlock (*Tsuga canadensis*)—those magnificent evergreens who used to define our woods. As the invasive wooly adelgid penetrates more deeply into our forests, the hemlocks fall in droves. If you go to any stretch of old woodland, you will inevitably see these trees, dark phantoms with dying limbs, backlit against the vibrant green of the forest. Like the hemlocks felled outside my cabin that winter at the camp, their demise has meant a wholesale change in our forests. It is a sharp grief for those who love the woodlands. But the hemlocks are also the only tree that bears this mythical mushroom. So as the hemlocks fall, the reishis boom.

A Psychedelic of the Spirit

Reishi mushrooms have been collected as medicine for millennia. The longest written record of medicinal use comes from China, where they have been prized for over two thousand years. Known in Chinese as *Ling zhi,* or "spirit plant," the Asian species of reishi (*Ganoderma lucidum*) is considered to be an elixir for the spirit incarnate. In traditional Chinese medicine, this vibrant wild mushroom is cherished for its ability to nourish the heart and safeguard shen. Not unlike the western concept of a soul, *shen* is the Chinese word for the part of a person's individual spirit that animates the body—bringing the spark of life into physical form. Our shen is housed within the heart, and its presence shines forth from our eyes. You can tell when someone has well-anchored shen; their eyes sparkle like a body of water. The disruption of, or disconnection from, our shen can manifest as anxiety, moodiness, poor memory, and a dullness about our eyes. Most of us know that far-away look intimately and probably have seen it in our own worn visage from time to time. Disconnection from our individual shen, and the heart that houses it, is epidemic in our culture. But it's not just to our inner shen that reishi helps us connect.

In Chinese medicine the character for shen has several different meanings. One way to make sense of the multiplicity is to understand that there are two different shens. There is our little shen, the aspect of our individual soul's light that animates our current selves, and our big Shen (with a capital S)—that much wider spirit or oversoul from which our individual souls arise. Some people like to use the term *higher self* to describe this part of us, but I prefer the term *wider self*. Reishi, as a medicine, can help nourish our small shen, our own individual beam of light, so effectively that we can become aware of, and interact with, the vaster Shen from which we come. When we nourish our little shen, we form a direct connection with the eternal aspect of ourselves, the one who observes the ever-changing weather of birth, death, and rebirth. It is no wonder that another ancient name for reishi is the "immortality mushroom."

Reishi's actions within our physical body mirror its more metaphysical inclinations. In contemporary and traditional herbalism, reishi is heralded as a powerful tonic of longevity. It is considered, among other things, to be an adaptogen (a substance that helps our bodies deal with stress), an immunomodulator (a medicine that supports both depressed and hyperactive immune systems to find their natural balance), an antiviral, a liver protector, and a nervine (an agent that soothes our nervous system). Traditionally used in China and Japan for a whole host of conditions including asthma, hepatitis, and hypertension, reishi has a deep affinity for our lungs, as well as our hearts. It is also a popular anti-cancer remedy, used in both prevention and treatment as well as to protect against the negative side effects of chemotherapy and radiation.

You won't find this in any book (other than this one), but reishi's medicine has one more quality that has always stood out to me. Reishi is a psychedelic. We've inextricably linked the term *psychedelic* to certain plants and mushrooms that contain psychoactive or hallucinatory compounds, but a true psychedelic is much more than a group of molecules that sets your world spinning. At its essence, the word *psychedelic* means "consciousness expanding or revealing." Psychedelics can be anything that changes our perspective, opening the garden gates of our psyche so that we can experience the world more fully. Sunsets can be psychedelic. As can a thoughtful conversation with a friend. Or that moment when your eyes lit upon the woods and you swore, for a second, you saw a stag.

I've found that most mushrooms are psychedelic in nature. We see them, and our mind stretches to understand. *How could this being, made of skin and breathing oxygen, crop up from the ground overnight? And who is this exactly? Round like a disc, or big as a pufferfish, or shiny and lacquered like an antique Chinese cabinet. Is it sea creature, dirt creature, human creature, or other?* Mushrooms constantly push us to expand our minds; they demand that we come up with new ways of interacting with the ineffable. Mushrooms have captivated our senses, taken spore in our language, and informed our rituals of spiritual connection for a very long time. Without us chewing on a single cap, the entire family of fungi turns our perception upside down.

As a shen-expander, part of reishi's innate Dao is to help us connect into a wider, more mythic state of being. Though much more subtle than a medicine like psilocybin, reishi has the ability to shift our perception, changing our experience of reality. On a physical level, reishi helps our body become healthy vessels that can hold and nurture this connection to our own wider self. On a spirit level, reishi helps to bring the energy and perspective of these wider selves into our everyday minds so that we can see the light that shines through all things. Drunk as a decoction, reishi can invoke feelings of expansion, interconnection, and a truly shimmering reality. Over the years I've had many experiences of sipping on reishi tea and clearly entering into an altered state of being. I remember one day in particular; I showed up to teach a class on flower essences at my previous alma mater—the Chestnut School for Herbal

Medicine—and was so elevated from a cup of fresh reishi that, my now dear friend, Juliet Blankespoor said to me, "If I didn't know you any better I'd think you were high!"—to which I replied, with an irrepressible effervescence, "I *am*—on reishi!"

Gathering a Wider Perspective

Mushroom gathering is not like wildcrafting plants. The window for collection is often short. You normally want to head out after a rain, and if you don't catch them right away, some mushrooms can fade within a few days. Unlike most plants, mushrooms don't always grow in the same places every year, so it takes a practiced eye to spot them. Mushrooms are, by nature, unpredictable. One year you might have a flush and the next it is as if they have become ghosts. Many mushrooms come and go with the rain, more ephemeral than rainbows. Even just attempting to have a relationship with mushrooms will begin to change the patterns of your perception, shaking you from your slumber so you can see the tricks of light that exist everywhere.

When we collect plants, we call it harvesting. But when it comes to mushrooms, it's a hunt—luck, skill, and a bit of courtship are needed. Reishis, like many mushrooms, enjoy hiding. There have been countless times when I went out to hunt reishis from a stand I knew and had frequented several times, only to have them disappear. Ask most serious mushroom collectors, and they will tell you that finding reishis, or any other mushrooms, is a mystical process. Two successful friends of mine, free spirits with equally long tangles of hair who head out to the field each day with a single avocado for lunch, make their entire living gathering wild mushrooms. They say that the key to their success is not so much that they know the best spots to look, but that they always start by standing at the entrance to the woods and feeling into the reishi first, calling out to them, shen to shen.

Even the most strait-laced of mushroom gatherers will attest that there is a magic to mushroom hunting. It's helpful to know all the tips and tricks, but the truth is, most of the time, the mushrooms find *you*. There is something innately tricksterish about mushroom consciousness. They will lead you off the trail, down the embankment, over river stones, and deep into the heart of the woods. They call like sirens, pulling you away from the predictable paths of moving and thinking to send you down an almost imperceptible deer track, a faery trail through a fabled wood meant to deliver you somewhere entirely new.

Earlier in the season, I had gone out to scout the reishi-rich spot I was hiking to now. Before the solstice, I had walked the entire length of this particular creek of tumbled hemlocks, crawling through a dark labyrinth of large stones to find *the* tree. Stretching between two boulders with its roots bridging a small channel of water flowing between, it looked like the mythical world tree, guarding the entrance to the Otherworld. Having anchored itself in the soil on either side of the upright stones, it seemed to be giving birth to the small waterfall beneath it. Dark, wide, and dying from a great height, this hemlock emanated all the power of a gatekeeper. There was no denying that medicine collected from this place would be potent. Hemlocks, like all evergreens, are signs of eternal life. I couldn't help but wonder as I touched the tree and promised to return in a few weeks—what happens when the green that never fades begins to disappear completely? What is born when that which is evergreen dies?

You cannot become a mushroom hunter without becoming a devotee to the power of death and its ability to bring forth life. Working with mushrooms is understanding that, on a molecular level, death is the building block of life. As author, cultural activist, and palliative care worker Stephen Jenkinson so succinctly puts it, "Life doesn't feed on life . . . Death feeds life. Every rooted thing knows that and proceeds accordingly. Death is the life-giving thing."[10] Creating the newly available nutrients of compost and humus—death is the unseen element that keeps our world evergreen.

Mushrooms, unlike plants, do not provide us with housing, or cloth-ing, or even that much food. Most species of fungi are inedible, and some will kill you outright. Mushrooms are not here to build up our lives. They are here to tear it down. To dissolve the old. To decompose what you thought you knew or identified with and to open your mind to the possibilities that exist just beyond. As gatekeepers for the realm between life and death, mushrooms come with a very particular mes-sage for those of us born during this time of species loss and seeming decline. We are not just here to witness the end but to be a part of the beginning.

Ruin and Reishi

A month had passed since I had scoped out that reishi-laden hemlock sitting over the waterfall. I had thought about it nearly every day since, wondering how big the mushrooms had grown. Then, one morning in early July, after the rattle of the previous day's thunderstorm, I woke up and knew—it was time. Having never experienced the blessing of being a morning person, it was already past noon by the time I had eaten breakfast and gotten my backpack in order, replete with cloth bags and a sharp knife, a jar of water, and a soft handkerchief with a few dia-monds from my last foray to the lake bottom—gifts to be given to the reishi and the hemlock tree before harvesting.

I was already on my way out the door when I got a phone call from an old friend. We had been playing phone tag for a while, so I lingered on the porch to talk to her, drawing circles on the wood with my feet while a part of my mind inevitably drifted through the blue curves of the mountains up into the forest. Soon the call reached its conclusion, the closing as natural as a cloth napkin falling back into timeworn folds; the art of ending is second nature with old friends. As a last off-handed note, she asked me where I was headed that day. It was in this place of deep, almost unthinking naturalness, that I answered, "I'm going to visit a Reishi Tree."

The words dropped out of my mouth like nuts from the canopy. Where on Earth did they come from? How do they feel so whole? And why can't I help but be delighted by their arrival? I stood stock-still on the porch. I remember a butterfly landed on the zinnia next to me. It felt like the world had cracked open along an unnoticed seam. My friend, who is used to hearing about my outdoor expeditions but wouldn't know the difference between a hemlock and a pine, didn't notice the strangeness of my words. She wished me luck and signed off. The call ended, but I still stood there with the phone in my hand, stuck like resin to that place on the porch.

Reishi Tree? A Reishi *Tree*? There is no such thing as a *Reishi Tree*. What made me say such a thing? Even more curious, what was this *feeling* I now had inside my body? This prickling at the back of my senses? My eyes unable to focus—as if I was looking at something I couldn't yet perceive?

Words are incantations; they have the ability to put you under a spell. Just like enchantments, they not only *en-trance*, they also open a kind of *entrance* into a new reality. Language, how we change it, and how it changes us, is a way of shaping the future. The words we call upon directly influence how we see the world—and how we envision our futures. Bilingual speakers and polyglots can attest that you often *think* differently when you are speaking different languages—and how could you not? Our words create our reality. The lived experienced of a native English speaker, whose language is composed of at least 40 percent nouns (aka objects), will be completely different from a native speaker of the language that gave us *Puhpowee*.[11] The Ojibwe language, which is 70 to 80 percent verbs, creates a world where everything is always animated by the motion of living.[12] If we want our futures to change, we need to be willing to not only let our language evolve, but become craftsmen of a new tongue. The birth of a new word is the birth of a new *world*—and, like all births, there is a liminal space you must enter as this newness is coming into form.

I drove in a kind of cloudbank to the woods, still lost in that strange trance state of *Reishi Tree*, wondering what it meant and why I felt so altered by saying it. I was still floating in that cushioned place of curiosity when I left my shoes in a pile on the trailside and began making my way down to the creek. Barefoot and elated, I slid the last few feet onto the bank, climbed over the whalebacks of the large stones, and there it was above me—the dying hemlock perched over the crack of two time-grayed boulders, a gatekeeper giving birth to a waterfall. And there, just as I remembered it, were the reishis, lining the tree's spine in waves of sunset reds, polished to a high shine. The approach felt important, sacred. Hidden in the folds of the creek bed, I stripped off the rest of my clothes and leaned, head back, into the waterfall flowing from the tree's roots. The cold water streamed instantly down my face, over my chest and belly. The bright shock of it made the outlines of the day immediately crisper and more alive.

Refreshed and still dripping with cold water, I slipped my soft handkerchief of gifts into a pouch around my neck and hung my knife from a holster at my waist so I could climb the rocks unencumbered. The boulders housing the tree were too tall for me to scale directly, so I crawled in a wide circle around the falls, placing my feet carefully into the nooks and crannies of the stones. It took me several minutes to pick my way over the downed limbs and smaller gushes of water, but finally I was next to the magnificent hemlock and its watery precipice.

Sometimes messages appear clear as day—*go here, release this, speak your piece.* But more often, the intuitive hits we get are wooly enough that we can't understand their full import at first. We must allow the hours, days, or years to shift by so we can card what is thick, and maybe a bit burred, into meaningful strands. It is only once time has done its carding that we can begin to see that what felt like an indistinguishable tangle actually held the threads of a new destiny. The words *Reishi Tree* had shaken me, but I wasn't entirely sure why. It wasn't until I was able to get close, with one foot perched on a boulder and one on the netting of the hemlock's old roots, that the answer came. As suddenly as the punch of cold water, I understood. *This* was a *Reishi Tree.*

No longer a hemlock—that fallen giant and emblem of an era ended—nor just a substrate for a new flush of mushrooms. This tree, with the last of its hemlock lifeforce anchoring it to the rocks and the fibers of reishis' mycelium running through its core, had become transformed into something else entirely. It had undergone a powerful alchemical transformation and was now neither one nor the other. It was, instead, something entirely new and profoundly whole—a Reishi Tree. I leaned my bare chest against the tree's hull, harvesting knife in hand, resting in wonder before I cut a single mushroom.

I pressed my heart into the trunk and tried an experiment. Breathing deeply, I asked to feel the shen of this being. All at once, I could sense the ineffable uniqueness of this tree's spirit. Although I have been around many hemlocks in my life, in that moment, I understood immediately that this wasn't one of them, nor was it just some dead material upon which this mushroom consciousness bloomed. The whole being had been reincarnated into something else—a Reishi Tree. The phrase itself felt like an invocation, a spell, an invitation to stop identifying with what is dying, both in our world and in my own life, and to start embracing the potency of what is being born. To let go of everything that held me back from being my true self so I could embody the vibrant wholeness of what is to come. *This* was a Reishi Tree. And so are *we*.

The Way Beyond Death

When something begins to die—a person, a pet, a part of ourselves—we reflexively hold tighter, as if our grip can reverse the flow of time. When we experience a change inside of ourselves, we cling to the people that we once were. We default to retelling the worn-out fables of our lives simply because we aren't sure what the new story will be. We immerse ourselves so fully in trying to puzzle out the past that we miss the tiny spores of what is being born. Meanwhile, the tighter we hold onto what is dying, the more that river of renewal gathers force. Meanwhile, the flowers of the soil are waiting to help us transform. Meanwhile, as the giants of the past fall, the bloom of a new future is arising. *Puhpowee*. If we let it, that transformation into the next phase could even take place overnight. The art of becoming—like a mushroom—is innately mysterious. Right now on our Earth, we know the old ways are dying, but we do not know what will come to replace them. With *Reishi Tree*, we get a glimpse of how that transformation will take place.

Many things are ending in our world right now, but the greatest purge of all is the death of a worldview that could see the Earth, and all her creations, as anything less than a living, sentient miracle. As so many beloved beings depart from our Earth—the hemlocks, the chestnuts, the polar bears, the bees—their dying is a clarion call, an opening into another world. It is an invitation—singular, generous, magnanimous, and essential—to let the wider death that is happening sweep away what no longer works within us, to let go of all the beliefs that have kept us apart from the world so we can become a part of everything once more. It's clear that we can no longer live in the world our worldview has created. This world, the one we've been handed, the one that was drawn in lines of hierarchy and separation, has hit its expiration date—and we are the deliverers of both its demise and rebirth.

When a tree is isolated from the underground network of mycelia, it can become so weakened that it eventually dies. The ways in which we have separated ourselves from the Earth have not only sickened us, but sickened the whole interconnected world to which we belong. A few years ago a childhood friend of mine was going through an incredibly hard time. We all knew she was suffering, but when I saw her, I was most shaken by how dim her eyes had become. It was as if the lights had gone out in some deep place inside her soul. It was this, more than anything else, that scared me. I didn't know where her shen had gone, but I knew why it had left.

Our souls came here to be in relationship with the collective, collaborative light of this world. When we cannot see the Shen shining through all things, we lose connection to the light and purpose within.

When we cut ourselves off from this wider connection, we lose our own lifeforce. We become a forest of weakened trees, ready to fall. And yet—an older way of being still glows within us. Hidden like spores beneath the surface, this way of perceiving reality is ready to fruit once more.

One of the most commonly reported side effects of taking psychedelic drugs is the ability to see the energy of nature, like the aura of light that surrounds a tree. Part of what makes psychedelics so healing is how they help us perceive, with profound clarity, the aliveness of the world and the incredible fact that we belong to this miracle. In one John Hopkins study with psilocybin mushrooms, one-third of all participants said the experience was the single most spiritually significant of their lives.[13] Today, our natural ability to see this aliveness and interconnection has been so crushed by our mythologies of separation that sometimes we need the muscle power of entheogens—psychoactive substances—to roll this boulder off our hearts. But you do not need a hallucinogen to access this expanded awareness. It's there every time you feel the sunlight on your skin and soften. Or when you park the car to sit by a roadside of flowers and bask in your luck. It's there when you find a stone that looks like a face, or follow a bird into the brush, or trace the knot of a tree with your knuckle and wonder what whirlpool of wisdom lives there. It is in every mycelial moment of slowness, self-benevolence, and connection that reminds you that *you belong*. When you can see the animacy that surrounds you, the Earth will be right there, reflecting your light back in turn. It is moments like these, when the Earth's Shen touches our heart, that the very world changes before our eyes.

In NDEs (or near-death experiences) people often recount that dying was the most blissful experience of their whole life. They come back from these experiences steeped in wonder, reporting that death wasn't an ending at all, but an awakening. The feeling of dying, they say, was one of returning home after a long time abroad. When they come back to Earth, these people often return with a sense of how infinitely precious their individual life is and how blessed we are to be here on this planet.

In our culture today, we often see death as final, but those who have ventured past that threshold have come back to report that there is a way beyond death—and that way is to *come home*. When we come home to ourselves, to the world's animacy and this mirror of our own goodness, we illuminate the way forward. When we embrace self-acceptance as the force of ecological healing that it is, we can spot the deer track that will lead us away from this paved path headed for nowhere and allow us to start walking toward a true heaven on Earth. If death is just that which ultimately returns us home, then we have all the energy we need on the planet right now to remember our power and help this rebirth. When home is our ultimate destination, coming back to our belonging is a blessing that is as unstoppable as a mushroom bloom after a hard rain.

We, as children born into this world, are used to defining ourselves by what we have lost. Ours is a generation that has become intimately familiar with the fact that our living, as contemporary human beings, means bearing the weight of human-created extinction. For those of us who have been able to reopen our hearts to the precious beauty of our home, the pain of this culpability is immense. We cannot help but see ourselves as death bringers, forest cutters, trash creators, mine diggers. We have yoked ourselves to these definitions as a kind of punishment, inescapable and damming—and yet by doing so, we have bound ourselves to the very way of life that is dying instead of handfasting ourselves to what is being born.

We are not here to be agents of death; we are here to be angels of new life. We are here to be those who help doula humanity into the next phase of existence, by allowing a way of being that has cost us our life to crumble into dust. When we embrace self-compassion, that love for the light that lives within us, our connection to this web of luminosity becomes clear. Each time we come home to turn the lights on, inviting our shen back into our precious hearts, we support this rebirth. No matter how much we may long for the past, none of us was born at the wrong time. You were made for this era, and every time you return to yourself you will remember—you are here to become a Reishi Tree in a new world.

Becoming Reishi Trees

After a time of decay comes the turning point. The powerful light that has been banished returns.

—THE *I CHING*, HEXAGRAM 24

The legacy we've been handed is in decay. Many of us have felt it from the time we could walk—when we were told not to eat the blackberries that grew up where the powerlines were sprayed or that our favorite animal was on the endangered species list. We've known it since the patchy woods that was our sanctuary became a new storefront, while the herons disappeared from the creek.

Where I grew up, we had one large common green behind the long curve of duplexes. We were allowed to play there but were expressly forbidden from venturing into the overgrown field of the neighboring development. No one explained why we couldn't go there, except that we could get terribly sick if we touched the ground. That field took on a mythic hue of darkness in my mind. In my scariest dreams, I would wander back beyond the fence and blackness would swallow me whole. It wasn't until I got older that I learned the reason why I wasn't allowed to go into that far field. The decade before I was born, a company that made the stuffing for car seats had dumped all their waste there, officially turning that stretch of land into a Superfund site. What gave them the right to pour chemicals into that field, a field with a brook and a wood in the middle of a riparian lowland, I do not know. But a few years after I was born, a teenage girl who lived on the edge of the field got bladder cancer, and after that no child was allowed back there.

How common is this story? We know it as well as our ancestors knew their creation myths. We are the children of plastic plates and fields where we cannot go. The progeny of box stores that used to be marshes where the herons roamed. The children who learned to eat onion grass and thought it was a miracle and the children who stopped seeking miracles altogether because we were taught they didn't exist after all—but they do.

Blackberries grow in to reclaim thoughtlessly cleared land. Spring water still flows. Fungi remediate whole swaths of contaminated soil. Even our hope, staying alight, buoyed like a hawk on the unseen winds of belief, is a miracle. Miracles never ceased to exist; we simply stopped seeing them because our worldview didn't leave space for them to bloom.

We are in the midst of witnessing the evolving miracle of what grows up when the old structures of thinking start to fall. White-tailed eagles, previously thought to be extinct in England, have just returned to the country. After 140 years, the Te Awa Tupua River in New Zealand, the ancestral waterways of the Whanganui people, was finally granted the same legal rights as a human being—a decision that has set a precedent for the governmental recognition of landscapes as living entities in countries around the world. Such miracles show us that there is another way to live. One that is so much more expansive, delightful, rich, and colorful than what we've experienced before. When we compost the old, we allow newness to stir inside our soul.

Immortality is a funny word. Like the holy grail, people have sought it for millennia without fully believing that it is real. But our ancestors, those whose lives aligned with the curve of the earth, understood that immortality *does* exist; it just usually goes by another name—rebirth. Immortality is just another word for remembering that, though your body may rot, and the pillars of a culture may fall, there is an essence, a Shen, that remains beyond death. The bloom of an era may come and go, but the mycelial roots of our soul remain eternal. True immorality is witnessing the wheel of life-death-life and knowing that you have a role to play in the rebirth.

In the ancient Daoist practice of *neidan*, a discipline of inner alchemy, the goal was not to turn base metals into gold, but to accomplish your own transformation, to embrace the process of self-realization so fully that you could be reunited with your true light and become immortal.

These ancient practitioners believed you could overcome death, decay, and the forces of entropy, not by resisting them—but by embracing them so fully that a new kind of consciousness is born. As acupuncturist Lorie Eve Dechar illuminates in her book *Five Spirits: Alchemical Acupuncture for Psychological and Spiritual Healing*, the alchemical process shatters "no longer efficient systems," reorganizing them into "a new, more potent and complex wholeness."[14] Alchemy arises when we are willing to go into the mycelial depths, the places where things are broken and dying, to find the spark of gold in the darkness.

Gold was prized throughout the ancient world because it is a metal that never loses its luster. Unlike brass or copper, gold is as bright as sunshine from the day it is formed, to the day it is unearthed, until it is buried once more. In ancient Daoist alchemical texts, the spark of inner newness that arises from our willingness to go into the death-steeped depths is called the *golden flower*. "The flower is the self," Dechar describes, "the ungraspable light, both mortal and divine, that glows at the empty center of our being."[15] Once this golden flower arises, the inevitably of disintegration is reversed, entropy changes course, and life itself is reborn. Some people visualize this flower as a lotus, but I imagine it might look a bit like a reishi mushroom blooming from the heart of a hemlock tree.

True alchemy is taking what is broken down into parts, the baseness of what we've been handed, and spinning it into gold. It is the ability to transform the elements of what *was* into something utterly surprising in its wholeness. Mushrooms are experts at alchemy, turning death into new life; it is simply part of their Dao. Just like the mushrooms, we too have the capacity to alchemize this legacy of waning and turn it into something golden. As Dechar goes on to explain, "[Any] person who has endured this shattering without succumbing to bitterness, hopelessness and despair, who has transformed pain and suffering into compassion and an abiding, spontaneous joy and gratitude for the experiences of life, has been involved in an inner alchemical mystery."[16] Our willingness to consciously live through this time of hardship, to take that journey to uncover the golden flower of self-compassion, possibility, and hope within, is what will help us transform into the agents of alchemy we were meant to be for this world. As the traditional Daoist Alchemist Liu I-ming once described, only if we are willing to undertake this inner journey can we become true "companions of the Earth" once more.

We are the children of a new-old world. We are not just the dying hemlocks, nor are we the bourgeoning reishi—but an alchemical fusion of the two. We are clearing within our bodies what is no longer working, that which is already dying. We recognize it as self-doubt and judgement, illness, oppression, and stress. And we contain within us the spores of a new beginning—self-compassion, empathy, a relationship with the living world, and a deep trust in a wider process unfurling.

To be a Reishi Tree is to anchor in self-belief despite the legacy of doubt we've been handed. It is to know that you are worthy and that you have the alchemical tools you need to aid this rebirth. Just like the threads of mycelium starting within a hemlock tree long before the mushrooms can appear, this revolution begins at our heartwood, and it has already taken root.

To this day, I am still confused as to where and when and how the reishi will flower. Mushrooms, like birth itself, come in their own time, in their own mysterious ways. Ultimately, it is not for us to understand how this new era happens. Our task is simply to *be it* by embodying the profundity of the integration that is taking place within us now.

Midwives for a Dying World

Still resting against the tree to steady myself, I cradled a handful of reishis in one hand as the other, holding a sharp knife, loosened more of their softness from the hard bark. I cut each one tenderly. My feet threatened to slip on the wet roots as I worked, but every time I felt I might fall, I just leaned my body more heavily against the Reishi Tree, steadying myself for the task. Afterward, cradling the reishi fans in my arms, I climbed carefully down the boulders with their streaming water and transferred the mushrooms into my waiting pack. I gathered only a handful, just enough to boil down into a strong silt and then preserve in a large dropper bottle. Over my years of collecting medicine from the wild, I've learned that a small amount can go a long way in creating lasting change in people's lives.

I gazed up once more at the tree perched over the waterfall, that gatekeeper between the realms who had forever changed the way I looked at myself and the role I was here to play in this world. There were dozens of reishi still glowing from its bark. From down below, it looked like the trunk was strung with warm rice-paper lanterns. Each mushroom was its own bronze-orange light in the darkness of the forest. I felt my eyes shine over with tears, arising from some deep place inside. Beyond the din of the rushing water, I could hear them all humming goodbye, a choir of mushroom, water, tree, and light, singing a canticle of new life.

After gently transferring the mushrooms to the bottom of my pack, I sought the pieces of me that I had strewn along the creek bank and upper slopes of the forest. I put back on my clothes, letting the wet rope of my hair rest on my shoulders. I picked up my half-eaten lunch, my socks and shoes. I juggled them all in my hands so the reishi would remain unblemished in my pack. Once harvested, reishi mushrooms are tender as newborns, bruising easily, especially on the soft white undersides of their belly. As I made my way back to the main path and then down to where my car was parked, I walked as if I was carrying a baby in a cradle on my back; I was the bearer of something deeply new, precious, and important. Like birthing a child, this clarion call to become a Reishi Tree, to help create a new world by coming home to myself, may not be something I would see come to full fruition in my lifetime—but it made every step I took feel rich as sunlight. In that moment, I understood that carrying the spores of this new beginning was what my life had been designed for. I was a nurse log for the rebirth.

When a hemlock dies, the mycelium invades its every pore. At that point, the tree becomes more reishi than hemlock. Or, another way to say it is—the tree becomes both. As I reached my car, I realized that I was shifting from one persona—the wild woman who takes her clothes off and climbs boulders to harvest mushrooms—to another—the careful driver who buckles up before she edges on the gas, using her blinker for every turn on the deserted backcountry roads. I was both the sensitive-hearted child who loved to roam the hillsides of her mind and a grounded Earth advocate who can, when the need arises, transform into an extroverted guide. I was that student in herbal school on the first day, not knowing anything about plants, and I was the seasoned teacher who reached students across the globe. I was the person who still sometimes doubted her goodness, and the one who knew, beyond all doubt, that I had a precious gift to give this world.

The root of the word alchemy comes from the Greek *chemeia*, which means a "mingling or infusion." True alchemical processes are about reuniting the forces within, so that out of the disparate elements, you create something entirely new. In Daoism, it's said that once there was perfect balance and reciprocity between human beings and the world. As a part of the natural course of the cosmos, this unity was broken, the wholeness becoming polarized. This shattering caused humans to begin to live out of alignment with the natural laws of nature. According to Daoist beliefs, this polarization is not some original sin, or a tragic flaw in human nature, but an organic part of the cosmic process, the dream of a sentient Earth—because it is only through this division that the halves can come back together again to create a greater whole. In this way of thinking, the Earth orchestrated this dissolution, because She knew even more wholeness was possible. For ancient Daoists, alchemy happens when you let go of trying to recapture what was, that first completeness, and consciously move toward the unknown future, that dream of wholeness that can only be reached when we come home to the beautiful complexity of our own selves.

Right now, we are in a cultural moment when we are moving beyond duality in all its forms. Animate and inanimate. Good and bad. Endings and beginnings. Part of becoming a Reishi Tree is to grow beyond duality and its fatalism, to simply be with *what is*. You are sensitive and you are strong. You are introverted and you are an agent of healing for the Earth. You are the death that gives birth to life, and the life that will lead us from the path of death. You are the hemlock and the mushroom—the Reishi Tree perched over this great crack in the world.

So embrace the wild dichotomy within you. Hold with tenderness the part of you that doubts your goodness, and root down in the wider light that has never left you. Honor the part of you that is both tied to the destruction and that holds the seeds of the solution. Just like the hemlock perched between those two boulders, we came into this world knowing how to live between a rock and a hard place, to straddle this hard gap between what is dying and what is being born. Open yourself to the bridge that you are, and we can all cross from one side of this torrent to another. Each of us is a gatekeeper at the in-between; we are the midwives for a dying world.

You carry medicine; you are every bit as laden as a Reishi Tree, and your gifts are a healing balm that can expand the consciousness of this world. As the ancient Daoists understood, it is only when we forget our true nature that we fall out of alignment with the Dao. When we alchemize the death of our own internalized self-doubt and harm, we reunite our own wholeness and change the world from the inside out. When you live in a way that celebrates the sentience of the Earth and the precious gift of being yourself, you become a psychedelic that can expand the mind of human culture. When you embrace yourself as the Reishi Tree that you are, you call into being a wholly alchemical reincarnation of our current worldview.

An old world is dying—the world that was bogged down in self-doubt and disconnection, a world in which your preciousness could ever be in question, where who you are wasn't recognized as important medicine for the Earth. And a new world is being born—one where you know, innately, how good you are. One where you accept yourself so fully, you can finally access the gifts of innovation, kindness, connection, and understanding that were always meant to change the tide. The gifts that are like warm steady hands, here to midwife a new world.

At the deepest level, where the mycelia and the roots intertwine, you've always known that this is why you are here. That, in fact, everything has been leading you to this point. You picked up this book because you heard that call—like the song of mushrooms rising from the duff—to see yourself, to accept yourself, to love yourself for who you truly are, and from that place, to blossom. When we see ourselves in the mirror in the Earth, reestablishing a relationship with the glowing shen within us and the greater Shen of this living planet—we become a light for this world. The Earth asked you to engage in this brave work of inner alchemy because this is how new wholeness is created for us all. You took this journey to remember that you become a Reishi Tree—a being that seeds a new future on Earth—just by being your full self.

So, gaze out with kindness, and allow the tenderness of the world to enter you. Let the Earth show you how precious you are. When you are parched, go to the hillside and kneel down, drink deep from the benevolence that is there. A new-old way is bubbling up from beneath the surface, and you are a carrier of this miracle.

When things get hard, remember to search for yourself in the loving mirror of the Earth. Protect what is within you, ready to grow. Let your own inner world nourish the Earth. Embrace every knock in your life as a part of what makes you so unique. Trust your own time-lines. Celebrate the parts of you that are small, tender, fallible. Know that the world sees you and embraces every iota of who you are. You are forgiven. Your heart is big enough to hold it all. Every time you believe in a new possibility for your life and the life of this world, you feed the mysterious healing of the Earth. You are here to help seed a new future, and you don't have to do anything fancy to make that dream a reality except to commit to this profoundly alchemical journey of becoming yourself.

This is not the end; it is the beginning. Who you are is the gift you were meant to bring to this Earth. You are a Reishi Tree, and your presence here is exactly what is needed for this great rebirth.

Acknowledgments

GRATITUDE IS A form of nourishment for the world—and I have been deeply nourished by many sources of support in the creation of this book. Thank you to all the healers and teachers who have touched my life, including Sarah Thomas, Jeffrey Yuen, Robert Moss, and Shannon O'Neil. Gratitude for Juliet Blankespoor, my first teacher in the herbal world and dear friend. I've come a long way since I almost failed my tree quiz; thank you for believing in me and supporting me in all the ways you have. I am also deeply indebted to all the Indigenous authors, philosophers, and artists whose wisdom forms the bedrock of many of the disciplines that have informed my path. I would not be where I am today in my thinking, perception, or education without these teachers. Deep gratitude, in particular, to my college advisor Professor Molly McGlennen whose brilliance, graciousness, and guidance opened my eyes and set me on a path that would lead me into the rest of my life.

All healing happens in relationship. This book would not have been possible without all the different friends and companions who've taught me, challenged me, camped under the stars with me, and walked beside me through the many chapters of this journey. To everyone who appears in this book, named or unnamed, thank you for being a mirror in my life.

Deep gratitude to my beloved One Willow Team, past and present, for supporting me throughout the creation of this book and beyond. Thank you to Catelynn, Shannon, Andrés, Ann, Noel, and the indomitable Aleli—who has helped to steer this ship through so many shoals.

Heartfelt thanks to everyone who read parts of this book as it came into being, including Miranda, Juliet, Sylvia, Shannon, and my writing buddy Samantha Fey, who made this book incalculably richer through her feedback. Deep appreciation, as well, to all the wonderful folks at North Atlantic Books, including Allison Knowles, Keith Donnell, Trisha Peck, and Rebecca Rider.

Profound gratitude to my parents who have been my writing editors since day one and who have encouraged and affirmed me every step of the way. You helped make this book what it is today. I am so blessed to have such loving mirrors in my life.

Gratitude to all the students, clients, and readers who I've connected with over the years. You have taught me, buoyed me, and inspired me more than you will ever know.

This book, like all of life, is a co-creation. It would not exist if it weren't for all the guides I've encountered in the more-than-human world. To the plants and stones, creatures, and teachers in both the seen and unseen—thank you. My life is possible because of your love. And to the grandmother of these mountains, thank you for all the ways in which you hold me. Living here in your coves is a blessing beyond imagining. Thank you for showing me what benevolence and wisdom truly mean.

And finally, to John—*mo sheasamh ort lá no choise tinne*. Thank you for being a place to stand when I'm weary, the ground where I can rest.

Notes

Introduction

1 Wilma Dykeman and Douglas W. Gorsline, *The French Broad* (Knoxville: University of Tennessee Press, 1965), 269–270.

2 Bradley Thomas Lepper, *Ohio Archaeology: An Illustrated Chronicle of Ohio's Ancient American Indian Cultures* (Wilmington, OH: Orange Frazer Press, 2005), 110.

3 The phrase "the more-than-human world" was first coined by ecological philosopher David Abram.

4 George Constantz, *Hollows, Peepers, and Highlanders: An Appalachian Mountain Ecology* (Missoula, MT: Mountain Press Publishing, 1994), 45.

5 Robin A. Smith, "Study Reveals How Eastern U.S. Forests Came to Be," *Duke Today*, May 20, 2015, https://today.duke.edu/2015/05/easternforests.

6 Robin Wall Kimmerer, *Braiding Sweetgrass: Indigenous Wisdom, Scientific Knowledge and the Teachings of Plants* (Minneapolis, MN: Milkweed Editions, 2013), 229.

7 Xue Wang, Zhansheng Chen, Kai-Tak Poon, Fei Teng, and Shenghua Jin, "Self-Compassion Decreases Acceptance of Own Immoral Behaviors," *Personality and Individual Differences* 106 (February 1, 2017): 329–333, https://doi.org/10.1016/j.paid.2016.10.030.

8 Stefanie B. Waschull and Michael H. Kernis, "Level and Stability of Self-Esteem as Predictors of Children's Intrinsic Motivation and Reasons for Anger," *SAGE Journals*, January 1, 1996, https://doi.org/10.1177/0146167296221001.

9   Lyla June, quote from a class recording. For more about Patricia
    Davis and her wisdom, please see Patricia Anne Davis, "Living
    the Loving Way, a Reverent Revolution," Whole System Design
    Portfolio, Center for Creative Change, Antioch University, June
    2005.

Chapter 1: Garden Edges and Paradise on Earth

1   Wikipedia, s.v. "History of Gardening," last modified September
    1, 2021, https://en.wikipedia.org/wiki/History_of_gardening.
2   Gabor Maté, *When the Body Says No: The Cost of Hidden Stress*
    (London: Scribe, 2019).
3   "When the Body Says No—Caring for Ourselves While Caring for
    Others. Dr. Gabor Maté," YouTube, Uploaded by SCSASmithers,
    6 March 2013, https://youtu.be/c6IL8WVyMMs.

Chapter 2: Florida Inner Worlds

1   Zenaida Kotala, "Florida Declared a Global Biodiversity Hotspot:
    Orlando News," *University of Central Florida News | UCF Today*,
    July 2, 2018, https://today.ucf.edu/florida-declared-a-global
    -biodiversity-hotspot/.
2   Graham Harvey, *Animism: Respecting the Living World* (London: C.
    Hurst and Company, 2017), xi.
3   Robert Moss, *The Boy Who Died and Came Back: Adventures of a
    Dream Archaeologist in the Multiverse* (Novato, CA: New World
    Library, 2014), 176.
4   John Tierney, "Discovering the Virtues of a Wandering
    Mind," *New York Times*, June 28, 2010, https://www.nytimes.
    com/2010/06/29/science/29tier.html; Christine Dell'Amore,
    "Five Surprising Facts about Daydreaming," *National Geographic*,
    June 12, 2016, https://www.nationalgeographic.com

/news/2013/7/130716-daydreaming-science-health-brain/; David B. Feldman and Diane E. Dreher, "Can Hope Be Changed in 90 Minutes? Testing the Efficacy of a Single-Session Goal-Pursuit Intervention for College Students," *Journal of Happiness Studies* 13 (2012): 745–759, https://link.springer.com/article/10.1007/s10902-011-9292-4; Marjorie Taylor, Candice M. Mottweiler, Emilee R. Naylor, and Jacob G. Levernier, "Imaginary Worlds in Middle Childhood: A Qualitative Study of Two Pairs of Coordinated Paracosms," *Creativity Research Journal* 27, no.2 (June 2015): 167–174, https://doi.org/10.1080/10400419.2015.1030318.

5 Christine Judith Nicholls, "'Dreamtime' and 'The Dreaming'—An Introduction," *The Conversation*, January 22, 2014, https://theconversation.com/dreamtime-and-the-dreaming-an-introduction-20833.

6 Elina Helander-Renvall, "Animism, Personhood and the Nature of Reality: Sami Perspectives," *Polar Record* 46, no. 1 (January 2010): 44–56, https://doi.org/10.1017/S0032247409990040.

Chapter 3: The Seasons of Trauma

1 Jeremy Deaton, "Summer Is about Here. For That You Can Thank a 4-Billion-Year-Old Rock," *Washington Post*, August, 15, 2019, https://www.washingtonpost.com/weather/2019/06/20/summer-is-about-here-that-you-can-thank-billion-year-old-rock/.

2 Peter A. Levine with Ann Frederick (contributor), *Waking the Tiger: Healing Trauma: The Innate Capacity to Transform Overwhelming Experiences* (Berkeley, CA: North Atlantic Books, 1997), 2.

3 Levine, *Walking the Tiger*, 19.

4 Levine, *Waking the Tiger*, 12.

5 Yasmin Anwar, "Nature Is Proving to Be Awesome Medicine for PTSD," *Berkeley News*, July 16, 2018, https://news.berkeley.edu/2018/07/12/awe-nature-ptsd/; Dorthe Varning Poulsen, Ulrika K. Stigsdotter, Dorthe Djernis, and Ulrik Sidenius,

"'Everything Just Seems Much More Right in Nature': How Veterans with Post-Traumatic Stress Disorder Experience Nature-Based Activities in a Forest Therapy Garden," *Health Psychology Open*, March 31, 2016, https://www.ncbi.nlm.nih.gov/pmc /articles/PMC5193293/; James K. Summers and Deborah N. Vivian, "Ecotherapy—A Forgotten Ecosystem Service: A Review," *Frontiers in Psychology*, August 3, 2018, https://www.ncbi.nlm.nih .gov/pmc/articles/PMC6085576/.

6   Caroline Casey, "Way of the Trickster: Liberating Your Soul to Liberate the World," Shift Network live video training, July 17, 2018, https://theshiftnetwork.com/course/13138.

7   Wikipedia, s.v. "Theia," last modified October 7, 2020, https://en.wikipedia.org/wiki/Theia.

8   Levine, *Waking the Tiger*, 193.

Chapter 4: Those That Keep Their Leaves

1   Richard Gast, "Marcescence: An Ecological Mystery," *The Adirondack Almanack*, November 16, 2017, https://www.adirondack almanack.com/2017/11/marcescence-ecological-mystery.html.

Chapter 5: Tender Spring

1   Brené Brown, *Rising Strong: How the Ability to Reset Transforms the Way We Live, Love, Parent, and Lead* (New York: Random House, 2017), 4.

2   Harvard Health Publishing, "Optimism and Your Health," Harvard Health, May 1, 2008, https://www.health.harvard.edu /heart-health/optimism-and-your-health.

3   Brené Brown, *Daring Greatly: How the Courage to Be Vulnerable Transforms the Way We Live, Love, Parent, and Lead* (New York: Avery, an Imprint of Penguin Random House, 2015), 145–146.

4 Brown, *Daring Greatly*, 34.

5 Associated Press, "Poll: Nearly 8 in 10 Americans Believe in Angels," CBS News, December 23, 2011, https://www.cbsnews.com/news/poll-nearly-8-in-10-americans-believe-in-angels/.

6 Belinda Womack, *Lessons from the Twelve Archangels: Divine Intervention in Daily Life* (Rochester, VT: Bear & Company, 2015), 138.

Chapter 6: Drop Dosages

1 Deborah Rogers, "Inequality: Why Egalitarian Societies Died Out," *New Scientist*, July 25, 2012, https://www.newscientist.com/article/dn22071-inequality-why-egalitarian-societies-died-out/.

2 "Dr. Bach," The Bach Centre, accessed June 9, 2020, https://www.bachcentre.com/en/about-us/history/dr-bach/.

3 Wikipedia, s.v. "Indigenous Peoples of Florida," last modified July 11, 2021, https://en.wikipedia.org/wiki/Indigenous_peoples_of_Florida.

4 Darcie A. MacMahon and William H. Marquardt, *The Calusa and Their Legacy: South Florida People and Their Environments* (Gainesville, FL: University Press of Florida, 2004).

5 MacMahon and Marquardt, *The Calusa and Their Legacy*, 83.

6 MacMahon and Marquardt, *The Calusa and Their Legacy*, 121.

7 Robin Wall Kimmerer, *Braiding Sweetgrass: Indigenous Wisdom, Scientific Knowledge and the Teachings of Plants* (Minneapolis, MN: Milkweed Editions, 2013), 23–24.

Chapter 7: The World Sees You

1 Dale Neal, "Madison County's Bounty of Old Ballads," *The Asheville Citizen Times*, July 20, 2016, https://www.citizen-times.com/story/news/local/2016/07/20/madison-countys-bounty-old-ballads/86919840/.

2   Sarah E. Earp and Donna L. Maney, "Birdsong: Is It Music to Their Ears?" *Frontiers in Evolutionary Neuroscience*, November 28, 2012, https://www.frontiersin.org/articles/10.3389/fnevo.2012.00014/full; Colin Barras, "Humans and Birds Share the Same Singing Genes," *New Scientist*, December 11, 2014, https://www.newscientist.com/article/dn26694-humans-and-birds-share-the-same-singing-genes/; C. Claiborne Ray, "Do Birds Listen When You Play Music?" *New York Times*, June 19, 2017, https://www.nytimes.com/2017/06/19/science/do-birds-listen-when-you-play-music.html.

3   Christopher Chabris and Daniel Simons, "The Invisible Gorilla," *The Invisible Gorilla: And Other Ways Our Intuitions Deceive Us*, 2010, http://www.theinvisiblegorilla.com/gorilla_experiment.html.

4   "Plants Are 'in Touch' with the World around Them." The University of Western Australia, May 25, 2016, https://www.news.uwa.edu.au/201605258690/international/plants-are-touch-world-around-them.

5   Linda Hogan, *The Radiant Lives of Animals* (Boston: Beacon Press, 2020), 16.

6   Michael Erardand Catherine Matacic, "Can These Birds Explain How Language First Evolved?," *Science*, August 2, 2018, https://www.science.org/content/article/can-these-birds-explain-how-language-first-evolved.

7   Brené Brown, *Daring Greatly: How the Courage to Be Vulnerable Transforms the Way We Live, Love, Parent, and Lead* (London: Penguin Life, 2015).

Chapter 8: Young Forests

1   "Japanese Knotweed," New York Invasive Species Information, July 2, 2019, http://nyis.info/invasive_species/japanese-knotweed/.

2   Bill Plotkin, *Soulcraft: Crossing into the Mysteries of Nature and Psyche* (Novato, CA: New World Library, 2003).

3   *Wikipedia*, s.v. "Hiroo Onoda," last modified September 3, 2021, https://en.wikipedia.org/wiki/Hiroo_Onoda.

4   Suzuki Shunryū. *Zen Mind, Beginner's Mind: Informal Talks on Zen Meditation and Practice* (Boulder, CO: Shambhala Publications, 2011), 1.

5   Max Planck Florida Institute, "Persistent Sensory Experience Is Good for Aging Brain," *ScienceDaily*, May 24, 2012, https://www.sciencedaily.com/releases/2012/05/120524123209.htm; Marcel Oberlaender, Alejandro Ramirez, and Randy M. Bruno, "Sensory Experience Restructures Thalamocortical Axons during Adulthood," *Neuron* 74,4 (2012): 648.

6   Jaya Saxena, "The Case for Having a Hobby," *New York Times*, May 10, 2018, https://www.nytimes.com/2018/05/10/smarter-living/the-case-for-hobbies-ideas.html.

7   James Hillman, *The Soul's Code: In Search of Character and Calling* (New York: Ballantine Books, 2017).

Chapter 9: Willow Water

1   Elizabeth Venzin, "How Does Low Self-Esteem Negatively Affect You?" *PsychCentral*, March 1, 2014, https://psychcentral.com/blog/how-does-low-self-esteem-negatively-affect-you/.

2   Everett L. Worthington, Jr., "The New Science of Forgiveness," *Greater Good Magazine*, September 1, 2004, https://greatergood.berkeley.edu/article/item/the_new_science_of_forgiveness.

3   Worthington, Jr., "New Science of Forgiveness."

4   Wikipedia, s.v. "History of Aspirin." last modified August 11, 2021, https://en.wikipedia.org/wiki/History_of_aspirin.

Chapter 11: Chestnut Groves
and the Resprouting of Hope

1   National Park Service, "Hemlock Woolly Adelgid," Great Smoky Mountains National Park, June 18, 2015, https://www.nps.gov/grsm/learn/nature/hemlock-woolly-adelgid.htm.

2 National Park Service, "Hemlock Woolly Adelgid."

3 Susan Freinkel, *American Chestnut: The Life, Death, and Rebirth of a Perfect Tree* (Berkeley, CA: University of California Press, 2009), 17.

4 Freinkel, *American Chestnut*, 19.

5 Freinkel, *American Chestnut*, 20.

6 Marc D. Abrams and Gregory J. Nowacki, "Native Americans as Active and Passive Promoters of Mast and Fruit Trees in the Eastern USA," *The Holocene* 18, no. 7 (November 1, 2008): 1123–1137, https://doi.org/10.1177/0959683608095581.

7 Freinkel, *American Chestnut*, 72.

8 Max Dashu, *Witches and Pagans: Women in European Folk Religion, 700–1100* (Richmond, CA: Veleda Press, 2016), 50–52.

9 Wikipedia, s.v. "Witch-Hunt," last modified on September 19, 2021, https://en.wikipedia.org/wiki/Witch-hunt.

10 Ginger Strivelli, "Appalachian Granny Magic," In *Pagan Traditions: An Overview of Belief System* (The Witches' Voice Inc., January 8, 2001).

11 H. Byron Ballard and Lauryn Heineman, *Roots, Branches & Spirits: The Folkways & Witchery of Appalachia* (Woodbury, MN: Llewellyn Publications, 2021), 96.

12 Andrew F. Leuchter, Ian A. Cook, Elise A. Witte, Melinda Morgan, and Michelle Abrams, "Changes in Brain Function of Depressed Subjects During Treatment with Placebo," *American Journal of Psychiatry* 159, no. 1 (January 1, 2002): 122–129, https://ajp.psychiatryonline.org/doi/full/10.1176/appi.ajp.159.1.122.

13 Dashu, *Witches and Pagans*, 50.

14 Ursula K. Le Guin, "Speech in Acceptance of the National Book Foundation Medal for Distinguished Contribution to American Letters," *Ursula K. Le Guin*, November 19, 2014, https://www.ursulakleguin.com/nbf-medal.

15 Scott London, "The Ecology of Magic: An Interview with David Abram," adapted from *Insight & Outlook*, National Public Radio, Claremont, California, 1999, https://scott.london/interviews/abram.html.

16 David Abram, *The Spell of the Sensuous: Perceptions and Language in a More-Than-Human World* (New York: Vintage Books, 1996).

17 London, "The Ecology of Magic."

18 The American Chestnut Foundation, *Using Science to Save the American Chestnut Tree*, accessed July 27, 2020, https://www.acf .org/our-work/reforestation-projects/.

Chapter 12: The Reishi Tree

1 Paul Stamets, *Mycelium Running: How Mushrooms Can Help Save the World* (Berkeley, CA: Ten Speed Press, 2005), 11.

2 Norbertas Velius, Rita Dapkute, and Dainova V. Kupcinskaite, *Lithuanian Etiological Tales and Legends* (Vilnius, LT: VAGA Publishers, 1998).

3 Laima Vincė, *Mushroom Hunting in Vermont—Lithuanian Style*, Deep Baltic, October 12, 2016, https://deepbaltic.com/2016/10/12 /mushroom-hunting-in-vermont-lithuanian-style/.

4 Radeq Brousil and Tomas Zilvar, *The Mushroom Whisperer*, VICE Media, October 27, 2011, https://www.vice.com/amp/en_us /article/wdp5e9/Vaclav-Halek-makes-mushroom-music.

5 Robin Wall Kimmerer, *Braiding Sweetgrass: Indigenous Wisdom, Scientific Knowledge and the Teachings of Plants* (Minneapolis, MN: Milkweed Editions, 2013), 48–49.

6 Kimmerer, *Braiding Sweetgrass*, 49.

7 Stamets, *Mycelium Running*, 8.

8 Stamets, *Mycelium Running*, 12.

9 Stamets, *Mycelium Running*.

10 Stephen Jenkinson, *Die Wise: A Manifesto for Sanity and Soul*. (Berkeley, CA: North Atlantic Books, 2015), 371–372.

11 Luca Onnis and Morten H. Christiansen, "New Beginnings and Happy Endings: Psychological Plausibility in Computational Models of Language Acquisition," *Cognitive Science – COGSCI*, January 1, 2005.

12   Brenda Austin, "Language of the People Forever: Bay Mills Spins Thread Tying Ojibwa Communities Together," *Tribal College Journal of American Indian Higher Education*, November 16, 2011, https://tribalcollegejournal.org/language-people-forever-bay-mills-spins-thread-tying-ojibwa-communities/; Kimmerer, *Braiding Sweetgrass*, 53.

13   Johns Hopkins Medicine, "Hopkins Scientists Show Hallucinogen in Mushrooms Creates Universal 'Mystical' Experience," press release, July 11, 2006, https://www.hopkinsmedicine.org/Press_releases/2006/07_11_06.html.

14   Lorie Dechar, *Five Spirits: Alchemical Acupuncture for Psychological and Spiritual Healing* (New York: Chiron Publications/Lantern Books, 2006), 362.

15   Dechar, *Five Spirits*, 345.

16   Dechar, *Five Spirits*, 312.

Index

A

Aboriginal Australian cultures, 55–56
Abram, David, 234, 238
absolution, 192–193, 204–205
abuse, 33, 99
acceptance, 177–178. *See also*
 self-acceptance
accidents, 69–72
accomplishments, 127
acorns, 181–182
activism, 212
agriculture, 129
alchemy, 260–261, 264, 265
alcoholism, 177
alignment, 100
allelopathic roots, 196–198
American Chestnut: The Life, Death
 and Rebirth of a Perfect Tree
 (Freinkel), 225
The American Chestnut Foundation
 (TACF), 239
angels
 of flower essences, 133
 of new life, 258
 signs and, 69
 as unconditional love, 122
anger, 218
animals, trauma and, 75
animism, 53, 58, 81
Anthropocene extinction, 233
Apalachee people, 137

Appalachia
 author's home in, 31
 chestnut blight in, 223–225
 China and, 7
 Florida and, 46
 granny witches in, 229
 hemlock and adelgid in, 222–223
 logging of, 167–168, 170
 mica in, 1
 mushroom hunting in, 244
 music of, 147–148
 seasons in, 65–66
 spring ephemerals in, 106–107
arborists, 222
Aron, Elaine, 25
art, loss and, 79
aspirin, 200
audience, small, 127–128
Aven, 210–212, 214
awe, 160
axis, Earth's tilted, 67

B

Bach, Edward, 131
basket making, 202
beauty
 of becoming, 178
 living in our original, 14
becoming, 178, 195
beech trees, 92
beginner's mind, 179–181

beginning again, 169, 226, 251, 266
beliefs
    animism, 53
    dismantling, 172
    in the goodness of life, 112–114
    about human/Earth impacts, 197
    magic of, 234–235
    misaligned with our souls, 9–10
    preventing flowering, 132
    reality as changed by, 230
    self-defeating, 175
    about self-worth, 174
    stubborn, self-preserving, 176
belonging
    being seen and, 164–165
    being yourself and, 115–117
    connection and, 257
    deep feeling of, 60
    self-doubt as eviction from, 11
Ben Cao, 7–8
bigness
    in human history, 129
    of love and care, 212–213
    and medicine for deep issues, 134
    success and, 126–128
biodiversity hot spots
    Earth as, 67
    Florida as, 45
birding, 154–155
birdsong, 152–153, 155, 161–164
birth, 212–213, 262. *See also* rebirth
black-and-white thinking, 195
blackberries, 170
Blankespoor, Juliet, 107, 250
blessings, small, 141
blight, chestnut, 224–225, 239–240
blood, freezing of the, 74
bloodroot, 107
Blue Ridge Mountains, 1, 3, 222
body, emotions in the, 29, 87
Bohr, Niels, 55, 136
boundaries
    as an art form, 36
    as crossed by spirochetes, 29
    enclosing your sanctuary, 27

freedom via, 28
    gardens as teaching, 19–20, 24
    hazards of no, 27
    healing via, 29–30
    for highly sensitive people, 25–26
    in our relationships, 41–42
    for self and all, 40
    self-knowledge via, 35
    soft and hard, 32–34
    thriving within, 39
Braiding Sweetgrass (Kimmerer), 11,
    140–141
brain, human, 156, 180
bravery
    to love, 109
    vulnerability and, 108, 123
    of youth, 181
Brecht, Bertolt, 214
Brill, Steve, 157
Brooklyn
    gardening in, 21–23, 33
    walking in, 89–91
Brown, Brené, 108, 115–116, 165
business, 127, 128

C

California wildfires, 182
Calusa people, 137–138, 139
camping
    author's first solo trip, 105, 114–
        115, 117–121
    Florida canoe trips, 43–44, 138
car accident, 69–72
caregiving
    by nature, 11, 160
    of small things, 142–143
    what touches us, 212–213
Casey, Caroline, 79
caterpillar-to-butterfly
    transformation, 61
Chabris, Christopher, 156
change
    via boundaries, 39
    clinging in the face of, 255

as individual, 94
via metamorphosis, 61–62
of perspective, 234
and power of dreams, 54
quantum leaps, 136
via self-acceptance, 14–15
time needed for big, 99–100
via trauma, 68
charms, 230
chemeia, 264
cherishing the small, 142–143
Cherokee (Tsalagi) people, 2, 224
Chestnut School of Herbal Medicine,
3, 249–250
chestnut trees, 223–225, 239–240
childhood
healthy reflection in, 11
reclaiming inner world as, 57
remembering, 63
for sensitives, 46–47
subjectivity in, 57–58
Chinese medicine
and blockage of *Qi*, 217
reishi in, 247
shen in, 247, 248
stone medicine, 7
on trauma, 74
choice, trust as, 112
Claus, 240
communication
along mycelium, 245
along the vagus nerve, 217
between birds, 155
human/nature, 157–158
language of feeling, 160
with plants, 191
community
acceptance in, 176
holding space in, 214
sorrow of disconnect from, 164
confidence, 121
connection, 213, 249, 256
consciousness
dreams as access to, 55
in every action, 140

of nature, 12
of our inner worlds, 53
psychedelics and, 249
quantum leaps in, 136
Constantz, George, 7
control, 77–78
Cook, Frank, 156
coolness, 115–117
courage, 108–109, 123
creation, 53, 54
creativity
aligned with the world, 14
as contact with inner worlds, 52
daydreaming and, 54–56
Creek people, 43
Crescent Moon Bear, 84
Cryphonectria parasitica, 224
cultural regeneration, 179, 181,
238, 264
cypress roots, 52

D

Daoism, 7, 264, 265
Daring Greatly (Brown), 116
dark times, 214–216
Dashu, Max, 228
Davis, Patricia, 14
daydreaming, 46–47, 54–55, 63
death
as a beginning, 231
environmental, 256
as feeding life, 251–252,
260–261, 264
gifts within loss, 229, 231, 236, 237
holding space for, 212–213, 214
as a homecoming, 258
transformation of, 263
the way beyond, 255–258
Debbie, 240
Dechar, Lorie Eve, 261
deciduous trees, 94–95
decisions, 36
decomposition, 251, 252
despair, 237

diamonds, quartz, 125–126
difference, sacredness of, 50
Dillard, Annie, 34
disconnection, 164, 248, 256
dispositional optimism, 113–114
dissociation, 82
diversity
    via Earth's tilted axis, 67
    of emotions, 84–85
    honoring and healing via,
        50–51, 59
    of timelines, 95
DNA, 61
dosage bottle, 145
dreams
    hope and, 123
    of a new future, 233
Dreamtime, 55–56
duality, beyond, 264
dukuns (Balinese shamans), 234, 238
dysfunctional behavior, 197

E
Earth
    acceptance of, 165
    aliveness of, 6, 264
    as angelic guardian, 122
    animistic view of, 53
    asking for help from, 88
    blueprint for healing, 181–182
    deep participation with, 39, 65
    forgiveness as innate to, 198, 200
    gifts of, 140–141
    growth as law of, 195
    guided education on, 4
    healed via self-compassion, 14
    holding space with, 214–216
    impact of Theia on, 66, 67, 73
    importance of seasons to, 67
    as a mirror, 11–12, 13, 266
    as multitude of worlds, 49
    reliance on fungi, 245
    successional healing of, 169, 172
    tilted axis of, 67, 83

earth skills, 153–154, 191
Eastern Band of Cherokee, 224
Eastern hemlock, 222, 247
ecological grief, 237
ecological healing
    alchemy of, 265–266
    animism and, 54
    blueprint for, 181–182
    via boundaries, 40
    for Florida, 45
    via fungi, 246
    by honoring our inner worlds,
        49–51
    by pioneer plants, 170–171
    via self-compassion, 14–15
    smallness and, 138–139
ecology, defined, 51
ecosystems, mature, 169
ecotherapy, 76
education, 4, 237
Einstein, Albert, 55, 113
elders
    at Firefly, 154
    healing by, 229
    hemlocks as, 240
    Jeffrey Yuen, 7
    Mary as, 21
    mosquitoes as, 139
    nature as, 11, 12, 160
    Patricia Davis, 14
EMDR (eye movement
    desensitization and
    reprocessing), 72
Emerson, Ralph Waldo, 181
emotion
    allowing, 79–80, 81, 85, 204
    of belonging, 60
    in childhood, 11
    holding space for all, 214–216
    illness and, 132
    impact on highly sensitive people
        (HSP), 24–27
    and the moon, 84–85
    as registered in the body, 29, 87
    as root of pain, 8–9

empaths. *See* sensitive people
empathy, 12, 60
energy
    discharging, 219
    of emerging mushrooms, 245
    feeling your own, 28
    in flower essences, 131
    language and, 253
    of nature, 257
    quantum leaps, 136
    of release and forgiveness,
        205–206
    self-care and observation of,
        29–30, 49
    shamanism and, 81–82
    trauma's effect on, 75
    of trees, 12–13
    of unconditional love, 122
environmental damage, 199, 214, 256
ephemerals
    mushrooms as, 250
    spring, 105–109, 118
eras of life, 101
Estés, Clarissa Pinkola, 84
evergreens, 251
evil, 28
evolution
    for the Calusa people, 137–138, 139
    humans as newcomers to, 160
    via trauma, 68
eyes, *shen* as visible in, 247

F

fairy rings, 244
family, nature as, 152
fear, of witches, 228
feeling
    forgiveness, 205
    holding space for all, 214–216
    plant communication and, 191
    science vs., 160
    See also emotion
Fernando, 37–38
fight/flight/freeze impulse, 75

Finn, Perdita, 139
fire, 182
Firefly gathering, 154
Five Spirits: Alchemical Acupuncture for
    Psychological and Spiritual Healing
    (Dechar), 261
fixing vs. holding space, 213
Florida, 43–46, 52
flower essences, 130–135, 143–146
flowering, 132, 164
flowers
    lady's slippers, 111
    mushrooms as, 244
    spring ephemerals, 105–109
    trout lilies, 117–118
forests
    old-growth, 167–168
    planting, 183
    young, 168–169, 172, 180, 232
forgiveness
    asking Earth for, 205–206
    by the Earth, 192–193, 204
    freedom via, 200
    growth and, 204
    and law of growth, 195
    relationships and, 198
Foster, Russel, 67
freedom
    via boundaries, 28
    via forgiveness, 200
Freinkel, Susan, 225
friendship, 153
fungi, 244–245, 246

G

gardens
    author's work in, 21–22
    boundaries in, 19–20, 22–24, 31
    as enclosures, 27
    First Peoples' "wilderness," 36, 224
    as medicine for sensitives, 20
    popularity of, 23–24
    "success" in, 37
    time and patience in, 38, 100

gardens *(continued)*
    volunteer plants in, 170
    your life as, 35, 36, 41–42
gatekeepers, 27, 251, 252, 254, 263, 265
gender, 26
germination, suppressing, 196
gifts
    accepting our, 265, 266
    of being yourself, 109
    humility and mystery of, 140–141
    joy of giving, 142
    to the land, 186
    marcescence as, 95–97
    paying forward, 141
    place-based divination, 184–186
    power of, 40
    from the sea, 137
    time needed to realize, 100, 101
    in trauma, 73–74, 79–80, 83
    vulnerability as, 119
God's eye, 202
gold, 261
golden flower, 261
goldfinch, 151–152
goodness
    course correction via, 14
    of life, belief in, 112–114
    mica as mirror for, 7–8
    questioning our own, 9–11
    receiving, 140–141
    as seen by nature, 151, 152
    service through recognizing our, 12
    showing Earth your, 3
    See also worthiness
grace, 177
granny witches, 229
gratitude, 177, 206, 257
Great Smoky Mountains National
    Park, 107
green, 180
green wall, 156–158
grieving
    allowing, 81, 91–92, 216
    ecological, 237
    lost ecosystems, 169, 226–227, 233
    love and, 213

making a place for, 211–212, 214
    overwhelm by, 212
    possibility within, 237
    ritual for, 217–219
Griffin, 159
growth
    allelopathic suppression of,
        196–198
    amidst death, 259–260
    Earth as ruled by, 195
    resentment vs., 204
    self-judgement vs., 198, 199
guides, 4, 122

H

Halek, Vaclav, 244
Hansen, Matt, 117
happiness
    of giving gifts, 142
    hobbies and, 180
    of the wilderness, 138
hardscaping, 32–34
harvesting, 250
Harvey, Graham, 53
hawk, 163–164
healing
    by allowing feeling, 85
    author's journey of, 30, 49, 174
    via change of perception, 228,
        229, 234, 238–239
    of the Earth after Theia, 73
    energy, 28
    forgiveness and, 198
    by going *through*, 215
    nature as place of, 6, 86–88
    optimism and, 113–114
    perspective following, 85
    pioneering, 169, 183–184
    via self-acceptance, 3
    by sensitive people, 25
    spiral path to, 9
    subtle, 134–135
    successional, 171–172
    from trauma, 73–74, 79–85
    by witches, 228, 229, 230–231

heart, *shen* in the, 247
heart, strength of, 214
heartbreak
    embrace of, 60–61
    flexibility within, 195
    of species loss, 233
Helander-Renvall, Elina, 58
hemlocks, 221–223, 235–236, 247, 251, 263
herbalism, author's study of, 3–4, 107
Hew Len, Ihaleakala, 206
hiddenness, 150
highly sensitive person (HSP), 25–26
Highly Sensitive Sanctuary, 26, 40, 89, 170
The Highly Sensitive Person (Aron), 25
Hillman, James, 182
Hippocrates, 201
Hogan, Linda, 160
holding on, 95–97, 99, 255
holding space, 213, 214–215
homecoming
    to being loved and seen, 164–165
    healing via, 6–7
    to our inner worlds, 48–51, 56, 59–61
    reverie for, 62–63
    soul retrievals, 81–83
    as way beyond death, 258
homeopathy, 132
homesteads, old, 168, 226, 240
Ho'oponopono, 206
hope
    despair and, 237
    growth and, 241
    immortality of, 216
    Maybe Game, 242
    possibility and, 234
    vulnerability and, 119, 123
Hopewell mounds, 2
human world
    Anthropocene extinction, 233
    death and rebirth for, 258, 265
    distorted self-perception in, 11–12
    as evolutionarily young, 160
    gift economy of, 141

    grieving losses from, 226–227
    as invasive species, 174
    invisibility in, 150–151
    pessimism about, 10
    as Reishi Trees, 262
    resiliency in, 183
    self-hatred in, 197–198
    smallness in, 129
    spiritual flatness of, 44
    trauma to nature from, 171
    wholeness from division for, 264
    as young forests, 178–179
humility, 141
hypervigilance, 76

I

I Ching, 258
illness
    and abandoning yourself, 49
    emotional undercurrents of, 132
    and saying no, 29–30
imaginal cells, 61–62
imagination, 57, 63, 233–234
I-ming, Liu, 262
immortality, 260
imposter syndrome, 115
"in," being, 215
Indigenous peoples
    Calusa people, 137–138
    controlled burns by, 182
    cultivation of "wilderness," 36, 224
    Dreamtime for, 55–56
    of Florida, 137
    mica's role for, 2
    nature awareness for, 157–158
    permaculture as practiced by, 23
    subjectivity in, 58
    understanding of the human world, 160
indolebutyric acid (IBA), 194
inner world
    consciousness as, 53–54
    creativity in contact with, 52
    daydreaming within, 46–47

inner world *(continued)*
emotions and the need of, 84–85
evolution in, 138–139
homecoming to, 56, 59–61
honoring/occupying your, 48–51, 63
importance of, 61–62
responsibility to reclaim, 57
innocence, 112, 115, 123
Instagram, 127
intuition, 254
Intuitive Plant Medicine, 19
invasive species
hemlock wooly adelgids, 223
humanity as, 174
knotweed, 173
as medicine, 176, 177, 179
succession and, 175
invisibility, 147, 150, 155
Irish keening tradition, 217
isinglass, 2

J
Jade Purity lineage, 7
Japanese myths, 84
Japanese tea ceremonies, 139–140
Jenkinson, Stephen, 251
jewelweed, 157
John, 26, 40, 71, 72, 170
joy, 122
June, Lyla, 14

K
keening, 217
Keewaydinoquay, 245
keyhole, going through the, 133–135
keystone species loss, 223
Kimmerer, Robin Wall, 11, 140–141, 245
kindness, small acts of, 141
kinship, with nature, 151–152
knotweed, 173, 176

knowledge
Ben Cao, 7–8
of place, 45
seed wisdom, 183
untapped, of mycology, 246
kudzu, 176–177

L
lady's slippers, 111
lambs, 121–122
landscapes as living entities, 260
landslides, 183
language, 253
Laurel, 148
Le Guin, Ursula, 233
leaves, marcescence and, 92–95
Lessons from the Twelve Archangels (Womack), 122
letting go, 93–94, 96, 98, 255
Levine, Peter, 68, 73
lichens, 171–172
life
cultivated day by day, 34
death as feeding, 251–252, 260–261, 264
force of, 53
language and, 253
participatory vs. acquisitive, 129
seasons of, 66
as seeing possibility, 238
as subjective sharing, 58
trauma as inevitable in, 77–78
lifeforce
animism and, 53
blood as foundation of, 74
connection and, 256–257
finding what serves our, 28–29
of flowering, 132
paradigm honoring all, 238
Qi, 53
understanding for healing of, 228
as wick, 228

Ling zhi (spirit plant), 247
Lithuanian culture, 244
logging, 167–168
loneliness
    in the author's life, 149
    as an illusion, 158
    and visibility to nature, 155
Lonesome Mountain, 147
longevity, 248
loss, mourning. *See* grieving
loss, species, 233, 256
love
    bigness of, 213
    bravery of deep, 109
    as a given, 159
    grief and, 219
    holding space for, 214–216
    of/by nature, 12–13, 160
    for the subtle and small, 140
    unconditional, 122, 161, 165, 193
loyal soldiers, 176
Lyme disease, 29–30, 174

M

magic
    of maybe, 234–235
    in mushroom hunting,
        250–251
    witches and, 232
Mandela, Nelson, 200
maples, 12
marcescence, 94–98
Mary, 21–22
Maté, Gabor, 29
materia medica, 7–8
mature ecosystems, 169
"maybe," power of, 234–237
Maybe Game, 241–242
McCartney, Paul, 55
medicine
    of being present, 171
    flower essences, 130–133, 134,
        143–146

invasive species as, 174–175, 176,
    177, 179
of newness, 180, 181, 184
reishi, 247, 248
stone, 7–8
subtle, small, 134
in us, 265
from willows, 200–201
of witches, 228, 230–231
    See also healing
memorials, 212, 214
metamorphosis, 61–62, 256
mica
    author's contact with, 1–3, 8
    Ben Cao for, 7–8
    as a mirror, 2, 3, 8, 9
microclimates, 95
mind, wandering in, 46–47
miracles, 193, 259–260
mirrors
    Earth as, 11–12, 13, 266
    invasive species as, 174
    mica as, 2, 3, 8
    mirror-gazing, 2
Mirrors in the Earth (Suler), 14
Mo Xi Shi (Membrane into the Source
    Stone), 8
monoculture, 129
moon, the
    birth of, 83
    emotions and, 84–85
    soul retrieval with,
        80–81, 83
Moss, Robert, 54
mother essence, 144, 145
mourning. *See* grieving
mushroom hunting, 243,
    246, 250
mushrooms, 244, 246–252, 261
music, 148, 152–153. *See also* songs
mycelium, 245, 263
Mycelium Running (Stamets), 246
mycoremediation, 246
mystery, 246, 251

N

napping outdoors, 163
nature
being seen by, 151–152,
157–158, 159
consciousness of, 12
as elder and mirror, 11–12
growth as law of, 195
healing via, 5–6, 49, 76, 86–88
living entity status for, 260
multiplicity of views on, 50
mycelium as nervous system
of, 245
noticing, 156
resiliency in, 77
seeing the energy of, 257
timeline of, 100
NDEs (or near-death
experiences), 257
negative allelopaths, 196
negativity bias, 113
neidan, 260
nervous system
effect of trauma on, 73, 75
healing via nature, 76
mycelium as nature's, 245
overwhelm, 26, 192
vagus nerve, 217
vulvodynia and, 8–9
newness
beginner's mind, 179
in cultural regeneration, 179–181
via death, 261
and the human brain, 180
medicine of, 169
soul-cleansing, 115
no, saying
challenge of, 27
illness and, 29–30
perception change via, 39
and self-knowledge, 35
"normal," 94
nugrybauti, 244

O

oaks, 50, 168
objectivity, 58, 59
observation
of cultural expectation, 47
of place, 36
ocean, life based on the, 137
Ojibwe language, 253
old-growth forests, 167–168
Oliver, Mary, 142
One Willow Apothecaries, 4, 195
Onoda, Hiroo, 176
optimism, 113–114
orchids, 111
overwhelm, 192, 212

P

pain
aspirin for, 200
choice and, 112
emotional roots of, 8–9
nature as balm to, 5–6
palo santo, 226
Paqos, 158
paradise, defined, 28
parenting, 11
path of life
choosing your, 34, 35
as a garden, 32–33, 36
individual timelines on,
95–101
as perfect, 4–5
small changes along, 136
trusting the wisdom of,
112–113
See also life
people pleasing, 27, 28
permaculture
land management via, 23
observation in, 35–36
"wilderness" gardens as, 36
permission, asking, 144

perspective
    change for healers, 238–239
    change via boundaries, 39
    as changed by trauma, 73
    death and change of, 256
    following healing journeys, 85
    healing via change of, 228, 229
    magic and change of, 234
    mushrooms and, 249
    psychedelics and, 249
    reality as changed by, 230, 234
    varied, on nature, 50
pets, 159, 160
physics, quantum, 135–136
pioneers
    in gardens, 170
    as sacred volunteers, 181
    willows as, 193–194
place
    deeply learning, 45
    place-based divination, 184–186
placebo effect, 230
pleasure, denial of, 59–60
Plotkin, Bill, 176
possibility
    as "acorn" of ourselves, 182
    beginner's mind and, 179
    of beginning again, 226–227,
      232–233
    death and loss of, 238
    dreaming and, 60
    Maybe Game, 241–242
    opening to, 231–232
    perception change and, 228, 230
    seeds of, 229
    within sorrow, 237
power
    of dreams, 54–55
    of little things, 128, 136, 141–142
    of maybe, 234–237
    of resiliency, 74
    of words, 253
    of your gifts, 40

premonitions, 69
present, being
    acceptance and, 177
    as being "in," 215–216
    during hardship, 215–216
    healing trauma via, 76, 215
    medicine of, 171
pride, 120
priests/priestesses, 25
primary succession species, 171
primitive skills, 153–154
pruning and weeding
    need for, 23, 35
    reclamation via, 32
    self-doubt about, 19–20
    as soft boundaries, 34
psilocybin mushrooms, 257
psychedelics, 249, 257
puhpowee, 245, 253, 256
punk culture, 115–116

Q

Qi, 53, 217
quantum leaps, 135–136
quartz crystals, 125–126, 142

R

rattles, 97
"realism," 233–234
reality, perspective as changing,
    230–232
rebirth
    death before, 258
    immortality as, 260
    as inevitable, 232–233
    Reishi Tree as, 255, 262
reception of gifts, 141, 142
regeneration
    cultural, 179, 181, 238, 264
    forgiveness and, 192, 196
    horticultural, 194

regeneration (*continued*)
   imagination needed for, 233–234
   mycoremediation, 246
Reiki, 28
reishi mushrooms, 246–250
Reishi Tree, 253–255, 258, 262, 263
relationships
   cultivating boundaries in,
      41–42
   ecological, 51
   forgiveness and, 198
   grieving, 91
   human/nature, 157–158
   mycelium's, 245
   for people pleasers, 48
   sensitivity and abusive, 25
   soft and hard boundaries in,
      32–34
   subjectivity and, 58–59
   toxic, 27, 28, 33
   with trees, 12–13
release, 93–94, 97
re-rooting
   chestnuts, 239–240
   old and new in, 203
   pioneering self-work for, 179
   willows for, 194
resentment vs. growth, 204
resiliency
   celebrating, 86.
   via ecotherapy, 76–77
   following trauma, 67
   in nature, 77, 183
   pioneer plants and, 171
   power of, 74
   vulnerability and, 108, 109
resourcing
   to bear heartbreak, 60–61
   in nature, 86–88
respect
   boundaries and, 40
   subjectivity and, 59
responsibility
   to reclaim inner worlds, 57
   self-compassion and, 12

resprouting, 203
revelations, major, 99–100
Revere, 148
re-wilding our inner world, 52–53
rhythm, internal, 95–100
riparian barriers, 194
Rising Strong (Brown), 108
risks, 109
rituals
   for grief, 217–219
   spells as, 230
rockhounding, 125–126
Rogers, Fred, 158
roots, 239
Ross, Charlotte, 223
Royal London Homeopathic
   Hospital, 132
Rumi, 77, 196

S

sacred, the
   difference as, 50
   marcescence as, 95
   volunteers, 170–172
salicin, 200
scent, 189–190, 225–226
science vs. feeling, 160
screaming, 219
seasons
   beauty of, 62–63
   collision leading to, 67, 68
   emotions and, 84–85
   marcescence and, 94–95, 96
   miracle of, 65
   resiliency and celebration of,
      77, 86
   timeline of, 100
secondary succession species, 171
seeds, 181–182
seen, being
   awe of, 160
   birdsong and, 155
   exercise for, 165
   healing disconnection via, 164

Indigenous understanding of, 157
in our goodness, 150–151
seers, 25
self-acceptance
and being seen, 165
belonging and, 115–117
gratitude and grace via, 177–178
healing via, 3, 14, 265–266
of our own timeline, 95–98
self-care, boundaries and, 29–30
self-compassion
being present and, 216
boundaries and, 20
ecological healing via, 14–15
journey of, xvi, 136
nature as serving, 12
re-rooting, 179
about timeline of healing, 96,
99, 100
self-doubt
alchemizing, 265
following trauma, 175–176
forgiveness and, 204
love vs., 175
persistent and hidden, 9–11
social media and, 127, 128
self-esteem, dysfunctional behavior
and, 197–198
self-hatred, 197
self-judgement
in the author's life, 192
on grief, 92
healing, 7
in the human world, 197–198
self/soul/spirit
appreciating the smallness of, 140
beliefs misaligned with, 9–10
boundaries for, 20–21
coming home to, 258
embracing the dichotomy
within, 265
flowering of, 132–133
gift of being yourself, 109,
115–117, 120–121
gifted to the Earth, 141

inner light of, 84
reishi as medicine for, 247
shen and the, 247, 256
soul retrievals, 81–82, 83
time and alignment with, 100
wider self, 248
sensitive people
author as, 24–25, 212
boundaries for, 20
children, 46–47
gifts/challenges of, 25–26
joyous participation by, 39, 60
selfishness for, 48
sensory gateways, 156
separation, mythology of, 257
service via self-compassion, 12
shamanism, 81–82, 234
shame
exposing, 165
mirrors dissolving, 13–14
over trauma, 68
Shannon, 98–99
Sharp, Cecil, 148, 150
Shaw, George Bernard, 61
shen (spirit in the physical body), 247,
256, 266
shoshin (beginner's mind), 179–181
signs, 69
Simons, Daniel, 156
size
of audience, 127–128
of dose, 133–134
search for bigness, 126–127
skepticism, 112
smallness
ecological healing and, 138–139
in the gift economy, 141
in human history, 129–130
keyhole medicine, 134
of our lived-in worlds, 139
reclaiming the power of, 136,
141–142
success and, 126–128
Smith, J. Russel, 223
social media, 127

Sodom, 148
soft boundaries, 32–34, 35
soil, 170
Somatic Experiencing, 68
songs
 Appalachian, 148, 150, 152–153
 of the birds, 152
 of the forest, 161
 of grief, 214
 human history of, 162
sorrow, 149, 164, 212, 237
Soulcraft: Crossing into the Mysteries of Nature and Psyche (Plotkin), 176
souls. *See* self/soul/spirit
The Soul's Code (Hillman), 182
species loss, 233, 256
The Spell of the Sensuous (Abram), 234
spells, 230–232, 255
spirit. *See* self/soul/spirit
spirochetes, 29, 174
spring
 angelic energy of, 122–123
 baby animals in, 121
 marcescence and, 98
 newness of, 115
 vulnerability of, 119
spring ephemerals, 105–109, 118
spring water, 44, 46, 52, 117
Stamets, Paul, 245, 246
stock bottle, 145
stones
 medicinal, 7–8
 quartz diamonds, 125–126
Strand, Clark, 139
strawberries, 140–141
strength
 of the heart, 214
 of holding on, 99
 of vulnerability, 108–109, 118–119
Strivelli, Ginger, 229
subjectivity, 57–59, 78–79
subtlety
 cherishing, 142–143

 in Japanese tea ceremonies, 139–140
 need for, 134–135, 136
success
 as bigness, 127
 "goodness" and, 47
 of reaching one person, 128
succession, 171, 175
successional cultures, 178
suicide, 210
Superfund sites, 259
Suppressed History Archives, 228
Suzuki, Shunryū, 179

T

tantric masters, 215
Te Awa Tupua River, 260
tea ceremonies, 139–140
teaching, overwhelm and, 192
tenderness, 109
thawing after trauma, 75–77
Theia
 Earth's absorption of, 85
 effect on the moon, 83
 healing following, 73
 name defined, 84
 seasons as born from, 66–67
therapy, 98–99
Thomas, Sarah, 7–8
through, as the way out, 215
tilted axis, 67, 83
time
 in a garden, 38
 of holding on/release, 95–98
 judgement about the "right," 93–94
 living on your own, 92–93
 for successional healing, 172
Timucua people, 43, 137
topsoil, 170
touch, 158
toxic relationships, 27
toxicity, flower essences and, 146

Trail of Tears, 224
transformation, 256, 260
trash, human, 44
trauma
    and being in the present, 171
    car accident, 69–72
    defined, 73
    evolution via, 68
    as a freeze, 74–76
    grieving, 92
    inevitability of, 77–78
    learning from, 67
    nature as place to heal from, 6
    PTSD and, 99
    self-doubt following, 175–176
    as shaping us, 86
    strength to bear, 60–61
    as subjective, 78–79
    symptoms of, 72
    vagus nerve and, 217
tree-felling, 221–222
trees
    chestnut trees, 223–225,
        239–240
    deciduous, 94–95
    energy of, 12–13
    hemlocks, 221–222, 235–236,
        247, 251
    palo santo, 226
    willows. see willows
trillium, 108
trout lilies, 117–118
trust
    joy of, 122
    trauma as violation of, 73
    in the wisdom of life, 112–114
Tsalagi (Cherokee) people, 2, 224
Tubman, Harriett, 55
Tula, 160

U

unconditional love, 161, 165, 193
uncontrollable events, 77–78

understanding, 172, 228
urban gardens, 21–22

V

vaccines, 133–134
vagus nerve, 217
Vassar College, 5–6
vernal, defined, 118
vinegar, preserving flower essences
    with, 145–146
viruses, 133–134
visibility, shame and, 165
visions
    discarded for the "real" world, 47
    mirror-gazing for, 2
    power of dreams, 54–56
    rattles as aiding, 97
    visionaries, 233
    words and, 253
visualizations, 62–63
vocalizing grief, 217, 218–219
volunteers, sacred, 170–172, 181, 215
vulnerability
    cherishing, 121–123
    courage of, 108–109
    empathy and, 60–61
    life as deepened by, 114, 119
vulvodynia, 5, 9, 49

W

Waking the Tiger (Levine), 68
walking, 89–91
wasps, 207–212
water, Florida's, 44
weaving, 202–203
weeds
    as invasives, 173
    location and, 35
    medicine in, 178
    as pioneers, 170
whales, 236
When the Body Says No (Maté), 29

wick, 228
wider self, 248
wikkiyaz, 231
wilderness
    First Peoples' cultivation of,
        36, 224
    Florida's, 45–46, 138
    as a garden, 36
    happiness/relief in, 138–139
    skills, 43–44, 153–154
wildflowers, 105–109
willows
    author's childhood
        relationship with, 190–191,
        194, 203
    basket making with, 202–203
    medicine from, 201
    as pioneers, 193–194
    scent of, 189–190, 192, 202
winter
    in Sodom, 148–149, 150
    walking in, 90–91
wisdom
    being present as, 216
    as kept by witches, 228–229
    of marcescence, 95, 96
    place-based divination, 186
    of seeds, 183
    slowly regrowing, 178
    trusting life's, 112–113
witches, 227–229
witch hunts, 228, 229, 230
Womack, Belinda, 122
Women Who Run with Wolves
    (Estés), 84
Wood Wide Web, 245
woodland ephemerals, 105–109
Woodstock, Our Lady of, 139
wooly adelgids, 223, 247

world, the
    death and rebirth for, 265
    language for a new, 253–254
    multiplicity of worlds, 46–47,
        49–51
    smallness of our, 139
worthiness
    belonging and, 164–165
    boundaries and, 36
    human doubt of our, 197–198
    of invasive species, 174
    mirrors reflecting our, 13–14
    of a Reishi Tree, 262
    as seen by nature, 151–152
    size and, 126–128
    tending the garden of self, 21
    See also goodness
wounds
    of being invisible, 164
    "hurt people, hurt people," 198
    Light entering via, 77
    self-punishment and, 200
writing
    as act of reclamation, 51–53
    as a journey, xv–xvi
WWII
    stranded Japanese soldiers, 176
    victory gardens, 23

Y

youth, 180
Yuen, Jeffrey, 7

Z

Zac, 202
Zen Mind, Beginner's Mind
    (Suzuki), 179

About the Author

ASIA SULER is a writer, teacher, Earth-intuitive, and ecological philosopher who lives in the folds of the Blue Ridge Mountains. She is the founder of One Willow Apothecaries, an Appalachian-grown company that offers handcrafted herbal medicines and educational experiences in herbalism, animism, ancestral healing, and Earth-centered personal growth. Asia has guided over twenty thousand students in more than seventy countries through her immersive online programs. With her writings and teachings, she helps people embrace their own unique medicine through a joyful engagement with the natural world. *Mirrors in the Earth* is her first book.

About North Atlantic Books

North Atlantic Books (NAB) is an independent, nonprofit publisher committed to a bold exploration of the relationships between mind, body, spirit, and nature. Founded in 1974, NAB aims to nurture a holistic view of the arts, sciences, humanities, and healing. To make a donation or to learn more about our books, authors, events, and newsletter, please visit www.northatlanticbooks.com.